HOLINESS
IN
WORDS

Heschel at Stanford University, 1963.
Courtesy of Stanford University News Service.

HOLINESS
IN
WORDS

ABRAHAM JOSHUA HESCHEL'S
POETICS OF PIETY

Edward K. Kaplan

State University of New York Press

SUNY Series in Judaica:
Hermeneutics, Mysticism, and Religion

Michael Fishbane, Robert Goldenberg, and Elliot Wolfson,
editors

Published by
State University of New York Press, Albany

©1996 State University of New York

For information, address State University of New York Press,
State University Plaza, Albany, NY 12246

Production by Dana Foote
Marketing by Theresa Abad Swierzowski

Library of Congress Cataloging-in-Publication Data

Kaplan, Edward K., 1942–
    Holiness in words : Abraham Joshua Heschel's poetics of piety / by
Edward K. Kaplan.
        p.   cm. — (SUNY series in Judaica)
    Includes bibliographical references and index.
    ISBN 0-7914-2867-2 (hardcover : alk. paper). — ISBN 0-7914-2868-0
(pbk. : alk. paper)
        1. Heschel, Abraham Joshua, 1907–1972. I. Title. II. Series.
BM755.H37K365   1996
296.3'092—dc20   95-42224
                                                                                CIP

10 9 8 7 6 5 4 3 2 1

How marvelous is my home.
I enter as a suppliant and emerge
as a witness; I enter as a stranger
and emerge as next of kin.
—Heschel, "On Prayer"

To those with whom I pray, members of the
    Newton Centre Minyan,
To my wife, Janna Kaplan, with whom I share all
    that can be shared,
To my children, Jeremy Joshua Kaplan,
    Aaron Emmanuel Kaplan, Simona Chava Kaplan,
    our future.

CONTENTS

Contents

 LIST OF
ILLUSTRATIONS

Cover: Heschel in 1972, Photograph by Joel Orent, Copyright.

Frontispiece: Heschel at Stanford University, 1963.
Courtesy of Stanford University News Service.   ii

Figures

 FOREWORD

The thunder of Sinai has long passed, and its dim echoes (such as exist) are muffled in texts and traditions. No flaming word pierces the silence and calls us to task with the kiss of inner-power. Who is the teacher for such times? Who speaks for the Spirit—and who speaks for the speakers? Our times have been blessed by the voice and life of Abraham Joshua Heschel, a man of Spirit, and his words and thought have been given new resonance through the devoted labors of Edward K. Kaplan. Once again—and in a new way—the theological and moral nuances of Heschel's spiritual passion can be heard. Kaplan has set our ear to sounds long-forgotten or never known. His work is no deposit of academic travail, but exemplifies scholarship as service in the highest sense.

A lifetime of listening has gone into the making of this book. Over many years, Edward Kaplan has contributed careful and perceptive studies on Heschel's poetic rhetoric, on his understanding of prophecy and prophetic consciousness, and on the moral life and its relationsip to mysticism and transcendence. They are now put to the service of a full-scale exposition of Heschel's thought and spiritual orientation. Key words and concepts are clarified with masterful pedagogy; themes and ideas are placed on the firm foundation of a philosophical anthropology; and the various patterns of concern are linked to their Western and Jewish sources. For Heschel wrote with the rhythms of a spiritual master—with deeply embedded layers of meaning from the multiple traditions which inspired him. Indeed his teachings weave many strands into a new texture, and only the most patient of expositions reveal their rich and remarkable content. The present book does just that, and in so doing inculcates a way of living through a way of reading and hearing.

Heschel's passion was promethean—no fire of the spirit was alien to him. He was imbued (in Kaplan's wonderful phrase) with a "radical reverence" for the holy possibilities of life and for the divine face hidden in all things. Indeed a central tenor of Heschel's concern was to reorient the modern person to this reverential and engaged relationship with life—and away from unthinking patterns encrusted by habit, obscured by disregard, or distorted by mendacity. The Bible is fundamental in this process. For Heschel believed that this text not only mediates the sacred, but vibrates with it. To read the Bible, therefore, is to be addressed by much more than its historical content or any given factual detail. It is rather to be addressed by a voice and a language; and in the patient attention to them and their claims, the reader is directed to the moral and spiritual content of Scripture. Heschel believed that this encounter could change a person, could redirect human passions and pathos. And so he wrote with care and concern about Scripture and its teachings. In a word: for Heschel the Bible expresses "God in Search of Man"—calling to the human subject, again and again, and in so many ways and forms, with the unyielding question, Where are you?

Edward Kaplan understands this passion of the master, and through his exposition helps the modern reader understand and assemble a personal response. What more can be said than that Heschel's voice resonates through this artful mediation? Indeed Kaplan's work captures the rhythms and energies of the speaker for the Spirit—and in the process becomes such a speaker himself.

Perhaps this is also the place to confess a memory which returned repeatedly in the process of reading this book. Many years ago, as a young boy, I sat in the presence of a great man with a piercing presence and a cadenced but commanding voice. That man was Abraham Joshua Heschel, and I sat mesmerized as he spoke of the sanctity of time—and watched the stack of index cards on his right hand gradually pile up on his left. As each card was lifted, and its contents spoken, I felt a new language and voice transferred to my inmost being. A teacher was teaching.

And now, with this book, a new audience may be found for his words. For this we must thank Ed Kaplan.

Michael Fishbane
Nathan Cummings Professor of Jewish Studies
The University of Chicago

~⟨ ∿ ACKNOWLEDGMENTS

There is no way adequately to recognize the influence of teachers, students, friendships, loves, and losses, during the almost thirty years since I first met Heschel and began to study his works. Perhaps those unnamed people who accompanied my journey to this book will find some echoes of my gratitude.

I began speaking with Abraham Joshua Heschel in 1966 while earning a doctorate in French literature at Columbia University. Through Heschel I learned to define my commitments through Jewish categories. Many other people influenced my development, by training, conversation, or the inspiration of their lives. First and foremost, my father, Kivie Kaplan (1904–1975), an idealistic businessman devoted to human rights. Our lives were inseparable from the ideals of the NAACP (National Association for the Advancement of Colored People) and the UAHC (Union of American Hebrew Congregations). My father shared his friends with me: among the multitudes, S. Ralph Harlow and Howard Thurman became my earliest mentors, preparing me for Heschel. Memories of these people and their families remain for me as a beacon.

My approach to Heschel was formed at Columbia University, where Michael Riffaterre exemplified the disciplines of philology and textual analysis. Teaching at Barnard College, Amherst College, and Brandeis University (where I have settled for the past sixteen years) provided intellectual communities, an indispensable context for my questioning. Decisive conversations with Michael and Mona Fishbane, from early along the way, helped strengthen many aspects of my life: moral and religious thinking, family, Jewish living, and essential friendship. I am grateful that Buzzy has honored our intellectual and spiritual dialogue by writing the foreword to this book.

The germinal insight underlying *Holiness in Words* first reached print in 1969, in my essay, "Prayer, Poetry, and Social Action" (*CCAR Journal*). Many people, in more recent years, provided enriching conversations: among them, Aharon Appelfeld, Harold J. Berman, Samuel Dresner, Arnold Eisen, John Merkle, Jacob Neusner, Fritz Rothschild, Sue Bailey Thurman, Arnold Jacob Wolf. As readers of earlier versions of the manuscript, Herb Dreyer, Michael Fishbane, Steven T. Katz, David Novak, Kenneth

Seeskin, Byron Sherwin, and anonymous readers for SUNY Press—and my wife, Janna, who offered astute criticisms at several stages—have been particularly helpful. Sylvia Heschel and Susannah Heschel have given me important encouragement for many years.

As this work has come to fruition, so has my intimate community: my children, Jeremy Joshua, Aaron Emmanuel, Simona Chava, and my wife, Janna. Her love and confidence—and critical intelligence—helped me clarify the path. To them, and to the Newton Centre Minyan, a community of prayer finally found, I dedicate this book.

My thanks to the editors of journals or anthologies in which previous versions of some chapters have appeared (complete references will be found in the bibliography):

William Scott Green, editor, *Journal of the American Academy of Religion,* for "Language and Reality in A. J. Heschel's Philosophy of Religion."

The University of Chicago for "Mysticism and Despair in A. J. Heschel's Religious Thought," *The Journal of Religion.* Copyright by the University of Chicago. All rights reserved.

New York University Press for "The American Mission of A. J. Heschel," in Robert Seltzer and Norman Cohen (eds.), *The Americanization of the Jews.*

B'nai B'rith Books for "Abraham Joshua Heschel" in Steven T. Katz (ed.), *Interpreters of Judaism in the Late Twentieth Century.*

"Metaphor and Miracle: A. J. Heschel and the Holy Spirit," *Conservative Judaism.* Copyright by The Rabbinical Assembly.

Excerpts from *The Prophets* by Abraham Heschel. Copyright © 1962 by Abraham Heschel. Copyright Renewed. Reprinted by permission of HarperCollins Publishers, Inc.

Excerpts from *Who Is Man?* by Abraham J. Heschel, courtesy of Stanford University Press.

Reprinted by permission of Farrar, Straus & Giroux, Inc.:

Excerpts from *The Earth Is the Lord's* by Abraham Joshua Heschel. Copyright © 1949 by Abraham Joshua Heschel. Copyright renewed © 1977 by Sylvia Heschel; Excerpts from *God in Search of Man* by Abraham Joshua Heschel. Copyright © 1955 by Abraham Joshua Heschel. Copyright renewed © 1983 by Sylvia Heschel; Excerpts from *The Insecurity of Free-*

⟨ℭℐ⟩ ABBREVIATIONS

Works in English by Abraham Joshua Heschel cited frequently, arranged chronologically.[1]

Books

Earth: The Earth Is the Lord's: The Inner Life of the Jew in East Europe. New York: Henry Schuman, 1950. Now: Farrar, Straus & Giroux, Inc.

Sabbath: The Sabbath: Its Meaning for Modern Man. New York: Farrar, Straus & Young, 1951. Expanded edition: Farrar, Straus and Co., 1963.

Not Alone: Man Is Not Alone: A Philosophy of Religion. New York: Farrar, Straus & Young; Philadelphia: The Jewish Publication Society of America, 1951.

Quest: Man's Quest for God: Studies in Prayer and Symbolism. New York: Charles Scribner's Sons, 1954; reprinted as *Quest for God*.

In Search: God in Search of Man: A Philosophy of Judaism. New York: Farrar, Straus & Cudahy; Philadelphia: The Jewish Publication Society of America, 1955. Hardcover also available at Jason Aronson.

Prophets: The Prophets. New York: Harper and Row; Philadelphia: Jewish Publication Society of America, 1962. Paperback edition, two volumes: New York: Harper Torchbooks, 1969; 1971.

Who Is Man? Stanford: Stanford University Press, 1965.

Insecurity: The Insecurity of Freedom: Essays on Human Existence. New York: Farrar, Straus & Giroux, Inc. 1966.

Israel: Israel: An Echo of Eternity. New York: Farrar, Straus & Giroux, Inc., 1969.

Passion: A Passion for Truth. New York: Farrar, Straus & Giroux, Inc. 1973.

---

1. Note on pronouns: Since Abraham Joshua Heschel wrote in English between 1942 and 1972, his use of the term *man* and its derivatives refers to all human beings, male and female. Similarly, "God" referred to as "He" makes no anthropomorphic claims.

Articles

"The Mystical Element": "The Mystical Element in Judaism," in Louis Finkelstein (ed.), *The Jews: Their History, Culture, and Religion* (1949). See bibliography for publication details.

"No Religion Is an Island": "No Religion Is an Island," in *Union Seminary Quarterly Review* 21, 2 (January 1966): 117–34. Quoted from the reprint in Harold Kasimow and Byron L. Sherwin (eds.), *No Religion Is an Island: A. J. Heschel and Interreligious Dialogue* (New York, 1991), pp. 3–22.

"Teaching Jewish Theology": "Teaching Jewish Theology in the Solomon Schechter Day School," *The Synagogue School* 28, 1 (Fall 1969): 3–33.

"On Prayer": "On Prayer," *Conservative Judaism* 25, 1 (Fall 1970): 1–12.

 INTRODUCTION

The Bible is *holiness in words*. . . . It is as if God took
these Hebrew words and breathed into them of His
power, and the words became a live wire charged with
His spirit. To this very day they are hyphens between
heaven and earth.
—Heschel, 1955[1]

In the two decades since Abraham Joshua Heschel's untimely
death (during the Sabbath night of 23 December 1972), contemporary religion still lacks thinkers and scholars for whom both
God and the human race are equally real. Heschel's writings con-
vincingly evoke the luminous presence of God; and his life combines prayer, faith, and nonsectarian social action. In the 1960s
he was the most prominent traditional Jew in the United States
committed to civil rights and political protest. For me particularly, he was a great artist. His poetic style enticed my yearning
for faith and his prophetic militancy gave substance to abstract
principles.

Claiming that "the Bible is *holiness in words*," Heschel writes
stirringly about God, inwardness, and ethics for agnostics as well
as for those who flourish within the categories of Scripture. His
works partake of the fascination with spiritual traditions attract-
ing North Americans since the 1950s. Zen Buddhist, Hindu, Sufi,
and, more recently, native American texts became available, and
people joined unusual groups in an attempt to overcome alienat-
ing aspects of organized religion. For Jews, the *Havurah* movement of the 1960s and 1970s fostered alternative communities of
worship and study that help mitigate, to a great extent, the shal-
lowness of synagogue routine. Translations of Jewish classics now
grace "spirituality" sections of commercial bookstores. In spite of
these advances, the unity of Heschel's mystical and moral vision
has yet to change our institutions.

The essays that comprise this book originated in a personal
perplexity: Why did Heschel appeal so strongly to me, a seeker of
faith attracted to mystical testimonies? I could trust the represen-

tative of Judaism who had the courage to admit: "Religion declined not because it was refuted, but because it became irrelevant, dull, oppressive, insipid."[2] Heschel's discourse was not banal or moralistic. He exploded clichés and slogans.

As a student of literature, I was captivated by Heschel's rhetoric. His prose combines various poetic devices—metaphor, assonance, rhythm—with incisive theological and philosophical polemics, aphorism, and bold ethical and political decisions. Other readers— Jewish or not, believers or those stalled at the threshold—also find in Heschel's writings a meeting place between human and divine.

He recovers the fervor of Judaism, the power of "piety," attachment to God. The Hasidic rebbes among whom Heschel lived as a child in Warsaw, Poland, combined wisdom, righteousness, and rigorous observance. He experienced his original theological insights within this culture whose language was Hebrew and Yiddish, and *halakhah* (Jewish law) its framework. Then, in 1940, he emigrated to the United States. Wrenched from his soil, he found a foreign idiom with which to usher readers into the holy dimension.

Heschel's books in English develop an artful strategy. His narrative of a modern mind in search of its soul evokes his own intuitions of God's presence—the Holy Spirit, or continuous revelation.[3] He is both witness and interpreter whose vibrant style "translates" (or transports) his knowledge of classical sources in Hebrew, Aramaic, and Yiddish—biblical, rabbinic, and Hasidic texts and oral traditions—into elegant, expressive English. Readers who do not know the originals might thus emulate Jewish piety and learning.

Heschel communicates directly with general readers, popularizing his knowledge for those without his erudition, prayer life, or historical experience. His discourse is multilayered, addressing several audiences simultaneously, although his academic debates remain implicit. Yet, in all frankness, his writings remain relatively unappreciated. He is quite quotable. But most people, untrained in literature or aloof to the nuances of spiritual encounter, find Heschel "hard to understand." That is why a careful study of his narrative is imperative.

The following chapters, the fruit of twenty-five years of pondering Heschel's works, share the goal of his own expositions: "By penetrating the consciousness of the pious man, we can conceive the reality behind it."[4] We face a double task: (1) to highlight the author's thought and organize it into some conceptual order; and (2) to experience intuitively the quality of his prose in order to possess, as it were, the writer's own devotional practice. I began by systematizing the formulas dispersed throughout his emotionally charged—and often baroque—literary style.

Holiness in Words is a reader's guide to transformation, not a plot summary. Since Heschel's method is phenomenological (an analysis of consciousness) and his practice literary (using style to surpass words), we analyze his *"poetics of piety"*—a theory and use of religious language in the service of spiritual maturity. A system of verbal expression and communication underlies his theology and ethics, and his rhetorical strategy aims to convert the reader's consciousness from egocentered to theocentric (or prophetic) thinking. The result should be "piety" (in Hebrew, *hasidut*), a way of living that includes "faith" and "action." Heschel's own moral, theological, interfaith, and political commitments flow from his ideal of piety.

The book begins with the life and writings. Chapter 1 surveys Heschel's American career as a "theologian, zaddik, and prophetic voice," including his youth and early adulthood in Poland and Germany. Literary style is the subject of chapter 2, "A Reading Strategy: Empathy with Critical Awareness," which demonstrates a method of slow reading and analysis. Becoming at ease with Heschel's rhetoric—his variety of narrative attitudes—allows us to appreciate his mixture of philosophical argument, lyricism, and aphoristic formula. (These two chapters are the most general. Appendix A lists readings and provides a curriculum for further study.)

The next three chapters examine the overall design of *Man Is Not Alone* and *God in Search of Man*, Heschel's foundational books of religious philosophy. A broad "macroreading" is complemented by a "microreading" of details that touch a reader's mind and intuitions. Chapter 3, "The Divine Perspective: Learning to Think Religiously," traces the path. Heschel's metaphorical language and the nonlinear organization of his books and essays deliberately challenge our usual manner of perceiving the world. He first evokes awe and wonder; then, after demolishing intellectual pride, he prepares us to receive divine inspiration.

Before examining Heschel's positions on specific religious and ethical controversies, we define his poetics of faith (see "Language and Reality," chapter 4). This is the key to his charisma as author and speaker. An analysis of metaphor explains how language can evoke the God side of religious experience. Opposing authoritarian legalism or fundamentalism, Heschel insists that biblical statements are not univocally literal but paradoxical, as he states, *more than literally true*. His argumentation effects what I call a "recentering of subjectivity" from the self to God. In this theocentric thinking, the Divine is the ineffable Subject of which human beings are the object.

Like Saadia Gaon, Jehuda Halevi, Maimonides, Blaise Pascal, and Franz Rosenzweig before him, Heschel is an apologist—but not to promote dogma or ideology. He seeks to convert our very consciousness of reality, in its emotional and rational aspects. The pivot is examined in chapter 5, "Mysticism and Despair: The Threshold of Revelation." We analyze a passage of poetic prose that "describes" an incursion of the Divine into human awareness. Heschel's literary frame reinforces his cogent interpretation of these wordless events. That is how he validates his claim that God is in search of us.

The next four chapters examine contemporary debates. "Sacred versus Symbolic Religion" (chapter 6), applies the recentering of subjectivity to hermeneutic, ethical, and ritual problems that continue to afflict contemporary Judaism. Heschel's repudiation of symbolism stands in stark opposition to philosophical anthropology, or sociological approaches, influenced by Martin Buber and other humanistic or liberal thinkers. "Prophetic Radicalism" (chapter 7) explains the basis of his civil rights and antiwar stands in the 1960s. He defines what I call a "sacred humanism" based on the conviction that every person is an image of God. The problem of evil, as well, is included in this study of reverence for humankind.

A radical, postmodern theology is perhaps Heschel's least explored legacy, and the most elusive. We begin to formulate it in "Confronting the Holocaust: God in Exile" (chapter 8); Appendix B delineates Heschel's understanding of Nazism in pre-War Germany and his responses to the horrors after he emigrated to the United States. Human responsibility is the key.

The preceding chapters explore the *exoteric Heschel*, a modern intellectual of European culture living within American religious and ethnic politics, who translates mystical piety and classical Judaism into contemporary philosophical and theological terms. Chapter 9, "Metaphor and Miracle: Modern Judaism and the Holy Spirit," uncovers the *esoteric Heschel*—himself inspired by the Divine as were the prophets, Maimonides, rabbinic sages, and mystics. Heschel's recently translated Hebrew articles claim (at least indirectly) that God still speaks to people.

Our concluding chapter, "Heschel's Unfinished Symphony," reminds us that faith is not the finale but the inauguration of a life voyage toward piety and ethical action. His works in English give access to authentic interpretations of tradition for those with little or no Jewish learning but who thirst for God or for stable meaning. Specialists, by mastering his rhetoric and religious thinking, can ferret out the relevant Hebrew and Yiddish origins of his English vocabulary, thus placing the author within a panorama of historical hermeneutics. Yet, in the end, we want, simply, to read Heschel who appeals to people of all backgrounds and attitudes.

This book, *Holiness in Words*, set as an academic study, is also an act of commitment. My hope is that readers can enter Heschel's world—with or without the golden bough of faith. His poetics of piety, prophetic radicalism, and phenomenology of holiness might help alleviate today's cynicism, moral confusion, and spiritual thirst. By becoming aware that *all* language is metaphorical, we open ourselves to the reality beyond words, beyond concepts, systems, ideologies. Even images of patriarchy give way before the Holy Spirit.

If one "source" of Heschel's thought can be located, it would be Hasidism, the legacy of its founder, the Baal Shem Tov. Heschel's study of spiritual life and action updates this tradition. He uses the term *faith* almost interchangably with *piety*, since a theocentric consciousness is the foundation of both. Yet piety, which includes cleaving to God in prayer and in sacred deeds (the *mitzvot*), is more indigenous to Judaism than faith. Piety, in Heschel's terms, is faith's fulfillment.

Heschel teaches us how to think and live religiously. He educates our love, fear, and trembling—beyond dogmas and creeds, beyond institutions or ethnic concerns. His works confront universal perplexities about meaning, death, evil, suffering—also joy, ecstasy, and celebration—helping us grapple with personal and group identity in a fragmented and often hostile world. Heschel expected Judaism to join other religions in bringing peace, justice, and compassion to the world. As we begin our journey, we meet a man rooted in—and uprooted from—history.

ABRAHAM JOSHUA HESCHEL IN AMERICA
Theologian, Zaddik,
Prophetic Voice

> A prophet is a man who feels fiercely. God has thrust a
> burden upon his soul, and he is bowed and stunned at
> man's fierce greed. Frightful is the agony of man; no
> human voice can convey its full terror. Prophecy is the
> voice that God has lent to the silent agony, a voice to
> the plundered poor, to the profaned riches of the
> world. It is a form of living, a crossing point of God and
> man.
>
> —Heschel, 1962[1]

Because of his combination of substance and charisma, Heschel
became a revered and controversial public figure in the United
States during the tumultuous 1960s. His prominence as a writer
was ratified in the mass media during that same period. In 1966
Newsweek wrote of him: "To recover the prophetic message of
ancient Judaism, Heschel has built up a rich, contemporary Jewish theology that may well be the most significant achievement
of modern Jewish thought,"[2] confirming Reinhold Niebuhr's pre-
diction fifteen years earlier that "he will become a commanding
and authoritative voice not only in the Jewish community but in
the religious life of America."[3]

Heschel's distinctive presence in the United States is a result of
his having integrated the spiritual and intellectual cultures of
three capitals of pre-World War II Europe: Warsaw, his birthplace;
Vilna ("the Jerusalem of Lithuania"), where he earned a high
school diploma from the secular, Yiddish-language *Real-Gymna-
sium*; and Berlin, where he attended a liberal rabbinic college and
the university. His complex personality, his originality and shortcomings, reflect these different sources of North American Jewry.

Born on 11 January 1907 in Warsaw, Abraham Joshua Heschel
Heschel (named after his ancestor, Abraham Joshua Heschel, the
rebbe of Apt) was groomed to lead the Hasidic dynasty of his

father, Moshe Mordecai Heschel (1873–1917), whose forebears included Dov Baer of Mezeritch (the "Great Maggid"), the principal disciple of the Baal Shem Tov, the founder of Hasidism; Israel Friedman of Ruzhin (1797–1850); and the Apter rebbe (1749–1825), who "was buried next to the holy Baal Shem."[4] His mother Rifka Reizel Perlow (1874–1942), also of distinguished Hasidic stock, was a descendant of Pinchas of Koretz (1726–1791) and Levi Yitzhak of Berditchev (1740–1793).

Heschel's aristocratic Hasidic pedigree (or *yikhus*) is vaguely known and still incompletely studied.[5] Reared in a devout community, Heschel was a child prodigy who mastered the extensive body of classical Jewish texts, particularly "the sea of Talmud." (His retention of texts from Bible, Talmud, Kabbalah, and Hasidic sources dates from his childhood.) Then he went on to earn his modern scholarly and philosophical credentials in Berlin, at the modern Jewish research and teaching institute, the Hochschule für die Wissenschaft des Judentums and at the Friedrich Wilhelm (now Humboldt) University.

An agonizing involvement in history accompanied this European education. Heschel completed his doctoral dissertation on prophetic consciousness in 1933 amidst events that remolded the world: on 30 January Adolf Hitler became Chancellor of Germany; on 27 February the Reichstag building was set on fire; the Nazis seized power in July. During that same period, even after Jews were eliminated from the German academic system, the University of Berlin finally accorded him the doctorate in December 1935.[6]

Writer and Teacher

From the very beginning, Heschel was a committed writer. Words would become his most effective weapon against hostile political and cultural forces. The very year he completed his dissertation he published his first—and perhaps most autobiographical—book, a collection of Yiddish poems, *Der Shem Ham'Forash—Mentsh* (*Mankind—God's Ineffable Name*), which combines compassion with human suffering and closeness to the living God.[7] Emblematic of his vision, the poem "*Ikh un Du*" (I and Thou), first published in the New York Yiddish periodical *Zukunft* (The Future) in 1929, proclaims an intimacy of human and divine surpassing the dialogical relation celebrated by Martin Buber: "My nerves' tendrils are intertwined with Yours, / Your dreams with mine. / Are we not one embraced in multitudes?"[8]

It has been observed that, after 1933, the systematic exclusion of Jews from Germany's cultural life revived latent Jewish creativity. Many assimilated Jews returned to the synagogue and enrolled in adult education courses in Judaism.[9] Publishing houses owned by Jews, forbidden to print "Aryan" authors, issued an impressive new list of books in Judaica. With a Ph.D. and a liberal rabbinical degree (he was ordained at the Hochschule in 1934), Heschel began to offer his knowledge to the general public in print and as a teacher.

In 1935 Heschel worked for a literary and artistic publisher in Berlin, the Erich Reiss Verlag, as editor of their series on Jewish thought and history. Heschel addressed readers directly in his 1935 biography of Maimonides and his 1937 biographical essay on Don Isaac Abravanel.[10] He complemented these retrievals of Jewish tradition with eight brief biographical essays on Tannaim (rabbis of the Talmudic period, among them, Yohanan ben Zakkai, Gamliel II, Akiba, Jehuda Hanassi) published in the Berlin Jewish newspaper, *Jüdisches Gemeindeblatt*, in 1936.[11]

Heschel's teaching paralleled his writing for the community. He gave lectures at the Berlin Lehrhaus. His theological career began in March 1937, when Martin Buber invited him to Frankfurt-am-Main as codirector of the Central Organization for Jewish Education and the Jüdisches Lehrhaus. It was there that Fritz Rothschild—who became Heschel's authoritative interpreter in the United States—first heard him present the Bible to a skeptical group of youth leaders. After their eventual emigration to the United States, the two men formed a lifelong professional tie.[12] In Frankfurt, Heschel consolidated his vision of Jewish renewal.

Then he was almost crushed by events. Heschel was expelled from Germany on 28 October 1938, with about eighteen thousand other Jews holding Polish passports. After a short stay at the frontier he returned to Warsaw, where he remained from November 1938 to June 1939 (one academic year), teaching at the Institute for Jewish Studies, a scientific academy of higher learning similar in orientation to the Berlin Hochschule. During this period he desperately sought a haven. Finally, in the spring of 1939, he received an invitation from President Julian Morgenstern to teach at Hebrew Union College in Cincinnati.[13]

Remarkably, amidst these uncertainties, Heschel maintained his spiritual center. Awaiting approval of a nonquota visa to the United States, he left Warsaw for London and wrote to Dr. Morgenstern on 28 July in his still-faltering immigrant English: "I would like very much to study the English language and to continue the work on a philosophical book on the prayer [sic]. Two chapters therefrom will be published before long." Heschel faced Europe's economic depression, fierce anti-Semitism, and the unknown future by preparing a book on Jewish inwardness.[14]

"A Brand Plucked from the Fire"

Heschel the refugee arrived in New York City on 21 March 1940, throughly familiar with Jewish culture and assimilation in Germany and Poland. Having long reflected upon various attempts at Jewish self-definition, secular and religious, as well as conditions of Jewish life in pre-War London, he rapidly concluded what Americans needed.

His thinking absorbed the Catastrophe and riveted upon redemption. In the early 1940s, he remained acutely aware, on a daily basis, that his family and the thousand-year-old Jewish civilization of Europe were being annihilated. Much later, in his 1965 inaugural lecture at the Union Theological Seminary, he defined himself as a survivor: "I am a brand plucked from the fire, in which my people was burned to death. I am a brand plucked from the fire of an altar to Satan on which millions of human lives were exterminated to evil's greater glory."[15]

Biblical values and reverence for each and every person would defy the genocide and the moral callousness that made it possible. His mission would be to preserve the essential principles of biblical religion: "the divine image of so many human beings, many people's faith in the God of justice and compassion, and much of the secret and power of attachment to the Bible bred and cherished in the hearts of men for nearly two thousand years."

Heschel the new American was an unusual prophetic voice. He had reached intellectual maturity in Europe and witnessed the cultural crisis following World War I. He saw the Nazi rise to power. And he had bridged the traditional and modern worlds without relinquishing his Hasidic ideals. Now he did not place in the Shoah—our century's major catastrophe—a source of Jewish energy, as did many postwar thinkers. Heschel's theology represents a passionate alternative to Judaism redefined by the Holocaust and the State of Israel.[16] It implies that Jewish survival does not require us to see ourselves, even triumphally, as victims.

On a more general level, Heschel recognized the perils of vicarious experience of any kind, moral or religious. American Jewry, despite its struggle with recent historical facts, could not derive enduring values and identity from events essentially foreign to its daily reality. Nor could Judaism survive without taking seriously the reality of God and God's immanence in Torah. He called Jews to their sacred mission to enhance religion and to redeem the world.[17]

Heschel's soul took root. His American career can be divided into three phases: (1) from 1940 to 1950 he defined the philosophical and theological foundations of contemporary values; (2) from 1951 to 1962 he elaborated a critique of Jewish philosophy and practice; and (3) from 1960 to his death in 1972 he became a prophetic activist. His writings and public appearances became like the divine tree of Kabbalistic legend: its roots in heaven, its branches and leaves on earth.

At Hebrew Union College in Cincinnati, where he remained from 1940 to 1945, Heschel was perceived as a traditionally observant but modern scholar committed to spiritual issues. There he refined his goal as writer and thinker: "how to share the certainty of Israel that the Bible contains that which God wants us to know and hearken to; how to attain a collective sense for the presence of God in the biblical words."[18]

Grateful for their having rescued him, Heschel nevertheless judged American Jews as being in the throes of a second Holocaust—he called it "spiritual absenteeism." He did not find enough leaders asserting the reality of God nor defending prophetic ethical imperatives. After the war, American Jews were relatively safe from anti-Semitism, gaining social and political power, moving to the suburbs, building synagogues and schools— all the while handicapped by reductionistic conceptions of Jewish tradition. For Heschel, the living God must not be reduced to folklore or symbols.

Rescuing the Jewish Soul

In America, Heschel soon realized that he could have an impact only through his writings. He would attack the sources of evil. During his first fifteen years in this country (1940–1955), Heschel's publications focus on prayer and piety and faith. By defining the inner life of religion, he sought to retrieve the Jewish soul (in Hebrew, *neshama*) from oblivion.[19]

Everything he subsequently wrote defies the twentieth century's spiritual crisis, of which Nazism was the most devastating, almost unspeakable, outbreak. But he did not broadcast his private agonies. He had tried unsuccessfully to convince Jewish leaders to help European victims.[20] His mother and two unmar-

ried sisters—Gittel and Esther Sima—perished in the Warsaw
Ghetto, while a third who lived in Vienna, Devorah Miriam
Dermer, was deported to Treblinka with her husband and mur-
dered in Auschwitz.[21] (His oldest sister, Sarah, had emigrated in
February 1939 to the United States with her family and her hus-
band, the rebbe of Kopitzhinitz—also named Rabbi Abraham
Joshua Heschel.)[22]

Heschel announced his understanding of the destruction of
European Jewry in the *Hebrew Union College Bulletin* of March
1943. He published an English version of a speech he had delivered to a Quaker group in Frankfurt, Germany, in 1938. Entitled
"The Meaning of this War," it began: "Emblazoned over the gates
of the world in which we live is the escutcheon of the demons.
The mark of Cain in the face of man has come to overshadow the
likeness of God."[23] Heschel blamed secular civilization—"us" not
"them," including Americans—for distorted values and a feeble,
ineffective response to events: "The outbreak of war was no surprise. It came as a long expected sequel to a spiritual disaster."[24]

His first scholarly publications written in (an impeccable)
English appeared between 1942 and 1944: "An Analysis of Piety,"
"The Holy Dimension," and "Faith."[25] For an essay on "Prayer,"
published in 1945,[26] the author signed his name as "Abraham
Joshua Heschel, Associate Professor of Jewish Philosophy, Hebrew
Union College"; by stating his full name for the first time, the
American academic had discreetly reappropriated his Hasidic
ancestry. In 1945, after moving from Hebrew Union College to
The Jewish Theological Seminary, he published another major
article, "The Mystical Element in Judaism."[27] These elegant
reflections on spirituality establish Heschel's post-Holocaust mission.

Heschel's manner of marketing his ideas, even then, was
quintessentially American. He understood that his credibility
would benefit from recognition by professionals outside as well
as within the Jewish community, so he placed articles in English
with the prestigious journals of Columbia University and the
University of Chicago and in Mordecai Kaplan's *Reconstructionist*,
which then reached a large, diverse readership.[28] Deprived of his
Yiddish-, German-, or Hebrew-speaking communities, Heschel
had become a translator of the Spirit.

Moreover, Heschel's literary style was, by necessity, addressed
particularly to outsiders. He understood that American readers
could not recognize his constant allusions (most of them without
direct citation of sources) to Jewish texts nor was their normal

experience conducive to intuitions of the Divine. His goal was to unveil, and to make verbally and imaginatively graphic, life's fundamental holiness.

The destruction of European Jewry made especially urgent his commitment to transplant the Kabbalistic tree of heaven to the new world. In a speech he gave in Yiddish to the New York YIVO conference in January 1945, he insisted that "romantic portraiture of Hasidism, nostalgia and piety, are merely ephemeral; they disappear with the first generation. We are in need of Jews whose life is a garden, not a hothouse. Only a living Judaism can survive. Books are no more than seeds; we must be both the soil and the atmosphere in which they grow."[29]

Heschel's first American book of spiritual rescue was an expansion in English of this speech, an essay entitled *The Earth Is the Lord's: The Inner World of the Jew in East Europe* (1950). Illustrated with exquisite woodcuts by Ilya Schor, also a Jewish refugee from Poland, this work is more than an idealization of Heschel's heritage and a *kaddish* (prayer for the dead) to a civilization lost; it outlines his theological system (in chapter 10, "Kabbalah"). His conclusion calls Jews to fulfill a prophetic task, as it joins the mystical and social dimensions of the tradition: "We are God's stake in human history. . . . There is a war to wage against the vulgar, against the glorification of the absurd, a war that is incessant, universal. Loyal to the presence of the ultimate in the common, we may be able to make it clear that man is more than man, that in doing the finite he may perceive the infinite."[30]

Heschel's reputation in the United States was established by 1951 when two more books appeared: *The Sabbath* and *Man Is Not Alone*.[31] At that time the author was recognized by America's leading Protestant theologian and social activist, Reinhold Niebuhr, as an authority on Judaism and religious insight. Heschel had become the paradigm of a Jewish theologian and prophetic witness.

A Zaddik for the 1950s

Mindful that American readers must at first share his spirit vicariously, Heschel the writer developed a rhetorical strategy meant to stimulate intuition. He sought to evoke what he called "the ineffable"—intimations of the transcendent that cannot be expressed in language. His narrative is both plain and poetic. His particular gift was to use language to surpass language so as to thrust readers beyond concepts—making us available to God's initiative.

Heschel is both stimulating and frustrating to read. His polyphonic style bristles with insights derived from biblical, rabbinic, Kabbalistic, philosophical, and literary knowledge. Yet at times his sentences become a virtuoso performance, verbal acrobatics. Some of his writerly excesses have led many readers to reject the thinker as a mere "poet." His artistry, however, plays a pragmatic role: pointing us to holiness—in the prayerbook, in the Bible, and notably in everyday living.

Heschel indeed completed "a philosophical book on the prayer" (as he had written to Morgenstern in 1939). He diagnosed American Judaism in *Man's Quest for God: Studies in Prayer and Symbolism* (1954), which includes his 1945 article on prayer and an English version of his 1938 address to the Quakers at Frankfurt. Two central chapters propose remedies for the illnesses of contemporary religious institutions. These judgments epitomize Heschel's dialectic method of inducing people to seek holiness.

Heschel's complementary approaches to prayer—one delivered to the (Conservative) Rabbinical Assembly of America and the other to the (Reform) Central Conference of American Rabbis—judged the practice of each audience in a manner each wanted the least to acknowledge. He warned his Conservative colleagues about the emptiness of their orderly services. He urged the Reform rabbis not to abandon *halakhah* (Jewish law) in favor of "customs and ceremonies." Both audiences expressed a mixture of outrage, embarrassment, and veneration. Heschel had pinpointed the theological crisis of both groups. Taken together, however, Heschel's two speeches promote a conception of Judaism as a *polarity* of apparently contradictory standards.

Heschel's message to the Conservative rabbinate began with a critique of current practice: "Has the synagogue become a graveyard where prayer is buried?" he asked.[32] "We have developed the habit of *praying by proxy*" (Heschel's emphasis).[33] Rabbis must face honestly the frailty of their faith: "I have been in the United States of America for thirteen years. I have not discovered America but I have discovered something in America. It is possible to be a rabbi and not believe in the God of Abraham, Isaac and Jacob."[34]

He then applied worship as a touchstone to criticize (some would say caricature) four approaches that subvert true religion: (1) the agnosticism that claims "that the only way to revitalize the synagogue is to minimize the importance of prayer and to convert the synagogue into a center"; (2) religious behaviorism, whose "supreme article of faith is *respect for tradition*"; (3) the view that prayer is a social act, "built on a theology which regards God as a symbol of social action, as an epitome of the ideals of the group";[35] and (4) a religious solipsism, which "maintains that the individual self of the worshipper is the whole sphere of prayer life. The assumption is that God is an idea, a process, a source, a fountain, a spring, a power."

Heschel countered with an imposing goal, citing an earlier work: "It is precisely the function of prayer to shift the center of living from self-consciousness to self-surrender."[36] People should strive to view reality from God's perspective, emulating the theocentric judgments of the Hebrew prophets. Already Heschel had defined his religious Copernican revolution; his works comprise a vast apologetics meant to recenter our consciousness from the self to God.[37]

This theology faced the realities of modern anguish. In response to the view that Judaism bestows "peace of mind" (as Joshua Loth Liebman or Norman Vincent Peale would have it) and makes us feel at home in the universe, he insisted that "we could not but experience anxiety and spiritual homelessness in the sight of so much suffering and evil, in countless examples of failure to live up to the will of God. That experience gained in intensity by the soul-stirring awareness that God Himself was not at home in the universe, where His will is defied, where His kingship is denied."[38]

Theological seriousness is imperative. Religious observance can provide the elements of a remedy: "To pray, then, means to bring God back into the world. . . . God is transcendent, but our worship makes Him immanent." Human beings have immense power and responsibility.

In North America as in Europe, before and after the War, skepticism had undermined the ability to recall God's self-expression at Sinai: "If [conviction in the reality of God] is lacking, if the presence of God is a myth, then prayer to God is a delusion. If God is unable to listen to us, then we are insane in talking to Him."[39] Heschel seems to have considered the 1930s and 1950s as spiritually equivalent. He of course holds to the objective reality of God; to many of us, however, if taken seriously, his demand might tempt one to relinquish any pretense to *religious*, as opposed to ethnic or political, identity. Such were the risks.

Heschel's admonition to the Reform rabbinate two days later also challenges agnosticism or atheism.[40] After expressing his gratitude to Julian Morgenstern, who made his emigration to the United States possible, he reassured his less traditional colleagues: "I, too, have wrestled with the difficulties inherent in our faith as Jews."[41]

In a rare autobiographical sketch, Heschel presented himself as paradigmatic of the Jewish journey to modernity. Scion of generations of rabbis, the young man had arrived in Berlin in the fall of 1927 to study at the university. One day he "walks alone through the magnificent streets of Berlin" and suddenly notices that the sun has gone down. He had forgotten to pray! "I had forgotten God—I had forgotten Sinai—I had forgotten that sunset is my business—that my task is to 'restore the world to the kingship of the Lord.'"[42] The East European Hasid, nourished in the hothouse of German academia, uprooted once again and transplanted to America, reminds liberal rabbis of their true origin: "There is something which is far greater than my will to believe. Namely, God's will that I believe."[43]

Rejecting the sociological view of observance as "customs and ceremonies," Heschel insisted on God's reality and the divine origin of the *mitzvot* (commandments). The current crisis of belief results from a false premise, namely, that the mind must first know God before obeying the law. So he urged his Reform colleagues to surpass rationalizations and "take *a leap of action* rather than *a leap of thought.*"[44]

Heschel is both "orthodox" and "liberal"—unsatisfactory to purists in both camps. To his Reform colleagues, he defended the metaphysical substance of ancestral practices: "In carrying out the word of the Torah [a Jew] is ushered into the presence of spiritual meaning. Through the ecstasy of deeds [a Jew] learns to be certain of the presence of God." He concluded: "For many years rabbis have in speeches delivered at conventions of the Central Conference of American Rabbis voiced their sense of shock and grief at the state of religious chaos prevalent in modern congregations, and have urged the members of this Conference to return to Jewish observance. May it be a *return* to a *halakhic* way of life, not to customs and ceremonies."[45]

Heschel thus broadcast his mission by 1953, thirteen years after his arrival on our shores. There is an instructive symmetry to this chronology. Twenty years before, he had completed his doctoral dissertation in Berlin and published his book of Yiddish poems in Warsaw. Now safe (if not secure) in the United States, he consecrated his bar mitzvah as a New American by denouncing vicarious Judaism. Faith in a real God can be achieved through tradition. At the same time, contemporary Jews must authenticate acts defined by *halakhah* through personal, inward experience. Such prayer can organize and inspirit an ethical life.

Heschel's works in English address believers and secular readers alike. As a twentieth-century observant Jew, he himself lived within tensions between religious confidence and a harsh historical realism. Both contemporary and traditional, he integrated universal religious experience with Jewish law as revealed at Sinai. His two foundational works of Jewish philosophy and theology, *Man Is Not Alone* (1951) and *God in Search of Man* (1955), led Heschel to be viewed as "a *zaddik* (or holy man) of the 1950s." *The Prophets* (1962) and *The Insecurity of Freedom* (1966) define the theological foundations of his activities as a "prophet of the 1960s." *A Passion for Truth* (1973), published soon after his death, outlines a paradoxical post-Holocaust faith and ethics.

Heschel had one model for contemporary religion: the God of pathos, Who cares passionately about the quality of human life. This bold confidence is at once a stumbling block, a challenge, and a gift. GOD always was and remains the source of Jewish energy: not large synagogues, community centers, money—nor deeply felt responsibility toward Israel. God is both the origin and the goal:

> GOD. Not an emotion, a stir within us, but a power, a marvel beyond us, tearing the world apart. The word that means more than universe, more than eternity, holy, holy, holy; we cannot comprehend it. We only know it means infinitely more than we are able to echo. Staggered, embarrassed, we stammer and say: He, who is more than all there is, who speaks through the ineffable, whose question is more than our minds can answer; He to whom our life can be the spelling of an answer.[46]

Heschel's life and writings comprise "the spelling of an answer." Prophetic truth rejects administrative solutions to the emptiness of contemporary life. Heschel's 1962 book *The Prophets* spans his career, as it assigns to moral action the fulfillment of theocentric thinking. His 1933 dissertation had defined a "religion of sympathy" as a response to God's pathos, the moral emotions expressed by the Divine reacting to human events. In both versions of the study, Heschel's phenomenological method—a detailed analysis of the prophets' identification with God's turning toward humanity—helps today's readers welcome inspiration.

Abraham Joshua Heschel writes as a Western philosopher, a Judaic scholar, a theologian, a Hasidic rebbe, and a poet who assumes an unshaking confidence in God's love for humankind. In addition, he emulates the Hebrew prophets' compassion and ethical radicalism. Now we seek to understand his conviction that words can become "a crossing point" between ourselves and God. Heschel hoped that readers would achieve communion—with the author, with their own depths, and with the Eternal.

A READING STRATEGY
Empathy with
Critical Awareness

Ashkenazic writers forego clarity for the sake of depth.
The contours of their thoughts are irregular, vague, and
often perplexingly entangled; their content is restless,
animated by inner wrestling and a kind of baroque
emotion.

—Heschel, 1950[1]

Heschel's varied writings seek not only to convince our intellect
but more so to transform our manner of perceiving existence. His
manner of philosophizing is "situational," relevant to the complete person in the world. Rather than establishing a system, he
is (in Richard Rorty's terms) an "edifying philosopher" who
brings readers to new ways of thinking.[2] The path is sometimes
difficult to grasp since his narrative voice can quickly switch
from criticism of commonly accepted categories, to subtle dialectics, to poetic passages that artistically perform the inner life.
Rich imagery collaborates with incisive reasoning in order to
wrench our minds, sometimes quite abruptly, from clichés to
original insights.[3]

Without claiming to present a guide to all of Heschel's books
and essays, we can observe the sweep of his concerns. He applies
the biblical view of humanity and nature in *Man Is Not Alone*, a
general philosophy of religion; in *God in Search of Man*, his Jewish theological masterwork, he focuses particularly on revelation
and observance. These two books constitute what I call his
"apologetics"—not the justification of a fixed system but a program to convert our minds and hearts to God-centered consciousness. Shorter books—*The Earth Is the Lord's*, *The Sabbath*,
and *Man's Quest for God*—examine the inner experiences of Jewish study, prayer, and holy celebrations.

The thinker also faced current events. Heschel lays the foundation for his social activism in *The Prophets*, an expanded transla-

tion of his 1933 doctoral dissertation written in Berlin. Readers daunted by its size (and *God in Search of Man*) may find Heschel's shorter essays of the 1960s to be more accessible. Most of them are collected in *The Insecurity of Freedom*. These writings give substance to media images of Heschel marching side by side with the Rev. Martin Luther King, Jr., in Selma, Alabama, his meeting with Pope Paul VI in Rome during the Second Vatican Council—or newspaper reports of his stirring addresses on Soviet Jewry, race relations, and his opposition to America's war in Vietnam.

Heschel's other books challenge prevailing notions of the absurd. His Stanford University lectures, *Who is Man?*, reinterpret philosophies of anguish and meaninglessness in light of biblical ideals of holiness. His lovesong to Zion, *Israel: An Echo of Eternity*, also ponders the value of religion in a post-Auschwitz era. Yet only in his final work—*A Passion for Truth*—centered on two abrasive dissenters, Søren Kierkegaard and Rabbi Mendl of Kotzk—did Heschel confess his own revulsion at the decay of institutional religion. This book expresses a biting irony more forcefully than Heschel's edifying, "spiritual" works.

How to Read Heschel

Heschel rejects the claim that any rational method or theological system can adequately prove God's reality. Quite the contrary. His philosophical arguments consistently undermine the pride and prejudices of speculation in which intellect seeks to fit God into preestablished concepts. Critics who have disparaged Heschel's "beautiful style" as mere ornament are unjust, and, moreover, they are naive readers of literature. Heschel's mixture of evocation and idea lends body to formulations which might otherwise strike only the surface of the mind.

This composite narrative trains us in a process he calls "depth theology,"[4] insights into a spiritual dimension that precede formulations or belief. Depth theology addresses today's seekers, ethical or spiritually minded, by placing Jewish doctrines and history into a personal context:

> Depth theology seeks to meet the person in moments
> in which the whole person is involved, in moments
> that are affected by all a person feels, thinks, and acts.
> It draws upon that which happens to man in moments
> of confrontation with ultimate reality. It is in such
> moments that decisive insights are born.

The literary stylist prepares us to develop s·ıch convictions, opening intellect and emotion to God's presence. His discourse assumes a universal core within us, what he consider: to be something of God's Holy Spirit (in Hebrew the term is *ruah ha-Kodesh*).[5] Scripture, prayers, and prescribed rituals also contain this power.

Depth theology helps readers develop empathy with the sacred content of religious writings. For example, people who pray with intention (*kavanah*) can project intimate feelings into ordained behavior often desiccated and rendered unconscious by habit. Spirit is also available to those deprived of faith—the majority. Religious language succeeds when diverse individuals achieve a tacit awareness of how God might enter their lives. Literary empathy can allow both doubters and believers to conceive the vital holiness contained in written prayers.

The expressive (or "poetic") aspects of Heschel's rhetoric are meant to nurture these intuitions of the sacred. Ideally, readers would respond personally to his words, appreciating their suggestiveness while analyzing the ideas they outline. Heschel's multilayered discourse seeks to open our minds to our hearts, to reconcile the rational and artistic dimensions of religious life, as it prepares us to meet God directly. In a sense, all readers share the dilemma of those without faith: "When placed before the Bible, the words of which are like dwellings made of rock, we do not know how to find the door."[6]

A theory of poetry is one guide to that door, and true poetic experience the key. His writerly strategies open the door to revelation and we enter a written universe replete with meaning, wonder, anxiety, and devotion. To use another image, his discourse conducts insight, as would an electric wire. This power is available through careful, responsive reading, for his expositions are neither simply factual nor merely edifying.

This is how he summarized his goal: "How does one rise from saying the word *God* to sensing His realness?"[7] Heschel was convinced that religious language can train us to perceive God's presence and inspire people of varying degrees of belief or skepticism. For those unable to share the certainty of his faith, studying his literary style—especially its effects on readers—may bring us closer to those who live in genuine piety.

The First Steps: Close Reading

Since Heschel's rhetoric is essentially pragmatic, it is easy to be either stymied or inspired. Above all, we should read with empathy and imaginative participation while not confusing his different techinques: rational argumentation, theological and philosophical aphorism, esthetic evocation, and spiritual insight.[8] Readers can distinguish between his several modes of discourse and then, consciously and critically, integrate them. Whoever we are, at whatever level of culture or ignorance, we begin with slow, patient reading, savoring the words.[9]

Some of Heschel's writings even reach the level of meditation, beyond their intellectual and ethical program. His style aims to arrest our everyday consciousness. Readers should pay deliberate attention to the choice of words, listening for some of Heschel's muted voices. Its rhythmic and metaphorical power resonates at many levels. Successful readers allow themselves to discover the unexpected (or latent) content of a passage. Holiness emerges as our mind welcomes insights and our heart embraces unexpected emotions.

New readers can begin with his shortest book, *The Earth Is the Lord's*, Heschel's spiritual autobiography. Illustrated with evocative woodcuts and divided into fifteen brief chapters, it serves as an introduction. Specialized terms are defined in footnotes. For example: *Wissenschaft des Judentums* (p. 8: Modern scientific research in Jewish history and literature); Litvaks (p. 22: Lithuanian Jews); *rebbe* (p. 22: The title of a Hasidic leader); *melammed* (p. 80: a teacher of children). No one should fear Jewish illiteracy.

Specifically, *The Earth Is the Lord's* explains his Hasidic ideals of study, prayer, and social responsibility—all of which are encompassed in the ideal of "piety" (in Hebrew, *hasidut*). His theological and ethical system emerges from its pages with limpid simplicity. Our challenge is to experience its wisdom, its familiarity with the sacred, and apply Heschel's ideals to daily life. We learn how to think religiously. From there we can hew paths to the longer, more complex books.

The sequence of chapters cultivates a rediscovery of Jewish spiritual tradition, beginning with the complete title: *The Earth Is the Lord's: The Inner World of the Jew in East Europe*. For many Jews, the allusion to Psalm 24, affirming God's sovereignty and ownership of creation, may be familiar from the Sabbath liturgy. The author then applies the subtitle to his value system: "We gauge culture by the extent to which a whole people, not only individuals, live in accordance with the dictates of an eternal doctrine or strive for spiritual integrity; the extent to which inwardness, compassion, justice and holiness are to be found in the daily life of the masses."[10] That is what the book is about—"spiritual integrity." It speaks not only about history, exterior facts, but more so it illustrates habitual Jewish life enriched with consciousness of the sacred.

We can carefully distinguish between what Heschel is doing and what he is not. Yet some of his oratorical mannerisms may interfere. One of his favorite techniques is to draw antitheses in order to make his point—sometimes within an entire chapter, often in each paragraph, and even within sentences. These dialectics can become monotonous and confusing, even irritating. More importantly, Heschel seems to reject one term in favor of the other. Yet his view is more nuanced than may at first appear. He usually appreciates *both* elements of the antithesis while favoring one.

In the preface to *Earth*, for example, he claims to value "daily life, habits and customs" over the production of books, buildings, and institutions. Heschel exaggerates these oppositions in order to emphasize his defense of inwardness.

The adventure in spiritual poetics begins with a slow, "microreading." Lingering upon the opening of chapter one, "The Sigh" (pp. 13–17), to understand the writer's attention to details, I will split up this paragraph, which introduces his basic antithesis of *time* versus *space*. It begins with an aphorism: "Monuments of bronze live by the grace of the memory of those who gaze at their form, while moments of the soul endure even when banished to the back of the mind."

This sentence balances the material and the spiritual dimensions of life without truly rejecting either. Even the "monuments of bronze" he apparently spurns can "live by the *grace* of those who *gaze* at their form." We feel that he, too, appreciates "*monuments*" just as he treasures, even more, "*moments* of the soul." Antitheses accumulate on the phonic and semantic levels of language. The words I have italicized establish a poetic equilibrium that contradicts his two exclusionary perspectives, paradoxically retaining both viewpoints.

The sentences that follow explain the terse contrast: "Feelings, thoughts, are our own, while possessions are alien and often treacherous to the self. To *be* is more essential than to *have*. Though we deal with *things*, we live in *deeds*." Rising from the stylistic to the intellectual level, the antitheses lead to a formula: "To be is more essential than to have." But we should not stop at the prescription. Now we reflect upon what it means "to be."

The second paragraph repeats and extends these antitheses: "Pagans exalt sacred things, the Prophets extol sacred deeds."

Then he begins to delineate the imponderable inner life of Jewish culture, as he quickly defines his goal to capture its nuances: "The Jews in Eastern Europe lived more in time than in space. It was as if their soul was always on the way, as if the secret of their heart had no affinity with things . . . the subtle shading of a thought, or a fervent gesture, which puts a situation, as it were, in God's quotation marks, is perhaps more suggestive of their essence." Eventually we should be able to imagine—and then experience spontaneously—a human event from God's perspective. We become successful readers when we can feel that "essence" in our guts.

It is both gratifying and frustrating that Heschel's writings— even the large books—lend themselves easily to this sort of "micro-reading"—that is, a word-by-word, sentence-by-sentence, meticulous attention to both form and content. At the very least, we can appreciate the artistic virtuosity of these sentences, their structural equilibrium, their picturesque and harmonious images.

Heschel's style can be esthetically gratifying: his phrases are melodious, his thoughts incisive. Slow reading can become a path to meditation. Durable insights may also form, as aphorisms flower in our memory.

There are pitfalls as well. If we dwell too long on the details, we may lose our track through the forest. That is why philosophically inclined readers complain that Heschel is "just a poet." Clear ideas become engulfed in a mist, as savory as it might be. Strangely, they assume that beautiful writing cannot coexist with critical thought. It would be more accurate to say that Heschel's metaphors enrich the content of his discourse by evoking analogies that speak simultaneously to imagination, senses, and judgment.

A Divine Perspective

Heschel's antitheses in fact broaden into an overview of Jewish cultural history. Chapter 3 of *The Earth Is the Lord's*, "The Two Great Traditions,"[11] compares the accomplishments of medieval Spanish (or Sephardic) Jewry and the later Ashkenazic or East European period: "Sephardic books are like Raphaelesque paintings, Ashkenazic books are like the works of Rembrandt—profound, allusive, and full of hidden meanings. The former favor the harmony of a system, the latter the tension of a dialectic; the former are sustained by a balanced solemnity, the latter by impulsive inspiration. . . . A spasm of feeling, a passionate movement of thought, an explosive enthusiasm, will break through the form."

Although Heschel seems to favor the mysterious gravity of Rembrandt, he admires Raphael's clarity of line. Even readers who do not relish these painters, or hold them in the mind's eye, recognize the opposition. On whichever side we find ourselves, we can surmize the validity of the other approach—although Heschel's own style accumulates "explosive" moments of insight. Implicitly he admits that his own organization is more "passionate" than linear.

As suggested, we can avoid misunderstanding this technique by construing Heschel's antitheses as an attempt to embrace the complexity of religious consciousness. (A tag more useful than "antithesis" would be *amalgam*.) Both poles retain their positive value, so that his apparent downplaying of Sephardic culture, for example, affirms that tradition as well. The contrast of "Sephardic order" versus "Ashkenazic depth" becomes a dynamic model of Jewish cultural pluralism. All in all, Heschel presents a fair and informative survey of intellectual and spiritual history. Experts can object to some of his rapid judgments, but his purpose is to scrutinize today's responsibilities.

Heschel's style teaches religious thinking. Another example: He interprets *pilpul*, intricate debate on Talmudic logic, sometimes judged to be oppressive and frivolous, as evidence of spiritual intensity: "The sense of the transcendent is the heart of culture, the very essence of humanity. A civilization that is devoted exclusively to the utilitarian is at bottom not different from barbarism. The world is sustained by unworldliness."[12]

This antithesis is more nuanced than may at first appear. Heschel does not denigrate "the world"; rather, he refines our conception of what it means to sanctify human life. (The term *unworldliness* alludes in a positive manner to the transcendent Creator as ultimately world affirming.) The author wants us to feel how poor, powerless Jews maintained a priceless spiritual and intellectual focus. We, too, might judge our culture from a divine perspective.

The practical implications converge in the final sentences of a later chapter, expanding limited, institutional self-definitions: "There is a price to be paid by the Jew. He has to be exalted in order to be normal. In order to be a man, he has to be more than a man. To be a people, the Jews have to be more than a people."[13] The word *people* has a double meaning: it is both a sociological and a sacred entity. Jewish ethnicity derives its values from its divine or transcendent origin. We fulfill our peoplehood by placing our acts within "God's quotation marks," as suggested in the opening chapter, "The Sigh."

The obstacles presented by Heschel's rhetoric can thus become opportunities. Close reading should prevent us from being rebuffed by his verbal play. Yet we have every right to question what it means to refer our commitments to "God's quotation marks." We can translate the metaphor: hypothetically, a divine consciousness can harmonize with ours. The Bible, commentaries, the prayerbook—and of course Heschel's own writings—all provide evidence of higher consciousness. Our intuitive grasp of "God's quotation marks" depends upon our habits and the values that shape, both implicitly and systematically, our actions.

Hasidic tradition is a model for today. *The Earth Is the Lord's* features Jewish mysticism as practiced by this eighteenth-century pietistic movement. The two central essays—"Kabbalah" and "Hasidism" (chapters 10–11)—map out his own ethical and metaphysical vision and anticipate his foundational books of religious philosophy, *Man Is Not Alone* and *God in Search of Man*. Slow reading of these two brief chapters should ready us for the fuller elaborations.

All Heschel's works interpret Jewish mysticism as a sacred ethics: "Inspired by the idea that not only is God necessary to man, but that man is also necessary to God, that man's actions are vital to all worlds and affect the course of transcendent events, the Kabbalistic preachers and popular writers sought to imbue all people with the consciousness of the supreme importance of all actions."[14] *The Prophets*, and Heschel's activism of the 1960s, confirm his conviction that God cares what we do. Our choices are of "supreme" consequence.

Ultimately, Heschel's goal was that of the founder of Hasidism. As he states at the very beginning of chapter 11: "Then came Rabbi Israel Baal Shem, in the eighteenth century, and brought heaven down to earth. He and his disciples, the Hasidim, banished melancholy from the soul and uncovered the ineffable delight of being a Jew."[15] Whatever our ability to bring God into our lives, we can strive to recover Heschel's own "ineffable delight of being a Jew."

Prophetic Call

The Earth Is the Lord's is a contemporary book, speaking sympathetically to secular minds. Its two final chapters, however, reverse expectations by attributing the accomplishments of Jewish modernity to its traditional antecedents. "'Guard My Tongue from Evil,'" and "The Untold Story"—consider spiritual and ethical progress as one and the same. His emphasis on inwardness and his belief in divine revelation do not exclude militant action:

> There arose the Enlightenment movement (Haskalah), Zionism, the Halutzim movement, Jewish socialism. How much of self-sacrifice, of love for the people, of Sanctification of the Holy Name are to be found in the modern Jews, in their will to suffer in order to help! The zeal of the pious Jews was transferred to their emancipated sons and grandsons. The fervor and yearning of the Hasidim, the ascetic obstinacy of the Kabbalists, the inexorable logic of the Talmudists, were reincarnated in the supporters of modern Jewish movements. Their belief in new ideals was infused with age-old piety.[16]

Heschel's ideal is pluralistic, not dogmatic—a symbiosis of religious vision and culture. We may recover the sacred kernal of secular Jewish commitments. "Piety" is the essence.

We further nuance his original polemic against material power (or "space") and against peoplehood as pure nationalism (one legitimate conception of Zionism). These contradictions are only apparent, for Heschel never repudiates worldly values completely. He builds upon our esteem for science, philosophy, and the arts. We can, he insists, infuse civilization with holiness, electrify our ethics and politics with prophetic passion.

The closing pages of *The Earth Is the Lord's* ring with alarm as Heschel judges contemporary religion: "We have helped extinguish the light our forefathers have kindled. We have bartered holiness for convenience, loyalty for success, wisdom for information, prayers for sermons, tradition for fashion."[17] These exhortations are bitter medicine, but the preceding chapters establish the standard. Knowledge of Jewish history can bolster our striving for loyalty, moral courage, wisdom, and holiness.

Finally, Heschel announces his (and our) prophetic responsibility. We remember that he delivered the original (1945) version of *The Earth Is the Lord's* in Yiddish at the YIVO conference in New York. As a witness to the Shoah, in which members of his family and several Jewish cultures of Eastern Europe, his own, were destroyed, he felt an almost apocalyptic urge to sanctify American Judaism: "A world has vanished. All that remains is a sanctuary hidden in the realm of spirit. . . . We of this generation are still holding the key—the key to the sanctuary which is also the shelter of our own deserted souls. . . . We are either the last Jews or those who will hand over the entire past to generations to come."[18]

Literary and Theological Insight

Heschel's other books also benefit from a slow reading in which elements of style lead to a broad view. His discourse combines the poetic with the propositional, discursive reasoning with spiritual intuitions, so that our minds may "abide in a state of awe." The texture itself of his "poetry" in prose increases a reader's self-awareness. The expressive particulars appeal to memories and desires with which we reverberate. The meanings, sounds, and images can then seize the initiative and transform the reader's soul.

Eventually we may learn to read religious texts (and Heschel's) with awe—a mode of religious thinking that embraces both the human side and the divine side of perception. At one and the same time, we intuit both God's presence and otherness: "It is the tension of the known and the unknown, of the common and the holy, of the nimble and the ineffable, that fills the moments of our insights."[19] We become an *amalgam* beyond the power of language to express. Our binary oppositions break down or become mixed.

That is why Heschel's longer expositions often revert to imagery, analogy, alliteration, and rhythm at crucial points. Forcing us to think in original ways, this technique probes the experiential foundations of previously unexamined ideas: "The issue at stake will be apprehended only by those who are able to find categories that mix with the unalloyed and to forge the imponderable into unique expression."

This is Heschel's dilemma: Logically speaking, it is impossible to "find categories that mix with the unalloyed," for the unalloyed is, by definition, unadulterated, pure—utterly transcendent. But poetically the task is possible.

Two paragraphs from *Man Is Not Alone* (from a section entitled "The Dawn of Faith") illustrate how the writer fleshes out his conceptual skeleton and plumbs our emotional depths. Prior to the paragraphs in question, the author lifts us "to a plane . . . where [God's] presence may be *defied* but not *denied* [emphasis added], and where, at the end, faith in Him is the only way."[20]

Symmetry organizes our concepts. The rhythm reinforces the subtle melding of antitheses.

Each paragraph consists of two parallel sentences, while the section as a whole works like a prose poem, evoking our sense of wonder within a conceptual framework. The first paragraph depicts the intuition and interprets it in structural terms while the second one reinforces the message with imagery:

> Once our bare soul is exposed to the omnipresence of the ineffable, we cannot bid it cease to shatter us with its urging wonder. It is as if there were only signs and hidden reminders of the one and only true subject, of whom the world is a cryptic object.
>
> Who lit the wonder before our eyes and the wonder of our eyes? Who struck the lightning in the minds and scorched us with an imperative of being overawed by the holy as unquenchable as the sight of the stars?

Dramatic adjectives in the first paragraph make abstractions concrete: our "soul" is *bare*, *exposed* and appears to the mind's eye as a vulnerable naked body. The "ineffable" is *omnipresent* and *shatters* us; its "wonder" is *urging*, endowed with stubborn desire. The second sentence interprets these evocations of the ineffable, beginning with an analogy: "It is *as if there were* [emphasis added] only signs and hidden reminders . . ."; the explanation appears at the end: "the one and only true subject, of whom the world is a cryptic object." Emotions feed back into the categories of subject and object, while the term *cryptic object* suggests the world's spiritual dimension.

The second paragraph translates the code. Echoing the voice from the whirlwind (Job: 38), Heschel anticipates the answer by asking metaphysical questions: "Who lit the wonder before our eyes and the wonder of our eyes?" One single sentence juxtaposes the world's sanctity and the marvel of my very consciousness: "*before* our eyes and *of* our eyes." The world and my eyes witness the same mystery.

The next sentences—"Who lit the wonder . . . ?" and "Who struck the lightning . . . ?"—thrust us beyond the beyond to introduce a personal presence, "Who?" Dramatic verbs make this intuition of divine will feel concrete: God "*struck* the lightning . . . and *scorched* us with an imperative." The abstract philosophical term *imperative* vibrates throughout our bodies while the repeated "*S*" sounds reinforce the impact. Our innate sense of God's concern should burst forth as would a lightning bolt, a traditional image of mental or mystical illumination.[21]

The picture should relate the author's keen wonderment to a secular reader's tangible experience. What is the imperative? The poetic style is calculated to make us feel "overawed by the holy as unquenchable as the sight of the stars." In the realm of logical prose, thirst is unquenchable, not star gazing. This endless thirst, however, is spiritual, not gastric. For the poet—as for many of us—stars are heavenly bodies and cosmic infinity a mystery to be revered.

Heschel's metaphors and analogies excite our unconscious loves and lacks, while, at the same time, they point beyond the merely human to the God side of the verbalized intuition. The energizing tensions of modern religion can be explained by this copresence of contrary ontological contexts: "For to have faith is to abide rationally outside, while spiritually within, the mystery."[22]

The very weave of Heschel's prose recreates the complexity of religious consciousness. His condensed juxtapositions, and even mixture, of reflection and affect lifts into awareness yearnings, moral and spiritual, which might otherwise remain tacit, unconscious—and uninterpreted. His eloquence should nurture the "hunger of the heart" that many consider to be evidence of God's presence within us.[23] The author's certainty derives from his encounters with the sacred while we, thirsting, continue to yearn.

Reading toward Community

Ideally, especially at first, we should read alone, in solitude. One of literature's greatest gifts is to release us, for those magic moments, from our mundane responsibilities. All the more fruitful when reading Heschel. His talent for nuances, and his skillful rendering of the higher reaches of religious thinking, require effort, concentration, and sympathy with his manner of reflection and feeling. Reading in solitude can become a form of meditation, of prayer, bringing consolation.

We might read Heschel as a spiritual discipline, giving a vocabulary to our inchoate inwardness. His lush prose may become devotional reading in its own right. Eventually we may form a friendship with the author's mind and heart. From a monological reading of his words (passive listening) we grow into dialogue or conversation. Then we may seize the initiative and think creatively. Yet a reader of Heschel cannot and should not remain alone.

Discussion of Heschel's writing provides a medium for building community. Just as traditional yeshiva students are paired with a partner (*haver*, friend or comrade), we can benefit from sharing and listening. Students read aloud to each other or to the group in order to grasp, and then highlight, the text's nuances. A "teacher" should not offer an authoritative interpretation. The group can work out its impressions and ideas; then a leader might help synthesize the insights or present an overview. That is how people involved in *havurot* (participatory fellowships or prayer groups) make religion alive.

As a higher goal, reading Heschel might follow the pattern of Jewish worship: a combination of privacy and togetherness. His writings speak first to the individual, in his or her earnest quest for God and for meaning. But Heschel's polyphonic discourse speaks to diverse attitudes. Conversation brings out the fullness of his articulation. The viewpoint is not so restrictive that only one "lesson" can be drawn. Open minds find surprises in his pages, perhaps also a threshold to faith. Reading can become another ritual leading to higher freedom.

THE DIVINE PERSPECTIVE
Learning to Think
Religiously

> Our problem . . . is how to share the certainty of Israel
> that the Bible contains that which God wants us to
> know and to hearken to; how to attain a collective
> sense for the presence of God in the biblical words. In
> this problem lies the dilemma of our fate, and in the
> answer lies the dawn or the doom.
> —Heschel, 1951[1]

As practice, Heschel's narrative aims to imbue readers with intuitions of the holy. As theory, it establishes a systematic scrutiny of the religious mind. Yet the goal of both is pragmatic: "By penetrating the consciousness of the pious man, we may conceive the reality behind it."[2] His analysis of metaphorical language forms the conceptual vocabulary of spiritual insight, since human awareness mediates the Divine. As the reader's distinctions sharpen, self-knowledge may increase, and openness to God.

Given that Heschel scatters his analysis throughout several books, interpreters must gather the strands together and arrange them into some order.[3] His apologetics appeals to our intellectual assent while attempting—in the final stage—to inspire belief and observance. His discourse follows Herbert Fingarette's explanation of the holy teacher: "The mystic's words are like [a psychoanalyst's] therapeutic interventions: they are designed to be effective in producing specific change, not to embody universal truths. The 'pattern' underlying the mystic's words is, in short, pragmatic, not logical."[4]

The key to Heschel's manner of thinking is a *recentering of subjectivity from the person to God*. We would read the Bible, for example, not to learn about Israel's search for the Divine, but rather to gain insight into God's active pursuit of the errant people; the Bible is not human theology but God's anthropology.[5] In fact, Heschel persistently evokes this "recentering to God." That is what makes Heschel "Heschel." We now examine some techniques for sensitizing readers to the holy dimension.

The Dynamics of Theocentric Thinking

System (or theology) is not Heschel's endeavor. He stirs the reader's consciousness by dwelling upon the inner life of piety, of those who live in intimacy with the Divine. His essay, "Depth Theology," asserts his fundamental distinction between theology (or "creed") versus original religious insight: "Theology is like sculpture, depth theology like music. Theology is in the books; depth theology is in the hearts. The former is doctrine, the latter an event. Theologies divide us; depth theology unites us."[6]

Heschel's antitheses, now somewhat familiar, form analogies to various arts. These images may at first cloud his precise analysis. But his focus on religious experience is clear. He carefully and deliberately seeks to lead our consciousness to theocentric thinking.

As a religious philosopher, Heschel submits our reflection on the problem of belief to another "Copernican revolution," extending the epistemological upheaval effected by Immanuel Kant, who turned philosophy on its head. Kant displaced our interpretation of reality from the sensory world to within the mind. By defining the "categories" intrinsic to consciousness, he would explain our perception of, for example, time and space. Heschel first explains how we normally think in anthropocentric terms. A person reflecting on religion is a self—a *subject*—in search of its supreme *object*, God. Then Heschel locates his view of reality *in God's consciousness*.

Depth theology displaces our focus from the human self to God as Subject. Heschel uses his analysis of Hebrew prophetic consciousness to establish a standard for contemporary religious thinking, to penetrate "a divine understanding of a human situation. Prophecy, then, may be described as *exegesis of existence from a divine perspective*" (Heschel's emphasis).[7] To accomplish such prophetic perception he manipulates today's idiom in order to recover "pretheological situations," the encounter of human and divine that precedes interpretation into creeds.

The narrative dialectically contrasts the Bible with Western philosophy. He systematically (and polemically) promotes biblical thinking over its subsequent "Greek" elaborations: "It was not the aspiration of Israel to know the Absolute but to ascertain what He asks of man; to commune with His will rather than with

His essence."[8] Heschel assumes revelation to be continuous and trusts that the Divine still manifests itself: "Man cannot see God, but man can be seen by God. He is not the object of a discovery but the subject of revelation."

By following Heschel's theory and practice of religious thinking, we should eventually experience ourselves as privileged objects of God's concern burdened with fearsome responsibilities. We may even receive God's initiative at the climax of our expedition. The doctrine of revelation, above all, must be "described" by reference to God as Subject.

It is the special power of figurative language to train this new, theocentric consciousness. Words can mediate the human and the sacred dimensions of reality. Heschel insists that "poetry is to religion what analysis is to science, and it is certainly no accident that the Bible was not written *more geometrico* but in the language of poets."[9] Philosophy of religion is the frame, poetry is the flesh and blood of Heschel's apologetics.

On the one hand, as a theologian, he conceptualizes the relationship between human and divine by using spatial analogies, the shift I call the recentering of subjectivity. On the other hand, as a writer, he nurtures religious insights by evoking his own intuitions in artistic passages that echo our loves, anxieties, and yearnings. Literary discourse overcomes the double bind.

Yet the process must surpass esthetics, which appeals only to senses and imagination. Heschel assumes that a metaphysical reality speaks through sacred language, and so worship provides the fullest opportunity. Regular prayer can redirect our consciousness of reality, as he explains in *Quest for God*:

> We do not step out of the world when we pray; we merely see the world in a different setting. The self is not the hub, but the spoke of the revolving wheel. In prayer we shift the center of living from self-consciousness to self-surrender. God is the center toward which all forces tend.
>
> Prayer takes the mind out of the narrowness of self-interest, and enables us to see the world in the mirror of the holy. For when we betake ourselves to the extreme opposite of the ego, we can behold a situation from the aspect of God.[10]

Genuine prayer can effect a shift from the self to God, one that he illustrates by the image of a wheel: God is the hub and my self-awareness is a mere spoke. Such structural descriptions are handy, and their author takes them seriously, but these analogies strike only the surface of the mind.[11] Conversion to religious thinking must combine abstract thought ("geometry") and acute emotion.

A Spiritual Itinerary

How do we integrate concepts and intuitions? Heschel's two expositions of religious philosophy—*Man Is Not Alone* and *God in Search of Man*—develop a strategy to absorb both emotion and value judgments into the path of religious perception. Both books sweep through Western philosophy and Judaic tradition from the author's Kabbalistic perspective. Their opening chapters explore the sense of the ineffable, stimulate a reader's capacity for awe and wonder, and lead us to a subtle awareness of living as objects of God's concern.

Each book begins by analyzing intuitions that comprise "radical amazement," a perception akin to the sublime. Awe and wonder should jar our thinking off the beaten track. The second half of each book reinterprets moral and religious principles in light of this transformed consciousness. At all stages, the author uses poetic devices to insinuate spiritual meanings into his demonstration.

The overall organization of *Man Is Not Alone* typifies the itinerary. Part 1, "The Problem of God," consists of seventeen chapters (pp. 1–176) that depict and analyze phenomenologically the radical conversion to faith. Part 1 establishes the foundation. The first eight chapters prepare readers for divine revelation (which can also be defined as mystical insight). The goal is reached in chapter 9 when Heschel evokes the rediscovery of our metaphysical identity as objects of God's concern. Part 2, "The Problem of Living," consisting of nine longer chapters (pp. 179–296), defines religion and morality from a Jewish perspective—one derived from inner experience as well as from textual traditions—biblical, rabbinic, Hasidic, and mystical. Now having deliberately suppressed the element of suspense, we can return to the beginning and carefully examine the book's rhetorical strategy.

A theory of language explains the interaction of the holy and the mundane. Heschel begins, paradoxically, with what cannot be adequately expressed. Chapter 1, "The Sense of the Ineffable," introduces the incongruity between words and subtle or exceptional experiences. Heschel extends Kant's notion of universal mental categories of space and time to *the ineffable*, which he considers to be an a priori category of consciousness, "as if there were an *imperative*, a compulsion to pay attention to that which lies beyond our grasp."[12]

Here secular and religious impressions cooperate. Creative activity is also inspired, in large part, by awareness of the limits of representation:

> What characterizes man is not only his ability to develop words and symbols, but also his being compelled to draw a distinction between the utterable and the unutterable, to be stunned by that which is but cannot be put into words. . . . The attempt to convey what we see and cannot say is the everlasting theme of mankind's unfinished symphony, a venture in which adequacy is never achieved.[13]

Heschel combines reasoning and metaphor to convince our minds: "mankind's unfinished symphony" names Hayden's familiar work in order to rouse our yearning for the transcendent.

This preliminary definition of the ineffable dimension of experience, completed by the symphonic image, directs our thought toward that which lies beyond words. Heschel then enlarges our ideas about what is real and questions all preconceptions: "Wonder or radical amazement, the state of maladjustment to words and notions, is, therefore, a prerequisite for an authentic awareness of that which is."[14] He wants to convince us that reality embraces more than what we normally know. That is how he fosters the reader's own radical amazement, opening thought to what concepts cannot grasp.

Heschel then makes another conceptual leap. He goes on to endow the Beyond with specific meaning and value: "What we encounter in our perception of the sublime, in our radical amazement, is a spiritual suggestiveness of reality, an *allusiveness* to transcendent meaning."[15] Feelings of reverence provoked by the ineffable demonstrate that such meaning exists.

We summarize the "logical" path followed thus far: (1) the world is perceived as an allusion; (2) specifically, to transcendent meaning; and (3) the content of which is life's preciousness. The author's conclusion is axiomatic, "a *certainty without knowledge*: it is real without being expressible" (Heschel's emphases). The boundary between philosophy and religion has been crossed.

The crucial transition occurs in chapter 5, "Knowledge by Appreciation." There Heschel's discourse becomes less intellectu-

ally incisive and increasingly poetic; reason yields its authority to
emotionally charged analogies. The lush imagery augments feelings of appreciation contained within the "sense of the ineffable." Distinctions between ordinary thinking and religious
insight become clearer as he condenses this phase of the argument in pictures:

> What is extraordinary appears to us as habit, the dawn
> a daily routine of nature. But time and again we awake.
> In the midst of walking in the never-ending procession
> of days and nights, we are suddenly filled with a sol-
> emn terror, with a feeling of our wisdom being inferior
> to dust. We cannot endure the heartbreaking splendor
> of sunsets. Of what avail, then, are opinions, words,
> dogmas? In the confinement of our study rooms, our
> knowledge seems to us a pillar of light. But when we
> stand at the door that opens out to the infinite, we
> realize that all concepts are but glittering motes that
> populate a sunbeam.[16]

This decisive passage demonstrates how Heschel uses poetic
devices to clinch his philosophical argumentations. In an analysis already tinted with emotion, he personifies the normal passage of time as "the never-ending procession of days and nights."
The expression of "wisdom [as] inferior to dust" uses a biblical
image of mortality to make tangible the notion that human
knowledge is frail. The ideas climax suddenly with an outbreak of
"solemn terror."

The dictionary helps unpack this complex insight. Emotions
comprise the substance of this cognition: "terror" is a state of
extreme fear, dread, devastating insecurity; whereas "solemn"
softens the horror with a touch of awe: religious ceremonies are
"solemn." The word *splendid* appears in definitions of "solemn"
and in fact enters in the next sentence: "We cannot endure the
heartbreaking splendor of sunsets." Of course this sentence does
not mean literally what it says; the author does not collapse. The
purpose of this hyperbole, and the glorious image, is to evoke
awe toward unfathomable Creation. Sunrise and sunset no
longer appear as monotonous cyclical processes but recall the
miraculous death and rebirth of existence. The conceptual breakthrough is indeed terrifying because it confronts us with all-sur-
passing mystery.

The poetic dimension of this passage probes the subtle modalities of our inner life and awakens not-yet-conscious insights. This is the chapter of *Man Is Not Alone* in which Heschel insists that "poetry is to religion what analysis is to science."[17] To complete the argument, a contrast between knowledge as "a pillar of light" that becomes "glittering motes that populate a sunbeam" closes the paragraph neatly. The loveliness of these images mitigates the shock of our mind's sudden humiliation.

Radical amazement bridges the chasm between finite concepts and ultimate meaning. The "negative" emotion thus leads to insight. Our consent to the sacred is reinforced by this frightful abandonment of reassuring notions. Admiration, reverence, and awe help us increasingly to appreciate the mystery in which we participate.

Now that he has begun to recast our ego-centered categories, Heschel engages a philosophical polemic: he criticizes the basic notion of a split between subject and object in order definitively to reject that manner of thinking. Our thoughts are again poised by (this time, literally) sharp antitheses:

> Our self-assured mind specializes in producing knives, as if it were a cutlery, and in all its thoughts it flings a blade, cutting the world in two: in a thing and in a self; in an object and in a subject that conceives the object as distinct from itself. A mercenary of our will to power, the mind is trained to assail in order to plunder rather than to commune in order to love.[18]

Heschel dramatizes the banal epistemological fact of a subject that requires an object of consciousness in order to think. Reason appears as a sadistic butcher and the process of concept formation as imperialistic attacks launched to gratify the will to power. Graphic imagery injects value judgments into an otherwise logical demonstration. Yet, the hyperbolic rebuff should not divert us from the positive lesson: communion is a higher form of knowledge.

The person who thinks religiously overcomes the subject/object split. Humility can reconcile us with the universe, so that we might view the self, not as an antagonist but as a member of a cosmic community:

> Where man meets the world, not with the tools he has made but with the soul with which he was born; not

> like a hunter who seeks his prey but like a lover to
> reciprocate love; where man and matter meet as equals
> before the mystery, both made, maintained and des-
> tined to pass away, it is not an object, a thing that is
> given to his sense, but a state of fellowship that
> embraces him and all things.

The cadence of Heschel's flowing, rhythmical sentence reinforces the message. Thinking displaces its focus from objects to a state of being in which an individual feels at harmony with the universe. This turning of the mind firmly distinguishes the hunter pursuing prey from the lover yearning to reciprocate affection freely proffered. Humankind and matter are "equals before the mystery," finite and mortal.

Now authentic religious thinking can begin—when the self leaves the center: "*To* our knowledge the world and the 'I' are two, an object and a subject; but *within* our wonder the world and the 'I' are one in being, in eternity. We become alive to our living in the great fellowship of all beings."[19]

Communion is the penultimate stage of pretheological awareness; we sense our kinship with the visible cosmos and feel its spiritual unity. An unheard-of significance begins to penetrate our consciousness: "Things surrounding us emerge from the triteness with which we have endowed them, and their strangeness opens like a void between them and our mind, a void that no words can fill."

At this delicate stage we turn our observation back upon our own mind and examine the dynamics of thinking itself. Heschel interprets as a religious insight our awareness of the "void"—the breach between consciousness and its contents—described by this scrupulous introspection (or phenomenology). For the discovery of a gap within consciousness can arouse an uncanny feeling for the true incommensurability between mind and reality. (Kant might speak of the discrepancy between "representations" and the "thing-in-itself.") The "strangeness" becomes a sense of estrangement from ordinary, "realistic" perception.

The next stage passes from this intuition of *impersonal* transcendence, beyond our ken, to a *personal God* Who relates to humankind. A specific interpretation enters the space between our sense of the ineffable and the divine message. We delve even more deeply into consciousness. For the "personal" aspect of Deity is but a metaphor of what we can perceive about ourselves.

We have clarified mind's function; now we examine its meaning and origin. Intuitions of estrangement advance our analysis of thought itself: "The self is more than we dream of; it stands, as it were, with its back to the mind. Indeed, to the mind even the mind itself is more enigmatic than a star."[20] Heschel compares consciousness with a star in order to concretize his abstract analogy. The image of an "enigmatic" star appeals to poetic appreciation at least as much as to scientific curiosity; its silence signifies.

Then Heschel makes another conceptual leap by claiming to perceive the divine foundation, a will of which our intelligence is but an echo. What is mystery to us alludes to superior truth. The self's enigma echoes the presence of a higher self, God, the source of human self-consciousness:

> Once we discover that *the self in itself* [my emphasis] is a monstrous deceit, that the self is something transcendent in disguise, we begin to feel the pressure that keeps us down to a mere self. We begin to realize that our normal consciousness is in a state of trance, that what is higher in us is usually suspended. We begin to feel like strangers within our normal consciousness, as if our own will were imposed upon us.[21]

That is how Heschel places a theological insight into the chasm he has made us sense within consciousness. He magnifies the self's imponderability by polarizing two views: that the human ego ("the self in itself") is either a "monstrous deceit" or "something transcendent in disguise." He prepares us to leap out of this antithesis.

At the end of chapter 6, "A Question Beyond Words," Heschel reconciles these two conceptions. He completes the transition from a mode of thinking centered *on* self to one centered on and emanating *from* God. The method involves an almost microsurgical removal of outer layers of his own self-awareness:

> Upon the level of normal consciousness I find myself wrapt in self-consciousness and claim that my acts and states originate in and belong to myself. But in penetrating and exposing the self, I realize that the self did not originate in myself, that the essence of the self is in its being a nonself, that ultimately man is not a subject but an *object*.[22]

The breakthrough is complete.[23] Until chapter 5 of *Not Alone* Heschel the philosopher anatomizes the finite self that asks questions about God; he does this in order to undermine our intellectual pride, deconstruct our self-centered epistemology, and make plausible the idea that God is the origin of human thought—as of Being itself. We can now think about God, and our world of experience, from a biblical perspective.

The decisive step toward certainty occurs in chapter 9, "In the Presence of God."[24] A series of vivid scenes highlights the transition from the emptying of mind to a revelation on God's part to our consciousness. A remarkable passage evokes this ecstatic invasion:

> Apathy turns to splendor unawares. The ineffable has shuddered itself into the soul. It has entered our consciousness like a ray of light passing into a lake. Refraction of that penetrating ray brings about a turning in our mind: We are penetrated by His insight. We cannot think any more as if He were there and we here. He is both there and here. He is not *a being*, but *being in and beyond all beings.*[25]

This quasiprophetic revelation spawns the spiritual awareness Heschel had described in his germinal article, "The Mystical Element in Judaism," which lends authority to his personal ideas through citations from the *Zohar*, the basic text of Jewish mystical tradition. *The Earth Is the Lord's* states the same theology and ethics in his own voice. God is both immanent and transcendent, not a being out there, beyond the world, but Being itself, a dimension of all existence. (For a detailed analysis, see chapter 5, "Mysticism and Despair.")

The Endless Tension

This foundational phase of Heschel's depth theology convinces us of the disparity between our minds and the sacred. We begin to welcome the possibility of God as Subject. The author's eloquence, when read with the sympathetic discernment of religious thinking, gradually becomes alive with God's presence. If readers identify with the implied author, they might begin to revere the world as an object of divine concern.

The poetic elements of Heschel's style energize the contradictions between finite experience clinging to language and the transcendent Reality to which it alludes. Its verbal grace ushers us beyond the beautiful to the holy: "Wonder is not a state of esthetic enjoyment. Endless wonder is endless tension, a situation in which we are shocked at the inadequacy of our awe, at the weakness of our shock, as well as the state of being asked the ultimate question."[26]

Such is the powerful paradox of Heschel's writing about the ineffable. Religious thinking maintains the "endless tension" between spiritual hunger and esthetic gratification. These contradictions allow him to introduce the holy dimension to those bereft of faith. Even religious minds remain, simultaneously, both inside and outside the Mystery sanctifying the world. Our quest for the Absolute—be it a personal God, Presence, or Being—endows reading with an elusive but compelling urgency. Heschel's analysis of the relation of language to divine reality prepares us even more methodically for God's initiative.

LANGUAGE AND REALITY
Toward a
Poetics of Faith

> Praying means to take hold of a word, the end, so to
> speak, of a line that leads to God. The greater the
> power, the higher the ascent in the word. But praying
> also means that the echo of the word falls like a
> plummet into the depth of the soul. The purer the
> readiness, so much the deeper penetrates the word.
> —Heschel, 1954[1]

What I call Heschel's "poetics of piety (or faith)" is a linguistic theory and practice—a rhetorical art in the service of spirit. His analysis of language as metaphor of the ineffable enables readers to interpret traditional texts, and retrieve their sanctity, while his narrative helps readers emulate his own prayerful awareness. Theological and philosophical categories provide points of reference, not the goal.

Heschel's expositions strategically combine abstract categories with imagery and vivid comparisons; he places the viscera back into philosophy and theology. Yet the coherence of his analysis has been insufficiently acknowledged. Not predictable in form, nor exclusively rational in intent, Heschel's writings have suffered from lack of scholarly attention mainly because he does not highlight his conceptual framework. Yet, close scrutiny reveals that his *use* of language follows a consistent *theory* that, dispersed among different works, is explicit and amenable to critical understanding.

Quest for God, God in Search of Man, and *The Prophets* investigate the poetic function of biblical language. "Poetic," in this sense, refers not to formal verse, prose sentences chopped into rhymes and rhythms, but to an imaginative manner of experiencing language. Words (and other signs, symbols, concepts—as Heschel loosely uses these terms) negotiate the frontier between God's will and human categories of discernment; without entering into technical distinctions, he points to the ultimate grounding: "The living encounter with reality takes place on a level that precedes conceptualization, on a level that is responsive, *immediate, pre-conceptual*, and *presymbolic*" (Heschel's emphasis).[2]

Against Fundamentalisms

Faulting dogmatic religion, Heschel defends God's ultimate reality. Yet he does not advance one single interpretation of the Sinai revelation and its rabbinic codification. He rejects ideology, from the monovocal interpretation of Torah and law by some Orthodox authorities to secular, "scientific" views of Scripture as a purely historical document, grasped through philology. His depth theology is more compatible with Conservative, Reform, and Reconstructionist developments, since he recognizes the ambiguous character of language. At the same time, he firmly refuses to reduce transcendent (or "ineffable") Reality to secular notions. Heschel himself stands "both outside and within" each community.

His most elemental assumption: we cannot read the Bible as *simple* fact; testimonies of divine communication require linguistic interpretation:

> The surest way of misunderstanding revelation is to take it literally, to imagine that God spoke to the prophet on a long-distance telephone. Yet most of us succumb to such fancy, forgetting that the cardinal sin in thinking about ultimate issues is *literal mindedness*. The error of literal mindedness is in assuming that things and words have only one meaning.[3]

Heschel does not construe the Bible as a flat description of events, but he will justify the validity of divine revelation. He insists that the prophets used figurative discourse to convey their essentially ineffable encounters with God.

With a characteristic play on words, Heschel describes biblical accounts as not less but *more than literally true*: "The prophets bear witness to an event. The event is divine, but the formulation is done by the individual prophet. According to this conception, the idea is revealed; the expression is coined by the prophet."[4] The words of Scripture are thus *not* "coextensive and identical with the words of God."[5] Their words mix the divine and the human as does the meeting that produced them: "Yet who shall presume to be an expert in discerning what is divine and what is but 'a little lower' than divine? . . . The spirit of God is set in the language of man, and who shall judge what is content and what is frame?"[6]

Literary hermeneutics subverts any sort of fundamentalism that allows an authority (a person or a committee) to define the word of God. *God in Search of Man* argues for the plausibility of supernatural revelation, while, at the same time, defending a relative freedom of interpretation:

> The savants are heirs to the prophets; they determine and interpret the meaning of the word. There is much liberty and much power in the insights of the sages: they have the power to set aside a precept of the Torah when conditions require it. Here on earth, their opinion may overrule an opinion held in heaven.[7]

Analysis of biblical language trains us to read religiously, allowing us access to Holy Spirit (in Hebrew the term is *ruah ha-Kodesh*), or God's continuing revelation. Heschel's manner of analyzing prophetic discourse balances human autonomy and submission to God's will.

Understanding metaphorical language prevents us from yielding to either extreme—orthodox or liberal. Given the necessarily inexpressible essence of the Divine, it would be absurd—indeed, idolatrous from the theological standpoint—to identify the "content" of a figure of speech with God's essence: "The word is the word of God, and its understanding He gave unto man. The source of the authority is not the word as given in the text but Israel's understanding of the text. At Sinai we received both the word and the spirit to understand the word."[8]

Ultimately, Heschel pushes readers beyond words to the Spirit within us that potentially understands. The very tension between what language can and cannot convey is the generative force of study, prayer, and insight: "The sense for the power of words and the sense for the impotence of human expression are equally characteristic of the religious consciousness."[9] The irreconcilable polarity of religious words, if perceived, subverts habitual patterns while it nurtures the bud of transcendent awareness.

The Limits of Language

Both the believer and the person without faith can meet at the gates of poetic empathy with religious language. That is why

Heschel first stresses God's transcendence in relation to rational categories. We should distrust the mirage of verbal adequacy. He trains us to depreciate "symbolic knowledge"—the substitution of words or concepts for reality—because it represents "an act of accommodation to the human mind."[10] Self-critical awareness of language as such is the premise.

Developing an analogy between concepts and images, he seeks to void religious language of its subordination to pictures. Words must not become icons of ineffable ideas: "Few of us are able to think in a way which is never crossed by the path of imagination, and it is usually at the crossroads of thought and imagination that the great sweep of the spirit swerves into the blind alley of a parabolic image."[11] Thinking literally may become idol worship.

Heschel attacks linguistic positivism that apprehends language as a sufficient expression of the clearly known. His real rival is dogma, since formulations of belief may disguise or obscure a concrete insight into God: "[The theoretician] does not seem to realize that idolization of ideas leads to an atrophy of the intuition of the ineffable; that God may be lost in our creed, in our worship, in our dogmas."[12] Depth theology subordinates formulas to the transcendent reality to which they allude.

The seeker should strive for nothing less than an actual relation to the living God: "There is hardly a symbol which, when used, would not impair or even undo the grasp or remembrance of the incomparable. Opinions confuse and stand in the way of intuitions; surveys, definitions take the name of God in vain. We have neither an image nor a definition of God. We have only His name. And the name is ineffable."[13] Mixing linguistic and sociological terms, Heschel warns institutional Judaism about substituting opinion polls for experiential self-definition and self-discovery.

Heschel's assault on concepts and imagery, verbal and graphic, does not, however, lead to an absolute refusal to communicate. His target is a naive apprehension of words as substitutes for direct verification of reality, natural or divine. In today's parlance, Heschel "deconstructs" the referential function of language. (This is not in itself a radical position. After all, who today would insist that words are identical with the reality or object they signify?) We cannot claim to know the Transcendent just because our words say so.

Given the deficiencies of religious discourse, then, one can adopt two basic attitudes. The most radical and uncompromising one is the *via negativa*, a refusal to render even a hint of the inef-

fable. Heschel appreciates this austere standard: "Silence is pref-
erable to speech. Words are not indispensable to cognition. They
are only necessary when we wish to communicate our ideas to
others or to prove to them that we have attained cognition."[14]
Silence, though metaphysically pure, does not allow for sharing.
Making mystery our rule would annul the community of verbal
communion and all religious literature. Some compromise must
be made with the Absolute in order to preserve culture—and Jewish tradition.

That is why Heschel does not shun conceptualization entirely.
Theology is a static point of reference, it is true, but it allows us
to interpret our intuitions: "creed is but the adaptation of the
uncommon spirit to the common mind. Our creed is, like music,
a translation of the unutterable into a form of expression. The
original is known to God alone."[15] The category of the "ineffable" stresses the God side, not the world side, of the event. Its
music remains.

His technique embraces a contradiction: he electrifies concepts
frozen by ideologies, using them to surpass themselves. This is
how he summarizes the fertile paradox: "It is precisely the challenge involved in using inadequate words that drives the mind
beyond all words."[16]

Poetic discourse is Heschel's solution to this logical bind, for it
can preserve the social cohesion of a common tongue while
exploiting the fluid relation of words to reality. At the borders of
speech we open ourselves to the positive value of silence: "To
become aware of the ineffable is to part company with words.
The essence, the tangent curve of human experience, lies beyond the limits of language."[17] Literary reading, through its
complexity, its music, its suggestiveness, points to a fuller realm
of being.

Heschel thus commits himself to a second approach to the
word's limits: a struggle to communicate the ineffable—the result
of an inward, individual encounter—in linguistic terms shared by
society. That is why his writings mix conceptual reflection with
evocative prose, with the express purpose of surpassing creeds or
systematic theology:

> Philosophy of religion must be an effort to recall and
> to keep alive *the metasymbolic relevance of religious
> terms*. Religious thinking is in perpetual danger of giv-
> ing primacy to concepts and dogmas and to forfeit the
> immediacy of insights, to forget that the known is but

> a reminder of God, that the dogma is a token of His
> will, the expression the inexpressible at its minimum.
> Concepts, words must not become screens; they must
> be regarded as windows.[18]

The religious thinker who enjoys insight and wants to communicate it must use conventional terms, with all their dogmatic connotations. Heschel's depth theology should actualize their nonsymbolic content. Its idiom is poetic discourse that can tangibly evoke that which surpasses all thoughts. A community can share its music and its meaning.

Windows to the Spirit

To summarize: ordinary denotative language tends to remove us from original insights; its function is to signify (represent) only the known aspects of reality. The successful denotative word is unequivocal and specific. Heschel firmly opposes an exclusively literal interpretation of the Bible, that is, when "literal" means to construe biblical images in a nonfigurative and precise sense.

Does this mean, however, that such statements are not to be taken seriously, that they have no "meaningful positive content"?[19] If this phrase means scientifically or systematically verifiable, then no, for that would require us to test the Bible from our secure human perspective. Heschel's poetic frame of reference rouses our audacity, requires intellectual flexibility and initiative, before religious thinking becomes possible.

Readers can develop literary tact, not limited to the prose of journalistic descriptions. To begin, we enter a world created by poetry. Its words are most often ambiguous, polysemantic, multivalent, and function through hints. Poetry is the most legitimate means of expressing religious insights:

> To intercept the allusions that are submerged in perceptibilities, the interstitial values that never rise to the surface, the indefinable dimension of all existence, is the venture of true poetry. That is why poetry is to religion what analysis is to science, and it is certainly no accident that the Bible was not written *more geometrico* but in the language of poets.[20]

Poetry can evoke realities that may not conform to expectations. Art and literature might even lead secular readers to infer how holy words are links between human awareness and God. In the right context, esthetics can prepare authentic metaphysical cognition.

There is a truth of poetry—not only a "poetic truth" (that is, a validity confined to the poem, the fantasy). Authentic poetry appears to be self-validating, defining its own standards: "When a great poet appears, he does not offer proof of his being a poet. His poetry speaks for itself, creating in us the power to appreciate its novel and exceptional vision of life at the price of abandoning established conceptions."[21] In general, artistic vision is a form of knowledge, an imaginative pledge to life transformed: "Great works produce rather than satisfy needs by giving the world fresh craving."[22]

Receptivity to the power of words involves above all respect for their autonomy. Heschel develops an analogy with moral discernment to illustrate the depths of language, suggesting that linguistic and human delicacy are connected:

> Yet to say that words are nothing but mental beasts of burden [that is, denotative signs] would be the same as to see in the person who carries our luggage to the train nothing but a porter. The essence of a person is not in carrying luggage, and the essence of the word is not in its being a sign. Let us distinguish between substance and function, between the essential nature of a word and its function, the mode in which it is used by us.[23]

Words have independent dignity and power. It is our responsibility to actualize their complexity. Poetry is especially resonant because its words can be polysemantic, expressing simultaneously several levels of meaning and value.

Using simple terms, Heschel starts to analyze the structure and function of metaphoric statements. To distinguish sharply between a literal, one-dimensional apprehension of words and a literary appreciation of their suggestibility, he defines *descriptive* and *indicative* words. As always, his linguistic concepts imply a manner of experiencing reality:

> *Descriptive* words . . . stand in a fixed relation to conventional and definite meanings, such as the concrete nouns, chair, table, or the terms of science; and *indicative* words . . . stand in a fluid relation to ineffable meanings and, instead of describing, merely intimate some-

thing that we can intuit but cannot fully comprehend. The content of words such as God, time, beauty, eternity cannot be faithfully imagined or reproduced in our minds. Still they convey a wealth of meaning to our sense of the ineffable. [Indicative words] call forth . . . not so much a memory, but a *response*, ideas unheard of, meanings not fully realized before.[24]

Both descriptive (or denotative) words and indicative words have "content" and "meaning." Though the level of apprehension is different, they are no less real within their own mode of experience. Yet the reader is more responsible for actualizing the content of indicative words: "The word is but a clue; the real burden of understanding is upon the mind and soul of the reader."

We read the Bible responsively. For example, the meaning of the assertion "God's word came to me" depends upon the reader's intelligence, skill, and flexibility. Religious statements require us to recognize their literary range: "It is only in similies that we can communicate when speaking of the ultimate."[25]

Empathy underlies a truly literary reading. By projecting our emotions into the words, readers actualize the text's semantic richness and, reciprocally, their own inner life. Such participatory reading can become ontologically validating:

What we encounter is the word itself, its unique intensity, the complex of meanings that surround it and that exist far beyond its dictionary meaning, of its strict relation to the object of which it is a sign. A word is a focus, a point at which meanings meet and from which meanings seem to proceed. In prayer, as in poetry, we turn to the words, not to use them as signs for things, but to see things in the light of the words.[26]

Prayer is, for Heschel, the fullest realization of poetic "reading," and it includes several phases of development. Prayer may begin as an act of empathy, as does poetry, identification with the content of a printed text. A self-aware worshipper, one who senses the richness of "indicative" words, can transform canonized routines into an original touch of the holy: "It is through our reading and feeling the words of the prayers, through the imaginative projection of our consciousness into the meaning of the words, and through empathy for the ideas with which the words are pregnant, that this type of prayer comes to pass."[27]

The next phase involves a crucial distinction. Worship surpasses imagination; Heschel avers that a metaphysical process actualizes an immanent force: "It is the spiritual power of the praying man that makes manifest what is dormant in the text. The character of the act of prayer depends on the reciprocal relation between the person and the word."[28] This contact is the consequence of Heschel's strategy to help readers confirm—in their minds and souls—his conviction that "words of prayer are repositories of the spirit."[29]

The Perspective of the Faithless

Heschel's poetics of faith accepts this challenge: "How does one rise from saying the word *God* to sensing His realness?"[30] Linguistic sensitivity can educate our ability to read poetically and mediate the contradictions of resistance, doubt, yearning, and trust. Even those without religious education may learn to converse with liturgical words by appreciating metaphorical suggestiveness. Regular prayer might help even those of skeptical disposition to enter a holy atmosphere.

Semantic paradox is the key, since religious declarations possess both positive and negative valences: "[A]ssertions that intend to convey the essence of reality or the aspect of mystery and grandeur are always understatements."[31] This "language of presence" evokes simultaneously two ontologically distinct dimensions: a reality surpassing human thought and an image of sublime value in a figure of speech. Hyperbole becomes litote.

Anthropomorphism is but one pole of the dialectic. By their very inadequacy, words that appear to "describe" God also elicit a sense of transcendence in relation to the known: "when taken to be allusions rather than descriptions, understatements rather than adequate accounts, they are aids in evoking our sense of His realness."[32]

The key, I repeat, to understanding how religious language expands consciousness is this paradoxical impression. Prayer is polar-valent, conveying simultaneously a (negative) sense of human limits and the (positive) richness of poetry. In prayer one realizes most acutely the outer limits of language:

> In no other act does man experience so often the disparity between the desire for expression and the means of expression as in prayer. . . . What the word can no longer yield, man achieves through the fullness of his

powerlessness. The deeper the need in which one is placed through this powerlessness, the more does man reveal himself in his essence, and himself becomes expression. Prayer is more than communication, and man more than the word.[33]

The paradoxical term "fullness of [human] powerlessness" expresses, in a concise, antithetical, poetic mode, an intuition, through words themselves, of the relationship between divine and human. On the one hand, language is powerless to communicate with the transcendent God; the very feebleness of our "means of expression" conveys God's unutterable grandeur. On the other hand—and herein lies the hope that poetic experience bestows upon the seeker—by this awareness of absolute disparity, we achieve a "fullness," a more forceful longing for the Absolute.

The seeker is full as he or she awakens to a sense of God's remote presence. True prayer unveils our "essence" and so "[we become] expression" by actualizing within our inner life the spiritual connections dormant in the printed text. Language perceived in this manner confirms the ineffable as a valid intuition of the Divine within human consciousness.

Furthermore, according to Heschel, prayerful insight, by its very intensity, actually participates in God's immanence. A metaphysical process has transpired: "It is the ineffable in us which reaches God rather than the expressed feeling. The unutterable surplus of what we feel, the sentiments that we are unable to put into words are our payment in kind to God."[34] Heschel uses the term *ineffable*—a concept erected in response to God's absolute grandeur—as a metaphor to evoke the Divine. The powerlessness of language, when pushed to its limits, becomes a plenitude of sensing the Beyond of human possibility.

Now we understand how Heschel's linguistic theory bridges the abyss that separates our mind from God. The categories of his depth theology have a double function: they pinpoint the limitations of dogma while helping us to surpass imagination: "in moments of insight the ineffable is a metaphor in a forgotten mother tongue."[35]

Heschel has thus explained theoretically, and demonstrated phenomenologically, how his much maligned concept of the "ineffable" actually works. (By now our analysis of poetry has superseded the naive or disingenuous view, viz., "If it is ineffable, why does he write so much about it?") The "ineffable" conveys a confined perspective, here perceived as contact with an outward form of (formless) God; "ineffable" is itself a metaphor of divine reality in an artistic idiom. The "forgotten mother tongue" is perhaps our awareness of having been created in God's image, the Edenic rapport with the Creator.

The positive aspect of the "ineffable," then, is its semantic function as a sort of negative attribute of God. Theocentrically understood, mystery "is not a *synonym for the unknown* but rather a name for a *meaning which stands in relation to God*" (Heschel's emphasis). [36] Recentering the origin of the substance "ineffable" from the human to the divine, Heschel shows structurally how a negative category can express positive meaning. Semantically blank, "ineffable" affirms God's presence through its indicative, poetic power. Confronting language's limits prepares us to think about "the meaning beyond the mystery."

In the final analysis, prayer becomes relevant when we can redirect our manner of apprehending its testimony: "Not the words we utter, the service of the lips, but the way in which the devotion of the heart corresponds to what the words contain, the consciousness of speaking under His eyes, is the pith of prayer."[37] According to a poetic reading of this statement, the expression "under His eyes" is not a literal, anthropomorphic description of God, but a mere hint, in figurative language, used to suggest the unutterable impression of living as an object of God's scrutiny.

The Structure of Biblical Metaphor

Heschel's mystical conviction that "the Bible is *holiness in words*" deserves further technical analysis. The analogy he uses to assert that God has spoken to us provides a model: "it is as if God took these Hebrew words and breathed into them of His power, and the words became a live wire charged with His spirit. To this very day they are hyphens between heaven and earth."[38] Language as "hyphen" between human and divine implies a formal connection between the two. An intuition of God's presence fulfills that contact.

Another analogy, a musical one. For Heschel, a poetic manner of reading can unlock the Bible as a source of truth: "We cannot sense [God's] presence in the Bible except by being responsive to it. Only living with its words, only sympathy with its pathos, will open our ear to its voice. Biblical words are like musical signs of a divine harmony which only the finest chords of the soul can utter."[39] The analogy "musical signs of a divine harmony" suggests the inner assent required by religious language, while emphasizing an intuitive, preconceptual, and nonverbal mode of perception.

Religious language, like music, can be analyzed. After all, the Bible is composed of linguistic signs—with a transcendent, or divine, referent. Passing from a theological to a structural approach, we now examine the two poles of religious discourse, its "natural" and "spiritual" contexts of meaning.

The structure of metaphor can help explain how language may link a person and God.[40] The metaphor is a concrete image that alludes to another reality, based upon some analogy between the two terms. The "vehicle" of the metaphor is the term (or image) that appears in the text, alluding to the "tenor," the absent reality or concept. Metaphor may be used to express something less known, abstract, or even unknown, by something more familiar: for example, "A mighty fortress is our God." A fortress alludes to one particular aspect of the Deity, seen from a definitely human perspective. The common quality that enables the metaphorical equation or comparison is the "ground" of the metaphor, here God's strength and stability.

Heschel depicts the "ground" of the biblical metaphor as a "hyphen between heaven and earth," since it hints to what is ultimately real. The vehicle and tenor themselves remain incomplete representations of their referents, for they must emphasize, in order to intensify them, only certain characteristics. In this sense as well, Heschel avers that religious assertion functions as *understatement*, for the vehicle of language can never completely express the divine tenor.

Heschel's approach resolves the thorny problem of biblical anthropomorphism—ascribing human characteristics to a Being whose essence transcends language and thought. A linguistically prepared reader can experience biblical narrative in its polar structure "which of necessity combines otherness and likeness, uniqueness and comparability, in speaking about God."[41] Because of this, all so-called descriptions of God are necessarily metaphorical, for the vehicle can never render the tenor accurately and positively. Furthermore, "otherness and likeness" are inseparable.

What happens, then, when God is "described" in human terms? Heschel's terminology helps liberate the nonanthropomorphic content of spiritual witness. He explains the theology of divine pathos, God's emotional concern for humankind—Heschel's own axiomatic idea—as understatement rather than hyperbole:[42] "The statements about [God's] pathos are not a compromise—ways of accommodating higher meanings to the lower level of human understanding. They are rather the accommodation of words to higher meanings. Words of psychological denotations are endowed with a theological connotation."[43] The use of anthropomorphic *expressions* does not itself demonstrate a belief in anthropomorphic *conceptions* of God.

It must be stressed that the metaphoric character of biblical language does *not* preclude authoritative religious insight. On the contrary, linguistic awareness should bring us closer. Reflecting on God's "emotions" as described in the Bible, Heschel severs the human analogy from the transcendent source: "Pathos is a thought that bears a resemblance to an aspect of divine reality as related to the world of man. As a theological category, it is a genuine insight into God's relatedness to man, rather than a projection of human traits into divinity, as found for example in the god images of mythology." The terms *resemblance* and *relatedness* refer to the ground of the metaphor, the quality shared by two disparate domains.

The "accommodation of words to higher meanings" involves an act of surpassing ordinary categories of thought and experience. The religious dimension cannot conform to our concepts; language as such is not metaphysically valid. Rather we read the prophet's evocative sympathy in light of the ultimate: "In the biblical expressions of divine emotions . . . the religious consciousness experiences a sense of superhuman power rather than a conception of resemblance to man." Theocentric thinking reverses our finite categories.

Knowing that a metaphor must choose only particular aspects of a reality in its analogy, we internalize its paradoxical dynamics. For religious assertions convey their own inadequacy with regard to God as such while, simultaneously, disclosing an aspect of God that a person might comprehend. Structurally speaking, a person relates to God as does the metaphorical vehicle to its tenor: both can touch only part of a reality from which they are, in essence, different. Language is a transitional object for the seeker of divine confirmation. All religious affirmation is metonymy.

Applying his theory of poetry, Heschel insists upon the uniqueness of prophetic inspiration. *The Prophets* (1962) maintains this view first developed in his 1933 dissertation. He traces a history of theories of poetic vision and locates its origins in the person: "Structurally, the experience may be described as an *object-object relationship*. Out of such inspiration, mysterious and overwhelming as it may be, no poet can derive the power of prefacing his words with the statement: 'Thus says the Lord.'"[44] Subjective in function, "poetic inspiration, though of great importance for the understanding of the poet's consciousness and the secret of creativity, is of no intrinsic significance for the evaluation of the [artistic] work itself." The poem, while it may transform our construction of reality, does not make an ontological claim other than the genesis of a work of art.

Prophetic inspiration, quite the contrary, originates in God's will. The prophet's words point beyond the human to a supernatural act: "In prophetic inspiration . . . the knowledge and presence of Him who imparts the message is the central, staggering fact of awareness. There is a certainty of having experienced the impingement of a personal Being, of another I. . . . Structurally, it may be described as a *subject-subject relationship.*" Using theocentric thinking, we can describe the significance of such inspiration as displaced from the human ego to the objectively transcendent made immanent by God's address to the person. Modifying Martin Buber's model, Heschel surpasses "dialogue" since it may appear to hand the initiative to the person. For Heschel, the divine tenor (God's "I"), not the vehicle, establishes its ultimate value.

The divine component of biblical metaphor is thus its only metaphysically "true" content. Language that refers to God is but a crude allusion to sacred reality. Heschel formulates the theocentric understanding of the ubiquitous biblical phrase "God spoke" in this way: "*what is literally true to us is a metaphor compared with what is metaphysically real to God*" (Heschel's emphasis).[45] This is another way of asserting the tenor's stability while affirming the contingent quality of the human vehicle. Heschel's theory of biblical assertions clarifies the structure of reality itself, so that our web of words can grasp the Transcendent.

Three Dimensions of Human Fullness

Heschel adds a third term—the world—to his linguistic *polarity* of human and divine. These theologically distinct dimensions are in fact *mixed*, though they can be analyzed structurally and sorted by binary categories. Heschel describes a sacred life as three dimensional; "every act can be evaluated by two coordinate axes, the abscissa is man, the ordinate is God. Whatever man does to man, he also does to God. To those who are attentive to Him who is beyond the ineffable, God's relation to the world is an actuality."[46] These geometrical analogies explain that people communicate with each other on the horizontal axis (the abscissa) while God functions vertically (the ordinate), intersecting human awareness at points of insight.

Ordinary language (or humanistic religion) is horizontal, pointing only to concrete objects in the world. By characterizing religious assertions as understatements, Heschel emphasizes what lies beyond words by displacing his emphasis from the negativity of language to its ultimate God side: "The speech of God is not less but more than literally real."[47] The presence of a sacred intuition in a word takes our consciousness to the vertical axis where the material meets the spiritual, the visible the invisible. Biblical language is that privileged *"meeting place."*[48]

Heschel's theory of language strives thus (1) to sensitize us to the disparity between human expression and God's reality—humbling thought and making theology more flexible, (2) and to specify the nature of our divine essence so that human beings will imitate God. Heschel's assault on symbolism—explored in chapter 6—applies this warning against reducing religion to esthetics: "The soul of the religious man lives in the depth of certainty: This is what God wants me to do. Where that certainty is dead, the most powerful symbolism will be futile."[49] The literal minded are condemned to worshipping their own projective portraits of divinity. Heschel's conversion of our consciousness should establish such "certainty"—about basic ethical, intellectual, and theological values.

This formula summarizes his standard of religious authenticity: "The self, the fellow man and the dimension of the holy are the *three* dimensions of a mature human concern. True love of man is clandestine love of God."[50] Mystical inwardness and prophetic action remain inseparable in "piety," religious living. All three dimensions are actualized: concern for the self and for the human family—both grounded upon, and ultimately derived from, God's unending question to us. But first, we face the most radical of challenges: the delicate threshold between mysticism and despair.

 V

MYSTICISM AND DESPAIR
The Threshold
of Revelation

We must first peer into the darkness, feel strangled and
entombed in the hopelessness of living without God,
before we are ready to feel the presence of His living light.
—Heschel, 1955[1]

Heschel's vision of human existence is both realistic and rever-
ent. His two foundational works, *Man Is Not Alone* and *God in
Search of Man*, respond to agnosticism, atheism, free thinking—or
secularized religion—with the witness of certainty and dynamic
faith. He interprets twentieth-century alienation as humanity's
anxiety without God, and so his narratives answer radical doubt
with an equally radical challenge: that of mystical experience,
direct confirmation of the Divine. This prophetic "passion for
truth" (the title of Heschel's final book) repudiates unreflective
cynicism and disbelief.

Heschel's blueprint for modern theology, his essay "The Mystical Element in Judaism," interprets the *Zohar*, the basic text of
Jewish mysticism, as a vision both inward and active.[2] Ultimately,
he seeks to awaken within readers "a yearning after the unattain-
able, [a need] to grasp with the senses what is hidden from the
mind [and] to experience as a reality what vaguely dawns in intuitions."[3] *Man Is Not Alone* completes his depth theology by defining the human condition—its needs, aspirations, and responsibilities—in a manner compatible with God's presence. The final
chapter, "The Pious Man," is a portrait of his model, "a mediator
who administers his life in the name of God." Heschel himself, as
American author, had become a contemporary zaddik and guide.

Out of the Darkness

Heschel's challenge to alienation reflects Blaise Pascal's condem-
nation of seventeenth-century France when people "diverted"

themselves in order to evade thinking about their frailty or "misery." Both Heschel and Pascal repudiate the rationalizations, psychological avoidances—and complacency—that weaken spiritual and moral courage. Before the Divine can enter our awareness, we must relinquish our pride.

Both apologists are expert rhetoricians who magnify human vulnerability. They understand that openness to God requires a relative emptying of the ego. Their critical analysis first undermines wish-fulfilling illusions. Like Pascal, Heschel casts us adrift. The meeting with God at its culmination begins with a sense of meaninglessness, leading to a productive dread (in Kierkegaard's terms, "fear and trembling").

As explained in chapter 2, "Reading Strategy," the apologist's discourse is pragmatic. Heschel and Pascal engage in logical argumentation in order to destroy shallow certainties and unquestioned ideas. We pay a stiff price for our mental armor and vanity. True—and this issue must be scrutinized in detail—Heschel's dialectics often appear incomplete and, at best, unconvincing by normal philosophical standards.[4] His critics consider that to be his obvious weakness. But depth theology can only prepare reason to surrender so that God may become manifest to our minds.

Again, Heschel strategically exploits a fecund paradox: readers must risk losing language itself, the most elementary of intellectual necessities. Words and theories are annulled. Yet he trusts that ultimate meaning appears beyond absurdity and despair. As an advanced stage of depth theology, destruction of concepts uncovers the positive side of nothingness:

> Only those who have gone through days on which words were of no avail, on which the most brilliant theories jarred the ear like mere slang; only those who have experienced ultimate not-knowing, the voicelessness of a soul struck by wonder, total muteness, are able to enter the meaning of God, a meaning greater than the mind.[5]

Rhetoric makes these abstractions concrete: the alliterations and rhythmic fullness of this long, powerful sentence articulate anxieties—and our tacit faith. For Heschel, even "ultimate not-knowing" and "total muteness" can lead to a "voiceless wonder," a mental letting go in which the Divine becomes available. Such terror is indeed solemn: it vibrates with an awesome transcendent presence.

Heschel's acknowledgment of risk is frighteningly clear: "We must first peer through the darkness, feel strangled and entombed in the hopelessness of living without God, before we are ready to feel the presence of His living light."[6] In this way Heschel dispels two complementary types of resistance to faith: dogmatic skepticism or dogmatic belief. In either case, we use the mind to surpass the mind.

This limit-experience is potentially universal. Mystics, atheists, or agnostics may experience utter darkness.[7] Nothing is more real, nor unfortunately more accessible to most people. The absence of God became an experience of Jewish history when Hitler's soldiers and bureaucrats annihilated six million Jewish individuals, destroying a European civilization over a thousand years old. When we gain the courage to embrace our own fragility, we might reach this nadir of the isolated soul—abandoned or misunderstood by loved ones, debased in our own eyes, hopeless, and alone.

Heschel is a critical thinker who probes our anguish, redefines it, and forges it into an instrument of redemption. *Man Is Not Alone* and *God in Search of Man* embark on a philosophical housecleaning procedure. At its outer limit stands a paralysis of belief and disbelief, the mind void of certainty, the self of any personal power. Even those who do not expect God to answer, if openminded, may engage his conviction that God is available. He faces readers with the horrifying possibility of a deathlike state of the soul.

Heschel's narrative will then push genuine anguish to the threshold of mystical piety. On the other side is theocentric thinking, which releases our essence as a cryptic image of God from the categories that had imprisoned or overshadowed it. As we yield our stubborn ideas we may conceive—through mind and action—the world's sacred dimension.

Recasting Mental Habits

Depth theology, first and foremost, derives its potency from the notion of *radical amazement*, a perception akin to the sublime: "Wonder or radical amazement is the chief characteristic of the religious man's attitude toward history and nature."[8] Amazement takes nothing for granted: being itself, the very fact of my existence, is unbelievable.[9] Radical amazement is a form of thinking with which we apprehend the world as an allusion to its deeper, spiritual significance.

Secular and religious awareness can meet at the gates of radical amazement, and from there they begin a spiritual odyssey. "Amazement" (or wonder) is a cognitive variant of awe, freeing us from ordinary assumptions about reality. As Heschel interprets it phenomenologically, "wonder" is a pristine intuition of the sacred mystery of existence. "Mystery" leads to the discovery of ultimate meaning, of God's presence beyond the obscure enigma of the world.

Both *Man Is Not Alone* and *God in Search of Man* systematically compare radical amazement with its opposite, philosophical doubt. This contrast segregates two parallel directions of the mind: "doubt" is concerned with self and its beliefs, while "wonder" focuses upon what is greater than the individual:

> There is no word in biblical Hebrew for doubt; there are many expressions of wonder. Just as in dealing with judgments our starting point is doubt, wonder is the biblical starting point in facing reality. . . . Doubt is an act in which the mind inspects its own ideas; wonder is an act in which the mind confronts the universe. Radical skepticism is the outgrowth of subtle conceit and self-reliance. Yet there was no conceit in the prophets and no self-reliance in the Psalmist.[10]

Heschel's antithesis is perhaps too harshly drawn. We remember, however, that this recurrent polemic device serves a constructive aim within its larger context. He intentionally emphasizes one element at the other's expense in order to subordinate secular philosophy to prophetic witness. He must demonstrate the limits of the former in pondering questions of ultimate import.

Speaking to modern minds bereft of faith, Heschel reinterprets our normal skepticism about religious ideas. We may be disappointed that he does not appear to take doubt as seriously as we do. Unlike Descartes, he rejects doubt (systematic or otherwise) as a valuable mode of understanding; only if we transcend the arrogance of cynical thought, Heschel avers, can we receive faith. He considers doubt to be incompatible with biblical thinking about reality.

Depth theology turns the negativity of "doubt" on its head, judging that uncertainty about meaning may signify something positive: chronic hesitancy may be "wonder" or "radical amazement" in disguise. The narrative has switched to the perspective of the uncertain believer. The radical amazement we yearn to enjoy indeed begins with a radical incapacity to believe confidently what we think we already know. But it ends in appreciation. The paradoxical dynamics of radical amazement—as opposed to Heschel's polemic presentation of it—takes fully into account the necessity of radical doubt.

Not surprisingly, his philosophical argumentation proves to be more pragmatic than logical. By undoing clichés, Heschel confronts us with the mind's finitude. However, terror at our nothingness might eventually reinforce our capacity to revere creation:

> What is extraordinary [usually] appears to us as habit, the dawn a daily routine of nature. But time and again we awake. In the midst of walking in the never-ending procession of days and nights, we are suddenly filled with a solemn terror, with a feeling of our wisdom being inferior to dust. We cannot endure the heartbreaking splendor of sunsets.[11]

Habit has frozen our awe before nature's astounding beauties that, although periodic, demonstrate to biblical thinking the working of divine concern. What appears to the routinized mind as a predictable physical phenomenon speaks to the religious person of God's glorious presence. Sometimes our ideas are so rigid, he claims, that only a violent dislocation will release intuitions of the holy.

Both believers and the faithless succumb to this habitual numbness. Only "solemn terror" can cure it. Heschel's combination of dialectics, biblical exegesis, poetic evocations, and personal testimony prepare that awakening, but in such a way that we are uplifted by "the heartbreaking splendor of sunsets."

Mystical Illumination

We now examine the culmination of Heschel's narrative of a consciousness in search of the soul. The chapter of *Man Is Not Alone* entitled "In the Presence of God" (chapter 9, pp. 67–79) defines the goal of his entire work: *the unity of inward piety and prophetic activism*. His apologetics pivots upon this transition from utter darkness to divine revelation (which I also call "mystical illumination"), demonstrating how God's self-disclosure leads the pious person (or mystic) to a moral and holy life.[12]

The argumentation preceding this decisive moment is meant to produce a "profound awareness of the incongruity of all categories with the nameless, unfathomable omnipresence of the mystery."[13] Heschel then pinpoints the helplessness that reflective people discover at times of crisis. He uses an image worthy of Kafka to express this excruciating state: the human condition becomes "a vast cage within a maze, high as our mind, wide as our power of will, long as our life span."[14] The self is emprisoned, as it were, by customary ideas, selfish desires, and temporality.

Those who question the meaning of existence can "either live on the sumptuous, dainty diet within the cage [or] look for an exit to the maze in order to search for freedom in the darkness of the undisclosed." Heschel's philosophizing should now bear fruit: we regurgitate the "dainty diet" of unquestioned clichés.

At this point in his demonstration, the author replaces rational discourse with highly condensed imagery and extended metaphor. We are caught in the vise of poetic logic, facing the endless labyrinth within. He appeals to our desire for freedom and encourages us to confront the "darkness of the undisclosed."

It is true that secular humanism, as well, can be an authentic form of courage in the face of the sightless night; Sartre's atheistic existentialism, for example, affirms the power of an alienated individual to create his or her destiny. Heschel shoulders this same loneliness, but with a further demand: that a person's commitment be directed toward and by *ultimate* reality.

Heschel's realism demands spiritual as well as moral courage. With a confidence given only to those who have, as it were, faced God, he pushes us beyond any humanly inspired hope. Those who have not yet discovered the Divine are plummeted into despair: "They have no power to spend on faith any more, no goal to strive for, no strength to seek a goal." Human volition is utterly stilled.[15]

Heschel's representation of mystical illumination (which he calls "revelation" or "insight") bursts through the apathy of radical self-alienation. It is the climax of his apologetics and bridges inwardness and religious living. The following passage from *Man Is Not Alone* evokes a filling of the void just described. It is one of Heschel's literary masterpieces and depicts—to the extent that is possible—an ineffable meeting with God. His breathless oratory conveys more than emotional conviction; it forms a prose poem rigorously organized to translate the supernatural event:

> But, then, a moment comes like a thunderbolt, in which a flash of the undisclosed rends our dark apathy asunder. It is full of overpowering brilliance, like a

point in which all moments of life are focused or a thought that outweighs all thoughts ever conceived of. There is so much light in our cage, in our world, it is as if it were suspended amidst the stars. Apathy turns to splendor unawares. The ineffable has shuddered itself into the soul. It has entered our consciousness like a ray of light passing into a lake. Refraction of that penetrating ray brings about a turning in our mind: We are penetrated by His insight. We cannot think any more as if He were there and we here. He is both there and here. He is not *a being*, but *being in and beyond all beings*.

The text's structure conveys its author's interpretation. Close analysis clarifies how Heschel intends to transform a reader's manner of thinking and capture his or her assent.

It begins with a typical comparison. Mystical insight is like a thunderbolt, rendering almost visually concrete the penetration of the soul (a dark cloud) by God.[16] The sky is ripped apart with a boom in an exquisite, yet painful, spectacle of prodigious strength. The image of "*dark* apathy" illustrates human emptiness and a total cessation of will—an abandon that could lead to passive despair, to death—or to God. Indifference is the most drastic contrary of the ego-assertion Heschel the philosopher constantly combats. Here he trusts that hopelessness will lead to a positive surrender.

The "undisclosed" then becomes manifest "like a point in which all moments of life are focused." The ineffable enters the soul in a flash, blinding normal thought but at the same time illuminating a heightened consciousness. He posits a simultaneous recall of past events viewed in an instant side by side. (People who imagine themselves falling to their death from cliffs or high buildings often fantasize a retrospect of their life.) Here, awareness of God accompanies this enhanced self-scrutiny; the divine presence "outweighs all thoughts ever conceived of" and gives life unheard-of focus: "There is so much light in our cage, in our world, it is as if it were suspended amidst the stars."

The world-prison metaphor is abolished as the inner illumination casts its brilliance outside; in other words, God endows the world with new meaning. A completely renewed vision of reality arises from depression and from the death of the old self: "Apathy turns to splendor unawares." This strikingly short sentence summarizes the mystical encounter, which Heschel insists has resulted from a revelation, God's movement toward the person: "The ineffable has shuddered itself into our soul."

Contrasted with the usual desire of the personality to possess God, the initiative, in this case, is clearly from the other side. In terms of literary technique, the image of a "shudder"—a physical as well as emotional sensation—signals to receptive readers the author's certainty.

The passage has gathered momentum, the rhythm quickens and climaxes. It now introduces a fundamental reorientation of the personality: "It has entered our consciousness like a ray of light passing into a lake. Refraction of that penetrating ray brings about a turning in our mind. We are penetrated by His insight." A religious Copernican revolution has taken place: a spiritual "turning" (in Hebrew, *teshuvah*) has transformed our awareness.

Heschel has completed his task: *the recentering of subjectivity from humanity to God*.[17] The normal subject-object perspective is reversed. Heschel's mystic, instead of gaining an insight into the nature of the Deity, becomes aware of being understood by God. (See Psalm 139: "O Lord, Thou has searched me and known me! . . .") The mystic is not absorbed into the divine Subject; rather, he or she now understands reality from a divine perspective. God is no longer utterly remote, transcendent, absent. The passage ends with this theological formula: "[God] is both there and here. [God is] *being in and beyond all beings*."

This is the theology to which the entire experience points: the confirming of God's simultaneous immanence and transcendence. God is no longer a concept, an abstract answer at the end of a chain of questions. Nor is God a "person," a "Being" susceptible to anthropomorphic translation. To the mystic God *is* Being. Not a static substance, a noun; God is a verb, a living force, as it were God-ing into our lives.[18]

Heschel further explores this divine incursion into human consciousness. The next paragraph displays the same combination of ecstatic evocation and rigorous sequencing. Heschel takes his place among the most effective mystical writers who convey their speechless, imageless contacts with the transcendent in dramatic sensorial language:

A tremor seizes our limbs; our nerves are struck, quiver like strings; our whole being bursts into shudders. But then a cry, wrested from our very core, fills the world around us, as if a mountain were suddenly about to place itself in front of us. It is one word: GOD. Not an emotion, a stir within us, but a power, a marvel beyond us, tearing the world apart. The word that means more than universe, more than eternity, holy, holy, holy; we cannot comprehend it. We only know it means infinitely more than we are able to echo. Staggered, embarrassed, we stammer and say: He, who is more than all there is, who speaks through the ineffable, whose question is more than our mind can answer; He to whom our life can be the spelling of an answer.[19]

Now the writer interprets the illumination more precisely. Intense kinesthetic reactions to revelation—the tremors, nerves quivering like strings, and, again, the shudders—produce an active response, an inaudible cry: GOD. The Ineffable Holy Name stands forth as real. Reversing Martin Buber's dialogical theology, Heschel's mystic becomes a thou of the Divine I.[20]

Readers can comprehend that mountain quake in more than a physical sense; we can imagine the pain and power condensed in a moment in which divine awareness might flash behind our minds. Yet I cannot imagine God; but can anyone? Heschel is not attributing a specific essence to God; rather, he is evoking human reactions to the Divine's self-expression. He insists that feeling is a response to an objective reality, that affect accompanies, and not invents this penetration of the sacred dimension: "Not an emotion, a stir within us, but a power, a marvel beyond us, tearing the world apart."

God's presence within the person's consciousness augments that self by disclosing its supernatural foundation; God actualizes the essence of the human being as divine image. We can only sing, praise: "holy, holy, holy; we cannot comprehend it." We worship, as the words of the Kedusha (the Sanctification) in our daily and Sabbath liturgy rise to the surface. Elsewhere a Heschel aphorism summarizes: to be truly human we must be more than human.[21]

Inward confirmation of God's existence, however, is not the homeland of this odyssey; quite the contrary. Our yearning for knowledge of the Divine, when surrendered, opens us to the ultimate question, that is, God's question to us. Heschel's mysticism, rather than resolving religious perplexities, creates greater problems. The solution is the problem.[22] Our true calling begins in a shared world. Piety—religious living—is our answer.

Faith, fortified by direct contact, clarifies the fuller challenge. The bare word "GOD" forms a message: "He . . . who speaks through the ineffable, whose question is more than our mind can answer; He to whom our life can be the spelling of an answer." Heschel's final sentence—incomplete because it contains no verb—is a synonym for God; a pure presence repeats the unending call to Adam, to all humanity: Where are you?

The Life of Piety

Heschel's "mysticism" (as I call it despite the author's admonitions) translates into a prophetic ethics. Reversing the seeker's quest for God, the pious person fulfills in a complete and spontaneous manner the recentering of subjectivity to God: "he is not aiming to penetrate into the sacred. Rather he is striving to be himself penetrated and actuated by the sacred, eager to . . . identify himself with every trend in the world which is toward the divine. . . . Piety is the realization and verification of the transcendent in human life."[23]

Heschel thus interprets modern alienation mystically. Rather than focusing upon our desolation, he identifies with God's relation to human history. He applies the rabbinic and Kabbalistic notion of *Shekhinah*—the presence of God's Indwelling, outcast, within the world—to his own sacred imperative: "God is, so to speak, involved in the tragic state of the world. . . . Not only for Israel [that is, the Jewish people] but the whole universe, even the *Shekhinah*, 'lies in the dust' and is in exile."[24]

This theology of the *Shekhinah* establishes an ethics. Prophetic urgency demands that we identify with God's eclipse and defy history's tragic message. According to Heschel, the mystic overwhelmed by God's presence must become involved with life at large: "The ultimate goal of the Kabbalist is not his own union with the Absolute but the union of all reality with God; one's own bliss is subordinated to the redemption of all."[25] This is no parochial vision.

Heschel portrayed this fulfilled intimacy with God from the very beginning of his American career. Again we have a blueprint. His very first article published in English, "An Analysis of Piety" (*The Review of Religion*, 1942) was transported verbatim to comprise the final chapter of *Man Is Not Alone*. Now entitled "The Pious Man," it completes the book by pointing contemporary readers to an ancient goal:

The pious man is possessed by his awareness of the presence and nearness of God. Everywhere and at all times he lives as in His sight, whether he remains always heedful of His proximity or not. He feels embraced by God's mercy as by a vast encircling space. Awareness of God is as close to him as the throbbing of his own heart, often deep and calm but at times overwhelming, intoxicating, setting the soul afire. The momentous reality of God stands there as peace, power and endless tranquility, as an inexhaustible source of help, as boundless compassion, as an open gate awaiting prayer. It sometimes happens that the life of a pious man becomes so involved in God that his heart overflows as though it were a cup in the hand of God. This presence of God is not like the proximity of a mountain or the vicinity of an ocean, the view of which one may relinquish by closing the eyes or removing from the place. Rather is this convergence with God unavoidable, inescapable; like air in space, it is always breathed in, even though one is not always aware of continuous respiration.[26]

Heschel believed that such confidence was available to everyone: "The momentous reality of God stands there as peace, power and endless tranquility, as an inexhaustible source of help, as boundless compassion, as an open gate awaiting prayer." With mystical understanding, we can revise our confining mental categories, resolutely attack the arrogance of dogmatic thought—philosophical or religious—and welcome the living God.

Heschel's paradigm helps us understand other twentieth-century spiritual activists, of whatever creed or belief.[27] The *Hasid* (for that is what "the pious man" means in Hebrew) is common to all religions, East or West. It is no accident that Protestants, Catholics, and Muslims responded deeply to the author of *The Prophets* and *God in Search of Man*.[28] Piety is the bridge.

The most comparable American figure is the Trappist monk Thomas Merton (1915–1968), who knew and admired Heschel, and resembled him in intellectual acumen, worldliness, emotional intensity, ethical militancy, and piety. For Merton, too, the mystical vocation is "a way of prayer, or of contemplation, *or simply living* [my emphasis], in which the direct action and influence of God tend to absorb the activity of our natural faculties, raising them to a habitually supernatural level. The characteristic mark of true Christian mysticism is not a succession of flamboyant experiences and phenomena, but a life of constant peace, recollection, absorption in God, charity, humility and, last but not least, balance and common sense, even in the midst of great trials, distracting duties, or heroic suffering."[29]

Resistance to Faith

Still, we must recognize that most people do not—and perhaps cannot—achieve such confidence. We should respect the inability to believe. As Maurice Friedman has keenly asked, how can Heschel's writings touch those readers detached from his manner of thinking? Can his viewpoint speak to those who cannot fathom his poetry, or rouse those who do not even yearn for faith?[30] Thinkers who reject Heschel's assumption that all people possess an inherent, a priori sense of the sacred will not let themselves be convinced.[31]

There is another way to approach these obstructions. What significance does Heschel attribute to spiritual blindness and to the moral callousness—feeble responses to evil and suffering—which may accompany religious obtuseness?

A biblical paradox helps explain why Heschel did not consider those contradictions to be final. The Hebrew prophets experienced God's silence, or even abandonment by God, as incitement to self-scrutiny on the immense journey. In the chapter of *The Prophets* entitled "Chastisement," Heschel interprets this drastic way to bring back wanderers. Hardness of heart—the root of all sin according to the Bible—can occasion a turning to God: "It seems that the only cure for willful hardness is to make it absolute. Half-callousness, paired with obstinate conceit, seeks no cure. When hardness is complete, it becomes despair, the end of conceit. Out of despair, out of total inability to believe, prayer bursts forth."[32]

Resistance to God, insensitivity to evil, is the opposite of freedom. The Bible considers guilt and punishment to exist on one continuum. Hardness of heart is both punishment and a source of surrender to God. Radical despair is the only cure for radical estrangement.

Heschel, like Pascal, has proposed a wager. For twentieth-century readers, hopelessness can become a positive intuition of human helplessness without God. Like Pascal, Heschel believed that confrontation with finite misery would awaken a devouring hunger for meaning. Such is the common goal of *Man Is Not Alone* and Pascal's *Pensées*. Conceit humiliated, arrogance quelled, the fragile and failing ego can be liberated: "Agony is the final test. When all hopes are dashed and all conceit is shattered, man begins to miss what he has long spurned. In darkness, God becomes near and clear."[33]

My teaching has confirmed the plausibility of these views. It is often the privilege of a college professor to encounter discerning students who formulate difficult insights without affectation. So I end with these words, written by a wise participant in one of my classes:

> Despair, then, is a transition between two states of being. Since we are striving for some kind of all-inclusive meaning to our lives, the tension between the irreconcilable opposites of faith and meaninglessness challenges us. The tension, the distance felt, is despair. In despair we are neither here nor there; we are in the "wasteland, wilderness, darkness." It is a state likened to death for we are separated, detached from an earlier fixed point, and we seem to pass through a realm that has none of the attributes of either state. We are "stripped of pretention and conceit" and humiliated by our "tragic insufficiency." We enter an abyss, a "spiritual blackout" of submissive apathy. We are lost, wandering and blind. However, some of the basic principles of religious teaching— self-emptying humility and detachment—are obscurely present in this state. We are no longer surrounded by self-deception or self-love: the landscape of our soul is a desert, but it is not barren. We desperately cry out for a hope that is beyond us, for we know that alone we cannot make that desert a fertile field. This submissive, disinterested self-denial, although excruciatingly painful, is the first step in the surrender to God. It is the seed of salvation and can be a splendid moment according to Heschel.[34]

Our assent to Heschel's answer does not necessarily bind us to an exact alternative of creed or suspicion. Somewhere between those two extremes emerges a prophetic task: it is the redemption of humanity by itself.[35] No waiting in stillness for the final Messiah; no surrender to the absurd—nor to meaninglessness, brute power, or chance. Amidst the tentative joy of faith and the bleak numbness of abandon lies the vision of a holy life.

The Divine may be essentially transcendent, concealed, or "God" may be a figment of our aspirations. God may be silent or God may be "Nothing"—in the mystical or atheistic denotations of the term. Whatever the truth, Heschel defines a path to follow, one committed to the present and to the future. Empty or full, we respond to different moments of that journey. Heschel's mysticism trusts that despair can become the birth, not the grave, of a significant, and perhaps sacred, renewal.

SACRED VERSUS SYMBOLIC RELIGION
Social Science
or God's Will?

> The service of God is an extremely concrete, an
> extremely real, literal, and factual affair. We do not
> have to employ symbols to make Him understand what
> we mean. We worship Him not by employing figures of
> speech but by shaping our actual lives according to His
> pattern.
>
> —Heschel, 1954[1]

Heschel's depth theology—his narrative journey toward presymbolic, preconceptual cognition—readies us for the gift of certainty. Although his confidence can erect stumbling blocks to those unreceptive to faith, he insists that we must surpass symbols in order to encounter the ultimate. His touchstone is authentic prayer: "We have lost the power to pray because we have lost the sense of His reality. All we do is done for the sake of something else."[2]

The itinerary from despair to mystical illumination demonstrates that there is no equivalent for direct apprehension of God. This bold standard underlies the author's surprisingly vehement opposition to symbolism in Judaism. Fully aware that Kabbalistic mysticism (especially in the *Zohar*) flourished in a plenitude of figurative expression, Heschel defended a polemic position, a minority opinion, insisting that symbolism was foreign to Judaism's foundations.[3] He was swimming against the prevailing academic current in order to repudiate images as a means of spiritual renewal.

Heschel's (somewhat quixotic) campaign against "symbolism" (a term he applies quite broadly) has two cultural contexts: philosophical anthropology current in European academic circles in the 1920s and 1930s, when Heschel was a student; and liberal religion as practiced in Germany and North America before and after World War II, when Heschel was a professor and writer. We begin with the scene of his strongest formulations.

As a prophetic witness in the United States, Heschel denounces secularization. He labels as "symbolism" religion shrunk to rationalizations: "Symbolism is so alluring because it promises to rehabilitate beliefs and rituals that have become meaningless to the mind. Yet, what it accomplishes is to reduce belief to make-believe, observance to ceremony, prophecy to literature, theology to esthetics."[4] Modern Judaism was in danger of demoting depth theology to anthropology or psychology. Ritual acts are not "symbols" of ethical or cultural values, speaking only to intellect and emotion.

His most forthright attack appears in a chapter of *Quest for God*, originally presented in 1952 at an interreligous symposium of theologians and artists who shared an enthusiasm for mythic forms.[5] True to his dialectic stance, Heschel denounced images (or concepts) used as substitutes for God's reality.

> It has become a truism that religion is largely an affair of symbols. Translated into simpler terms this view regards religion as a *fiction*, useful to society or to man's personal well being. Religion is, then, no longer a relationship of man to God but a relationship of man to the symbol of his highest ideals: there is no God, but we must go on worshipping His symbol.[6]

At stake is the very integrity of institutions that maintain the faith. For Heschel, a communicative God is the only given: "[The Bible] is built upon a rock of certainty that God has made known His will to His people. To us, the will of God *is neither a metaphor nor a euphemism* but more powerful and more real than our own experience." Heschel is *not* an "existentialist" who validates theology through consciousness. His "rock of certainty" derives from his "ontological presupposition" of divine revelation to humankind.

How do we reconcile his claim that religious language is metaphorical versus this attack against sacred imagery? Vicarious religion—not language or symbol as such—is the danger. Within the Jewish world, Heschel targets Classical Reform, Kaplanian Reconstructionism, and some tendencies in the Conservative movement as having fostered secondhand observance. He understands these tendencies of American thought as extensions of neo-Kantian rationalism, popularizing Salomon Maimon's notion "that only *symbolic knowledge* is possible."

Heschel prepares seekers to resist the comfort of symbols and ideologies by analyzing prayer and the *mitzvot* (divine commandments encoded in Jewish law) as "indicative" language. The sacred canon combines semantic limits, poetic powers, and God's presence, underscoring the relativity of human expression (the vehicle) while expressing God's will (the divine tenor). Symbols can mediate our disbelief or ambivalence, but we must eventually surpass them.

Spirit versus Symbol

Heschel's poetics of faith and piety—as explained in chapter 4—preserves both God's transcendence and human freedom. His theory of symbolism translates his conviction that Jewish law (*halakhah*) contains immanently what God had "spoken" at Mount Sinai—but without betraying either the divine imperative or critical reflection. Condemning substitutes for authentic faith, he overstates his case in order to electrify our passion to reach beyond the known:

> Those who are in the dark in their lonely search for God; those to whom God is a problem, or a Being that is eternally absent or silent; those who ask, "How does one know Him? Where can one find him? How does one express Him?" will be forced to accept symbols as an answer.[7]

In practice, Heschel's writings do provide ample clues, and some consolation, to "those who are in the dark in their lonely search for God." His rejection of symbolism as an insidious deceiver is not a profession of pure silence but a warning to the weary traveler. His polemics against symbolism brings home to seekers his own trust that God is available.

An elementary linguistic analysis can fend off idolatry: "The essential function of the critic is to protect such ideas [that is, theology or dogma] from pretension and inflation, resulting in either visible or verbal iconography. A sacred venture is always in danger of ending in blasphemy."[8] Critical knowledge of the manner in which one interprets experience approaches the threshold: "To the pious man knowledge of God is not a thought within his grasp, but a form of thinking in which he tries to comprehend all reality."[9] Heschel's phenomenology of piety—his analysis of theocentric consciousness and action—completes his poetics of piety as a humanistic discipline of the spirit.

Religious insight distinguishes between two opposite types of representation: (1) the *real symbol* "because it is assumed that the Divine resides in it or that the symbol partakes to some degree of the reality of the Divine"; (2) and the *conventional symbol* that "represents to the mind an entity that is not shown, not because its substance is endowed with something of that entity but because it suggests that entity, by reason of relationship, association or convention, for example, a flag."[10] Recalling our analysis in chapter 4, the "conventional symbol" is another name for metaphor, implying a merely syntactical relation between vehicle and tenor.

Jewish observance shuns the "real symbol." Heschel insists that "there is no *inherent* sanctity in Jewish ritual objects. [They have] no symbolic content."[11] In fact, by differentiating between form and content in acts of worship, we approach God's initiative more closely. Cultic devices and ceremonies are vehicles of metaphors with a primarily psychological function: "The purpose of ritual art objects in Judaism is not to inspire love of God but to enhance our love of doing a *mitzvah* (religious act)."[12] Such emotion is crucial but carries no metaphysical status.

The *mitzvah* (or sacred deed) represents in the domain of external behavior what the biblical metaphor bestows to the person's inner consciousness. Both can be apprehended as a vehicle having a meaning in and by itself—as, simply, literary or cultural metaphor—or both can be experienced as pointers to the Presence ultimately beyond: "The primary function of symbols [or symbolic language about religion] is to express *what we think*; the primary function of the *mitzvot* is to express *what God wills*. Religious symbolism is *a search for God*, Jewish observance, a *response to God*" (Heschel's emphases).[13]

In this way Heschel displaces his analysis of the ritual or deed from the person to the Divine: "Ceremonies are created for the purpose of *signifying*; *mitzvot* were given for the purpose of *sanctifying*."[14] The *mitzvah* sanctifies since it actualizes in the world the divine concern. In other words, acts or objects created by persons possess no inherent sanctity, but they derive their power from the living God. Our participation in the *mitzvah* that they signify can become individual responses to God's "personal" will, as it were, addressed to me. God as Subject enters our "leap of action."

Heschel's distinction between "symbol" and "*mitzvah*" should thus prevent us from replacing the ineffable with an icon. Our deeds are vehicles of a metaphor that points to divine will. Sheer physical interaction with a ritual object, as gratifying as it might become subjectively, does not as such constitute a full response: "Symbols have a psychological, not an ontological, status; they do not affect any reality, except the psyche of man. *Mitzvot* affect God. Symbols evade, *mitzvot* transcend, reality. Symbols are less, *mitzvot* more than real. . . . Whatever is done in religious observance is an original act."[15]

These strictures apply equally to all branches of modern Judaism—Orthodox, Conservative, Reconstructionist, Reform, or secular. Although poetic intuition may unveil God's presence within inherited texts, Heschel cautions against an exclusive reliance on acts of worship: "Let us be frank. Too often a ceremony is the homage which disbelief pays to faith. . . . Judaism does not stand on ceremonies. . . . [Heschel's ellipses] Jewish piety is an answer to God, expressed in the language of the *mitzvot* rather than in the language of *ceremonies and symbols*."[16] We worship to surpass worship; as Heschel says, "I pray because I am unable to pray."[17]

Heschel's premise is clear: the Bible rejects "all visible symbols for God." Even the universe qualifies only as a veil of the Divine. Separating himself from some Kabbalistic mystics, who might consider the world as an emanation somehow *continuous* with the Godhead, he accents the separation of the divine "essence" from its manifestations: "The world speaks to God, but that speech is not God speaking to Himself. It would be alien to the spirit of the Bible to say that it is the very life of God to be bodied forth. The world is neither His continuation nor His emanation but rather His creation and possession."[18] For Heschel, *transcendence* must be acknowledged before God's *immanence* becomes available.

Law and Inwardness

Both liberal and normative Judaism can find God within prescribed rituals, and Heschel maintains that *halakhah* (Jewish law) can for both fulfill this vital bond. The traditional Jew, who considers his or her obligations to be divine commandments, fulfills a *mitzvah* as a response to God's will as revealed through language, not to a human authority or symbolic interpretation. Religious acts—be they cultic or ethical—allude to the Subject beyond representation. A full response to God adds an overflow of holiness to the fulfilled *mitzvah*, the outward conduct.

Symbols, scripture, and liturgy cannot be experienced in only one dimension—either as coming directly from God or exclusively from the human side. Depth theology fosters the spirit of tradition by interpreting the *mitzvot* as opportunities to absorb the holy within prescribed forms. Yet he exposes fundamental shortcomings of the Orthodox or Conservative conceptions by promoting inward piety against mechanical or rationalized performance: "Religious behaviorists" (as he caricatures Jews who obey only the law) ignore the subjective in favor of the external act.

Consciousness is the criterion by which to evaluate religious deeds; it is an inward standard of reference. From Heschel's perspective, an observant person can be analyzed as if he or she were a sacred poem: human intention meets divine intention. As he writes in *The Prophets*: "Prophetic consciousness . . . does not spring from the depths of the human spirit; it is based upon anticipation or inclusion of man in God."[19] In structural terms, the human vehicle (the action), by alluding to its tenor (God), actualizes within us a holy presence (the ground of the metaphor).

Ritual obligations can revive our awareness of a sacred mystery, God's involvement with human choices. Heschel's theory of the *mitzvah* challenges legalistic fundamentalism as well as religion defined by sociology—the two still current extreme prototypes. Beyond secular or dogmatic preconceptions, he reproaches the "popular misunderstanding" of traditional observance he calls "religious behaviorism":

> As an attitude toward the law, it stresses the external compliance with the law and disregards the importance of inner devotion. . . . You do not have to believe, but you must observe the law; as if all that mattered is how men behaved in physical terms; as if God were not concerned with the inner life; as if faith were not indigenous to Judaism, but *orthopraxis* were. Such a conception reduces Judaism to a sort of sacred physics, with no sense for the imponderable, the introspective, the metaphysical.[20]

That is why Heschel tends to emphasize the inner life. He assumes the sanctity of *halakhah* and, as would a reader of biblical metaphor, he highlights the metaphysical simultaneity (and perceived tension) between external performance and inner response: "No religious act is properly fulfilled unless it is done with a willing heart and a craving soul. You cannot worship Him with your body, if you do not know how to worship Him in your soul. The relationship between deed and inner devotion must be understood . . . in terms of polarity."[21] Conversely, an observant person who does evil, violates this integrity of inner and outer.

Heschel's recentering of the reader's consciousness again enables us to probe, through literary empathy, the intimate sanctuary of faith. Intention (or *kavanah*) removes our will from the self and directs it toward its divine origin: "*Kavanah* is awareness of the will of God rather than awareness of the reason of the *mitzvah*. Awareness of symbolic meaning is awareness of a specific idea; *kavanah* is awareness of an ineffable situation."[22]

Religious observance enriches our responses to life as it dares our minds to surpass utilitarian accounts, be they psychological, sociological, or esoteric: "A *mitzvah* is performed when a deed is outdone by a sigh, when divine reference is given to a human fact. In a *mitzvah* we give the source of an act, rather than the underlining of a word."[23] The "sigh" is Heschel's evocative way of voicing the holy dimension to which the act refers, its "source." These are "God's quotation marks."

We should emphasize, however, that Heschel does not promote inwardness, untrammeled spontaneity, to the detriment of Jewish law. Those critics who accuse Heschel of neglecting *halakhah* are simply not reading him carefully. With equal force, he repudiates an exclusive focus on feeling and intention as substitutes for obedience: "Prayer becomes trivial when ceasing to be an act in the soul. The essence of prayer is *aggadah, inwardness*. Yet it would be a tragic failure not to appreciate what the spirit of *halakhah* does for it, raising it from the level of an individual act to that of an eternal intercourse between the people Israel and God; from the level of an occasional experience to that of permanent covenant."[24]

Authentic Judaism—be it modern or traditional—is itself "pluralistic" in that it both reveres inherited ritual and welcomes unplanned emotions. Heschel conceptualizes this intersection of spheres as a "polarity" between *halakhah* and *aggadah*. (What he calls "polarity"—the dynamic tension of opposites—is really a mixture, an amalgam.)

Quest for God puts these views together in its central chapters, "Spontaneity is the Goal" and "Continuity is the Way" (examined above in chapter 1). *God in Search of Man* defines the complementarity of *halakhah* and inwardness more intently, and with ample documentation from the classic sources.[25] Heschel's ability to capture the nuances of personal devotion can be explained by his own "halakhic way of life."

Buber's Atheistic Theology?

A biographical incursion uncovers the original context of Heschel's surprisingly harsh opposition to symbolism. His first loyalty was to the living God—and to the Sinai revelation, law, and sacrament. The prevailing approach he opposed was called "philosophical anthropology," a humanistic interpretation of culture established by Wilhelm Dilthey (1833–1911). Later in the 1920s, the eloquent neo-Kantian philosopher, Ernst Cassirer (1874–1945), published three exhaustive volumes on language, myth and religion, and theory of knowledge as "symbolic forms." This encyclopedic humanism had been popularized and eventually filtered down into the ideology of American educators and religious rationalists.[26]

In Germany, before emigrating to the United States, Heschel had confronted this view in Martin Buber (1878–1965), at the time Europe's celebrated Jewish thinker, and himself, like Cassirer, a former student of Dilthey's. Heschel's "dialogue" with Buber (a genuine sharing of views) defines two opposing conceptions of Judaism in the twentieth century: prophetic theology derived from divine revelation versus religion as interpreted by social philosophy.

Time and place: 1935 in Berlin. Heschel at age twenty-eight had recently completed his dissertation on prophetic consciousness. He first met Buber around 1929–1930 and attended several of his lectures in Berlin. In 1935 Buber mailed Heschel a copy of his paper, "Symbolic and Sacramental Existence in Judaism"—a comparative analysis of prophetic ethics and Hasidism he had delivered at the 1934 Eranos conference on East-West Symbology and Spiritual Direction.[27] Heschel's answer defines their radical separation—while striving to maintain a productive relationship.

At issue in their debate was the status of symbol in the Hebrew prophets. For good reason, their conflict of interpretations was potentially devastating. Heschel remained respectful but firmly objected to Buber's apparent reduction of prophecy to a symbolic manner of conveying a moral lesson. To put it briefly, Heschel con-

sidered Buber's "theology" to be at best a philosophical anthropology, despite its religious overtones:

> The focus on the category 'sign' is certainly very
> important and will clarify many things. But it seems
> questionable to me when you define, in this sense,
> the totality of prophetic existence ("he lives symbolic-
> ally . . . he himself is the sign," p. 350). Is that not a
> generalization, instead of determining its prevailing
> uniqueness? Yet, not only methodologically, but also
> in principle, I would like to object to a conception
> according to which the prophet's existence in toto, as
> well as the particulars of his activity, should have no
> intrinsic value, but only value as sign. There is a last
> question, and I must confess that I would not endure
> it to experience the event as a mere illustration, —to
> have no meaning, to be just a *sign* of meaning [*Sinn-
> bild*].
>
> "Biblical man, and with him the biblical God, craves
> for the spirit to express itself more perfectly, more sub-
> stantially than in the word only, but that it [that is, the
> spirit] become incarnate," p. 347.
>
> But what is the advantage of such an incarnation? Is
> the [*crossed out*: reproduction] image more perfect than
> the [*crossed out*: original] being?
>
> You presuppose a need for signs and symbols. Then
> why should we not incarnate God himself and symbol-
> ize him?[28]

In 1935—as much later in the United States—no issue was closer
to Heschel's heart than the actuality of God's direct communication to the ancient prophets. The divine pathos was primary.
Heschel's characterization of the elder's position might be over-
simplified, but his citations are precise. He was alarmed at what
he considered to be—at least potentially—Buber's subversive
message.

Heschel warns Buber how perilous it was for a Jewish thinker
to elaborate a theory of symbolic "incarnation"; his interpretation might associate Hebrew Scripture with a Christian typology,
whereby the prophets of Israel can be interpreted as predicting
the coming of Christ. At the very least, the primal reality of God's
initiative might be forgotten or reduced to ethical insight.

Such was the complex inauguration of a dialogue that continued long after Buber chose Heschel, the following year, as co-director in Frankfurt-am-Main of the Center for Adult Jewish Education and the Jüdisches Lehrhaus. For Heschel, the prophets fulfilled their sympathy with God by becoming an "object" of the divine "Subject." That is how the young man established his lifelong, though irenic, polemic against Buber's dialogical philosophy.[29]

Further historical hindsight helps explain Heschel's fierce opposition to compromises with the divine origin of Jewish tradition. He advances a key debate, years earlier, in which Franz Rosenzweig (1886–1929), in an essay entitled "Atheistic Theology," had reproved Buber's earlier approach to the biblical God as essentially sociological in conception.[30] This was a critique of contemporary religion that Heschel, in the United States, often recommended to his students.[31]

Rosenzweig had objected to Buber's apparent view that God was an entity realized through human communication, and that ritual obligations (the *mitzvot*) derived not from revelation but from human dialogue. (In point of fact, Buber insisted on the reality of the divine Thou—although he did subordinate the Law to human initiative.) At stake for both Rosenzweig and Heschel was the primacy of the Divine, the validity of the *mitzvot*, and obedience to God's will. It was well known that Buber was not an observant Jew—that he was in fact hostile to ritual obligations— and that he did not consider Jewish law to be sacred. Heschel asserted that *halakhah* derived its power from God's revelation at Sinai.

Heschel judged that Buber's approach to the prophets had substituted a human "symbol" for the transcendent Subject. Heschel would always insist upon a theocentric explanation of biblical witness: "Prophetic experience is the experiencing of a divine experience, or a realization of having been experienced by God."[32] In 1935, Heschel feared that Buber, with whom he would be compared as the century's preeminent Jewish philosopher, despite his sensitivity to the inner life, might foster a universal (or even secularized) religion, depriving Judaism of its specificity.

Poetics and Observance

Our modern mind still asks, Can ritual transform us? Are there but two doors to the sanctuary—either trust that God cares about our ceremonies or surrender our brains to legalistic authorities? Understanding the complexity of religious language voids this fixed alternative. Heschel supports both critical awareness and chastening the ego. His poetics of the *symbolic* dimension of Jewish celebrations helps people actualize their *sacred* dimension.

The "symbolic" or customary meaning of ritual can be distinguished from its spirit. Heschel's analysis confirms our intellectual autonomy, our demand for verification through experience, while broadening our concepts. He stands against the fashion of "customs and ceremonies" that claim no metaphysical status:

> Jewish festivals do not contain any attempt to recreate symbolically the events they commemorate. We do not reenact the exodus from Egypt nor the crossing of the Red Sea. Decisive as the revelation of Sinai is, there is no ritual to recreate or to dramatize it. We neither repeat nor imitate sacred events. Whatever is done in religious observance is an original act. The Seder ritual, for example, recalls; it does not rehearse the past.[33]

At the same time, the religious calendar is not just a script for community performances. Ceremonies, insofar as they fulfill duties defined by revealed law, provide forms that respond to God's will: "Jewish piety demands their fulfillment regardless of whether or not we comprehend their symbolic meaning." We are potentially able to perceive God's presence by striving to perform rituals with *kavanah*, inward participation and intention. Paradoxically, by experiencing ceremonies as *pointers*—not as "real symbols" of divine mystery—we can approach holiness.

The Sabbath represents our most complete, and most accessible vehicle of sanctification. The Seventh Day may appear to be a "real symbol," possessing inherent holiness: "Judaism teaches us to be attached to *holiness in time*, to be attached to sacred events, to learn how to consecrate sanctuaries that emerge from the magnificent stream of a year. The Sabbaths are our great cathedrals."[34] Heschel comes perilously close to contradicting his axiomatic opposition to spatial analogies of the holy. Time, not symbols, can partake of transcendence. Indeed for Heschel, as for all observant Jews, the Sabbath bestows a "foretaste of eternity"; but time as such cannot "symbolize" the Divine.

Heschel explains how observance both conveys and veils the ineffable : "The idea of the Sabbath as a queen or bride did not represent a mental image, something that could be imagined. There was no picture in the mind that corresponded to the metaphor."[35] Instead, this vivid feminine presence in the Friday evening liturgy—the Consort of God and Israel—actualizes the vertical dimension of language, the axis of connotation and indication: "The idea of the Sabbath as a queen oɼ a bride is not a personification of the Sabbath but an exemplification of a divine attribute, an illustration of God's need for human love; it does not represent a substance but the presence of God, His relationship to man."[36]

The Sabbath Queen is a "vehicle" that "exemplifies" or "illustrates" one transitive aspect of God, making holiness available to our hearts. The image does not touch God's substance in itself but evokes only that sanctity accessible to intuition. Awareness of the metaphysical conflux of tenor and vehicle in the Sabbath amounts to a perception of God's transcendence: both distance and immanence meet in the liturgical image. The ground of the metaphor, the quality (or value) shared by the two terms, is our intimation of Eternity: "Such metaphorical exemplification does not state a fact; it expresses a value, putting into words the preciousness of the Sabbath as Sabbath."[37]

Yet symbolism has contradictory value even in Heschel's poetics of the Sabbath. For his analysis of the Bride or Queen, paradoxically, both ushers us to the threshold of transcendence while it, simultaneously, entices us with something less:

> There are two aspects to the Sabbath, as there are two aspects to the world. The Sabbath is meaningful to man and is meaningful to God. It stands in a relation to both, and is a sign of the covenant entered into by both. What is the sign? God has sanctified the day, and man must again and again sanctify the day, illumine the day with the light of his soul. The Sabbath is holy by the grace of God, and is still in need of all the holiness that man may lend to it.[38]

Ritual can fulfill the coexistence of God's intimacy and God's ultimate otherness. Observance renews the mutual covenant. In precious moments of prayer or celebration, human "vehicle" and divine "tenor" may feel as if they kiss, recentering our focus to the Divine.

Although Heschel's discourse exploits the ambiguous frontiers between art and the Holy Spirit, his theory insists upon their differences: "This is one of the aspects that distinguishes the religious from the esthetic experience: In a religious experience . . . it is not a thing that imposes itself on man but a spiritual presence."[39] Beauty as an intimation of divinity may also *exclude* God's presence: "An esthetic experience leaves behind the memory of a perception and enjoyment; a prophetic experience leaves behind *the memory of a commitment*."[40] The sacred thrusts inwardness into the world.

Perhaps the simplest explanation for Heschel's militant repudiation of symbols lies in his sensitivity to their power. He is well aware that esthetic delight, if manipulated as an end in itself, may subvert the sacred venture: "The quest for symbols is a *trap* for those who seek the truth. Symbols may either distort what is literally true or profane what is ineffably real. They may, if employed in the inner chamber of the heart, distort our longing for God into mere esthetics."[41] The symbol may eclipse religious truth if the vehicle is savored as an adequate representation of its ineffable referent. The deeper, presymbolic quest for God may be stymied by its own enchantments.

Only behavior—such as worship and ethical acts—can become metaphysically authentic. In the highest stages of religious thinking, language as a vehicle for spiritual insight dissolves. Heschel opposes above all the literal fallacy, the adequation of expression with reality. That is why his theory builds upon the irreducible tensions between the ineffable versus words. The actual life of one who meets God should be transformed.

Symbols have no foundation beyond visible experience. They are only stepping stones to the holy. Beyond Heschel's poetics of observance is an astounding metaphysical claim: "Great is the power of prayer. For to worship is *to expand the presence of God* in the world. God is transcendent, but our worship makes Him immanent. This is implied in the idea that God is in need of man: His being immanent depends upon us."[42] In literary terms, perceiving the ground of the biblical metaphor is a way of actualizing holiness within human experience. Three-dimensional worship can sanctify the world.

Becoming God's Symbol

The only vehicle that, for Heschel, literally embodies the Divine is a human being.[43] Perhaps the most challenging and, to my mind, the boldest of his linguistic concepts is his interpretation of the person as an image of God:

> The symbol of God is *man, every man*. God created man in His image (*tselem*), in His likeness *(demuth)*. How sig-

nificant is the fact that the term *tselem* that is frequently used in a damnatory sense for a manmade
image of God, as well as the term *demuth*, of which Isaiah claims (40:18) no *demuth* or likeness can be applied
to God—are employed in denoting man as an image
and likeness of God.[44]

Only a person is a "real symbol," partaking of God's substance as
well as God's function: "Biblical tradition insists that not only
man's soul but also his body is symbolic of God." These words are
denotative; they are not merely pointers to an ineffable concept
of "image." This "divine image anthropology" (as I call it) surpasses Buber's "symbolism" of the prophets, which Heschel
viewed as a didactic convention.

Yet how are we to reconcile Heschel's insistence that religious
language is wanting with this apparent deification of human
beings? We must construe such statements in a theocentric manner. Heschel's claims are *understatements* whose transcendent
meaning is understood only by God, not hyperboles of social or
psychological reality. His philosophy of religion represents an
"accommodation of words to higher meanings," not an inflation
of thought to the level of absolute fact. Hence, to consider a person as an image of God reflects the divine view of persons, not a
rational picture of humankind by itself.

Heschel's ethics, too, recenters subjectivity from the human to
the divine. This reversal of the usual manner of thinking should
inspirit our striving to imitate God, to actualize our essence as
imago Dei. For human beings are more than ordinary symbols:
"what is necessary is not to *have a symbol* but *to be a symbol*. In
this spirit, all objects and all actions are not symbols in themselves [that is, real symbols] but ways and means of enhancing
the living symbolism of man."[45] Freely chosen moral and ritual
actions can actualize the world's spiritual dimension. Only persons, in Jewish tradition, share that power with God.

What we might call Heschel's "sacred humanism" further distinguishes between image and God. Even as a "real symbol,"
never is the human vehicle identical and coextensive with the
tenor: "The divine symbolism of man is not in what he *has*—such
as reason or the power of speech—but in what he *is* potentially:
he is able to be holy as God is holy. To imitate God, to act as He
acts in mercy and love, is the way of enhancing our likeness. Man
becomes what he worships."[46] The human divine essence, the

quality we share with God, is a potential to be achieved, not a full actuality.[47]

Heschel's poetics of piety leads finally to the prosaic responsibility of living under the eyes of God. Since each and every human being is a divine image, we must revere every person as we revere the Creator: "The ultimate worth of man is due neither to his virtue nor to his faith. *It is due to God's virtue, to God's faith. Wherever you see a trace of man, there is the presence of God*" (Heschel's emphasis).[48]

Where does the unbeliever stand in relation to Heschel's sacred humanism? It is not necessary, I maintain, inwardly to accept his faith in order to identify with his ethical claims. Theocentric thinking can provide communication between certainty and agnosticism or doubt. Whether or not one truly understands what it means to be created in God's image, Heschel's poetics of faith and piety justifies the ethical potential of religious observance. We arrive at a theology of action.

Figure 1. Heschel, c. 1947.
*Photograph by Lotte Jacobi. Courtesy of the Lotte Jacobi Archive,
Dimond Library, University of New Hampshire.*

Figure 2. Heschel at his desk at The Jewish Theological
Seminary, c. 1952.
Photograph by John Popper.
Courtesy of the Ratner Center for the Study of Conservative Judaism.

Figure 3. Heschel at his desk at The Jewish Theological Seminary, c. 1960.

Photograph by John Popper.
Courtesy of the Ratner Center for the Study of Conservative Judaism.

Figure 4. Heschel and Augustin Cardinal Bea, New York, April 1963. Left to right: Rabbi Heschel, Rabbi Marc H. Tannenbaum, National Interreligious Affairs Director of the American Jewish Committee, Augustin Cardinal Bea.
Courtesy of the American Jewish Committee.

Figure 5. Selma-Montgomery, Alabama, 1965. Next to Heschel from right to left, Dr. Ralph Bunche of the United Nations, the Rev. Martin Luther King, Jr., the Rev. Ralph Abernathy.
Courtesy of The Jewish Theological Seminary of America.

Figure 6. Heschel in anti-Vietnam War protest at Arlington Cemetery, 6 February 1968. Left to right: the Rev. Martin Luther King, Jr., the Rev. Ralph Abernathy, Rabbi Maurice Eisendrath, President of the Union of American Hebrew Congregations, Rabbi Heschel.

Photograph by John Goodwin. General Board of Global Ministries.

Figure 7. Heschel teaching Rabbinical Students, 1972.
Courtesy of The Jewish Theological Seminary of America.

Figure 8. Heschel at his desk, August 1972.
Courtesy of Jacob Teshima.

PROPHETIC RADICALISM
Sacred Humanism
and Social Action

> The law demands: one should rather be killed than
> commit murder. Piety demands: one should rather
> commit suicide than offend a person publicly. It is
> better, the Talmud insists, to throw oneself into a
> burning furnace than to humiliate a human being
> publicly.
>
> —Heschel, 1963[1]

In the social domain, throughout the 1960s until his death in 1972, Heschel became a charismatic activist. On the level of appearances, he was recognized as the only traditional Jew (that is, with beard and skullcap) to take radical positions in matters of moral, political, and interreligious controversy. For Christians, especially, he seemed to resemble a Hebrew prophet, picturesque with his bushy white hair, his whiskers, vehement manner, and biblical oratory. Analysis of his poetics of social action demonstrates that, beyond the media images, Heschel's appeal was not artificial. The persona felt authentic because his message conveyed substance.[2]

Heschel's national influence began in 1960 when he adressed the first White House Conference on Youth, and he returned the following year to speak on Aging. In 1963 his denounciation of racism at the first National Conference of Religion and Race mesmerized the audience, and there he met the Rev. Martin Luther King, Jr. (The photograph of Heschel at the side of Rev. King on the 1965 Selma-Montgomery march is still distributed as a reminder of vibrant civil rights alliances now past.) Heschel was among the first to demand the rescue of Soviet Jewry. In Rome, working with Cardinal Bea who admired his biblical scholarship and sharp judgments, he represented the Jewish position at the Second Vatican Council, influencing the drafting of the declaration on the Jews in *Nostra Aetate*. From 1965 on, Heschel was a dramatic presence at press conferences and worship meetings protesting United States warfare in Vietnam.

Heschel's writings now supersede the person. While his passionate positions typify the noble decade of human rights movements and optimistic hopes for reconciliation, his oratory still calls. His writings maintain the spiritual core, addressing readers at a visceral, as well as intellectual, level. These contemporary biblical judgments combine repudiation of human evil and intimacy with the sacred.

Prophecy in the New World

Heschel's activism in the United States was authentically biblical; it derived not from "ethical monotheism"—a secular morality couched in the idiom of the Hebrew prophets, as laudable as it is—but from a convincing sympathy with God: "[The prophet's] life and soul are at stake in what he says and in what is going to happen to what he says. . . . Not only the prophet and the people, but God Himself is involved in what the words convey."[3] Heschel's depth theology applies a spiritual radicalism to current social and political problems.

In his last interview, taped shortly before his death, Heschel claimed that preparing his book *The Prophets* for publication (it appeared in 1962) had thrust him from his tranquil study into public action.[4] Yet his earliest writings in Europe demonstrate that he never separated spiritual and moral concerns. In 1933 he completed his doctoral dissertation on prophetic consciousness (*Das prophetische Bewusstsein*) and published a collection of Yiddish poems, *Der Shem Ham'Forash—Mentsh (Mankind—God's Ineffable Name)*, in which a mystic boldly questions divine compassion and justice.

As explained in chapter 1, in Berlin he joined the literate Jewish public in defying the Nazis.[5] Heschel's 1935 biography of Maimonides portrays a scholar who, at the end of his life, chose medecine and practical healing—Heschel called it "imitation of God"—over study and pure meditation.[6] After emigrating to the United States in 1940, Heschel adapted these models of spiritual activism to conditions in his new homeland.

The Prophets defines the theological foundation of ethics, as it extends the 1933 dissertation. This large, somewhat disorganized book—but highly readable when approached with care—contrasts human and divine responses to evil and analyzes the structure of prophetic consciousness. The author defines a "theology of pathos"—the assumption that God is emotionally involved with history—from which he derives his own commitments. The book speaks to three separable audiences: academic, theological, and political.[7]

On the most practical level, *The Prophets* contains insights and formulations he applied to contemporary events, based on his studies of Amos, Hosea, Isaiah, Micah, Jeremiah, and Habakkuk (chapters 2–8). The prophets are spiritual radicals of ancient Israel who challenge today's cynical expectations. When the author stepped into the public arena, delivering speeches, engaging in protests—and attending numerous committee meetings—he drew some of his most striking phrases and judgments from this erudite book.[8]

The rhetoric of *The Prophets* draws readers into its passionate, situational way of thinking. Alliterations and energetic cadences stir up feelings that flesh out the analysis. Above all, the prophet derives his power from God's involvement with humankind, and his utterances sound exaggerated to us only because our moral outrage is so feeble. The style helps us sense God's infinite sympathy:

> The prophet is a man who feels fiercely. God has thrust a burden upon his soul, and he is bowed and stunned at man's fierce greed. Frightful is the agony of man; no human voice can convey its full terror. Prophecy is the voice that God has lent to the silent agony, a voice to the plundered poor, to the profaned riches of the world. It is a form of living, a crossing point of God and man. God is raging in the prophet's words.[9]

The ethical and the divine live in symbiotic discord, for God cares actively for people and is more dismayed by evil and suffering than we normally allow ourselves to be. The God of Israel is not the Unmoved Mover of the philosophers, but the Most Moved Mover of the prophets, according to Fritz Rothschild's felicitous formulation.[10]

Heschel's analysis of prophetic inspiration shares the goal of his analysis of prayer, ritual, and the *mitzvot*: to recenter thinking from the self to God. Depth theology has political implications. The social activist who uses God as model may thus judge events according to theocentric standards:

> God is the focal point of his thought, and the world is seen as reflected in God. Indeed, the main task of pro-

> phetic thinking is to bring the world into divine focus. This, then, explains his way of thinking. He does not take a direct approach to things. It is not a straight line, spanning subject and object, but rather a triangle—through God to the object. . . . The prophet is endowed with the insight that enables him to say, not I love or I condemn, but God loves or God condemns.[11]

Again, tridimensionality defines authentic religious consciousness. The writer conveys a dynamic relationship with God while imitating, in his own voice, a radical ideal of justice and compassion. Its implications are potentially subversive, to the point of castigating institutional religion itself.

Heschel's Stanford University lectures, published as *Who Is Man?*, translate this prophetic outlook by transforming polemically the terms of philosophical anthropology.[12] Explaining why ethics and theory cannot be separated, he philosophizes in order to surpass philosophy:

> Philosophy, to be relevant, must offer us a wisdom to live by—relevant not only in the isolation of our study rooms but also in moments of facing staggering cruelty and the threat of disaster. The question of man must be pondered not only in the halls of learning but also in the presence of inmates in extermination camps, and in the sight of the mushroom of a nuclear explosion.[13]

Philosophy of religion must include situational thinking, in which speculation absorbs its historical—as well as individual—circumstances. Humanity is not an abstraction. Nor can scholarship remain detached: "Philosophy cannot be the same after Auschwitz and Hiroshima."

Prophetic thinking analyzes human choices using a standard of uncompromising truth. In the 1960s, Heschel's decisions often angered or intimidated complacent or defensive citizens, but inspired those who sought to reconcile progressive politics with a longing for faith and biblical ideals. The effectiveness of his witness—for Christians as for Jews—was due to the fact that he did not collapse spiritual imperatives into tactical ethics. The biblical God remains our ultimate judge.

Reverence for the Divine Image

At the foundation of what I call Heschel's "sacred humanism" is a theology that demands reverence for human beings as *literally* (body and spirit) an image of God.[14] (See chapter 6, final section.) The "human" is not a synonym of weakness and corruption but "a disclosure of the divine, and all men are one in God's care for man. Many things on earth are precious, some are holy, humanity is holy of holies."[15] The precept has substance, as he continues: "To meet a human being is an opportunity to sense the image of God, *the presence* of God." This mystical core—transcendence within the human—defines prophetic ethics. Each and every person is sacred. Heschel derives this theology of the person from the Bible, rabbinic and Kabbalistic interpretations—all of which testify to the living God of concern.[16]

Given the horrors of daily life, this is an astounding doctrine, and one that violates common sense. How little proof we possess that being human is a privilege, almost a miracle. But Heschel does not segregate moral value from piety, since God and humankind are inextricably, metaphysically, intertwined.

Heschel's witness to human holiness takes particular poignancy in North America's post-civil rights era. Distrust and hatred between ethnic communities now appear to be normal. This is not the place to analyze how insecurity—especially among African Americans and Jews, each as marginalized citizens—has pitted one group against the other. Heschel stands out among the numerous Jews who understood that the destiny of African Americans and Jews is one and the same. The Hebrew Bible confirms a kinship deeper than economics and politics.

Heschel's 1963 keynote address to the National Conference on Religion and Race, which inspired many clergy men and women to participate in the great march on Washington, proclaimed a continuity from the Bible to the present: "At the first conference on religion and race, the main participants were Pharaoh and Moses. Moses' words were: 'Thus says the Lord, the God of Israel, let My people go that they may celebrate a feast to Me.' While Pharaoh retorted: 'Who is the Lord, that I should heed this voice and let Israel go? I do not know the Lord, and moreover I will not let Israel go.'"[17] Heschel grounds his judgment on theological insight and it is absolute: "*Racial or religious bigotry* must be recognized for what it is: *satanism, blasphemy*" (Heschel's emphasis).

Reverence for the person is the norm. The rhetoric communicates it by combining sentiment and analysis; its pragmatic aim is to mobilize a reader's ethical consciousness. For true "piety" joins heart and mind in an experience of the sacred—or its absence.

An analysis of the three following paragraphs clarifies how an imaginative sympathy with the afflicted can lead to ethical and religious commitment. The poet's lyrical rhythms, the theologian's insight, and moral analysis harmonize in this modern prophetic consciousness. Law and piety are one:

> My heart is sick when I think of the anguish and the sighs, of the quiet tears shed in the nights in the overcrowded dwellings in the slums of our great cities, of the pangs of despair, of the cup of humiliation that is running over.
>
> The crime of murder is tangible and punishable by law. The sin of insult is imponderable, invisible. When blood is shed, human eyes see red; when a heart is crushed, it is only God who shares the pain.
>
> In the Hebrew language one word denotes both crimes. *Bloodshed*, in Hebrew, is the word that denotes both murder and humiliation. The law demands: one should rather be killed than commit murder. Piety demands: one should rather commit suicide than offend a person publicly. It is better, the Talmud insists, to throw oneself alive into a burning furnace than to humiliate a human being publicly.[18]

The first paragraph is like a biblical verse that emphasizes the mute anguish fostered by social oppression. Compassion for victims of poverty—an economic fact—leads to identification with their inward suffering. A thrust of empathy—anger at the living conditions of the poor, especially the Black poor—moves us because of the author's deliberate positioning of images, repetitions, and verbal rhythms. He interweaves high style—for example, "dwellings," "cup of humiliation" (a renewed biblical metaphor)—into the contemporary example; he protracts the long, flowing sentence, as if in lamentation.

The second and third paragraphs specify a theological judgment. Here we observe how Heschel absorbs classical Jewish sources into a secular sensibility. Human compassion merges with God's pain, as he says later: "Seen from the perspective of prophetic faith, the predicament of justice is the predicament of God."[19] This leads to the Talmudic authority (footnoted in another statement to *Berakhot* 43b[20]) in the third paragraph: "one should rather commit suicide than offend a person publicly." We should not underestimate Heschel's radical position. It is hard to imagine greater devotion to the sanctity of another person.

Returning to our phenomenological analysis, Heschel's narrative has recentered our focus from physical to spiritual distress. This does not mean, however, that Heschel considers economic conditions to be less significant than humiliation. His goal here is not to offer specific social or political solutions but to arouse spiritual indignation. Our sacred humanity is at stake. He sensitizes readers outside the community to the inward degradation of African-American citizens so that we may commit ourselves, whatever the circumstances, to revering God's image in every person. Empathy should lead to action.

Prophetic Ethics versus Expediency

Implicitly repudiating a so-called death-of-God theology in which the holy is a frail product of imagination, Heschel develops an eclipse-of-humankind theology that asserts personal responsibility. Applying traditional texts, he takes citations from the *Zohar*, to assert that human beings and God affect each other.[21] Individuals have the power, and of course the responsibility, to augment or to inhibit the divine presence: "The fate of God is bound up with the fate of Israel [that is, the Jewish people throughout the world]. 'Ye are my witnesses, and I am God.' [Heschel, quoting rabbinic sources, supplies the interpretation:] 'When you are My witnesses, I am God; and when you are not witnesses, I am not God.' We are witnesses, and we sin if we do not bear witness."[22] It is as if we can remove or welcome the Divine by our own free will. Heschel's radical exegesis of Isaiah 43:12 (as glossed in Midrash) gives us daunting power: "In this world God is not God unless we are His witnesses."[23]

The essays and speeches collected in *The Insecurity of Freedom* (1966) perform that almost theurgic partnership. The biblical notion that the individual is infinitely precious clarifies problems related to youth, the aged, and the medical profession: "According to a rabbinic dictum, 'he who saves one man is regarded as if he saved all men; he who destroys one man is regarded as if he destroyed all men.'"[24] To surpass the cliché, he amplifies infinitely the code of reverence for the person, every person, regardless of their identity. Heschel's sacred humanism makes our parochial conscience universal.

For example, the essay "Religion in a Free Society" defines modern faith as a challenge. Religion is not relaxation, not a remedy for anxiety, but a call to action. Dissatisfaction gives it force:

> Religion is spiritual effrontery. Its root is in our bitter sense of inadequacy, in a thirst that can only be stilled by greater thirst, in the embarrassment that we do not really care for God, in the discovery that our religious need is utterly feeble, that we do not feel any need for God.[25]

We begin to perceive our closeness to God, paradoxically, by experiencing the frailty of our devotion to the Ultimate. Humility, then, contributes to moral courage. Individuals, and the religious establishment that propagates their influence, must defy complacency of any kind.

Responsibility is our inescapable inheritance as free citizens. We find the prototype of his Vietnam era slogan—"In a democratic society, some are guilty, all are responsible"—already in *The Prophets* (1962).[26] Particularly in the United States, affluence requires us to make courageous spiritual and ethical decisions. Heschel admonishes religious institutions that have accommodated too comfortably, and individuals who avoid daily spiritual discipline:

> The insecurity of freedom is a bitter fact of historical experience. In times of unemployment, vociferous demagogues are capable of leading the people into a state of mind in which they are ready to barter their freedom for any bargain. In times of prosperity, hidden persuaders are capable of leading the same people into selling their conscience for success. Unless a person learns to rise daily to a higher plane of living, to care for that which surpasses his immediate needs, will he in a moment of crisis insist upon loyalty to freedom?[27]

Medical professionals must recognize human inwardness. Physicians should exercise moral, as well as technological, skill: "A patient is a person in crisis and anxiety, and few experiences have such decisive impact upon our ability to understand the meaning of being human as the way in which the doctor relates himself to us at such times."[28] There is a spiritual standard whenever human beings are involved: "The doctor is not only a healer of disease, he is also a source of emanation of the spirit of concern and compassion."

Heschel's 1960 address on "Children and Youth" opens with a judgment on American culture. He comes right to the point. Alienation—an unhealthy introversion and lack of meaning—is our enemy:

> The problem of our youth is not youth. The problem is the spirit of our age: denial of transcendence, the vapidity of values, emptiness in the heart, the decreased sensitivity to the imponderable quality of the spirit, the collapse of communication between the realm of tradition and the inner world of the individual. The central problem is that we do not know how to think, how to pray, how to cry, how to resist the deceptions of too many persuaders. There is no community of those who worry about integrity.[29]

Heschel examines the total context of each problem in order not to blame, but rather to guide educators. The Bible defines the goal of parenting:

> The mainspring of tenderness and compassion lies in reverence. It is our supreme educational duty to enable the child to revere. The heart of the Ten Commandments is to be found in the words *Revere thy father and thy mother*. Without profound reverence for father and mother, our ability to observe the other commandments is dangerously impaired. The problem we face, the problem I as a father face, is why my child should revere me. Unless my child will sense in my personal existence acts and attitudes that evoke reverence—the ability to delay satisfactions, to overcome prejudices, to sense the holy, to strive for the noble—why should she revere me?[30]

The situation of elderly people also receives a prophetic audit. Heschel judges their problems from his theocentric perspective. Instead of fulfilling their potential as divine image, old people also experience alienation: (1) The sense of being useless to, and rejected by, family and society; (2) a nagging emptiness and boredom; and (3) loneliness and the fear of time. He suggests that we alleviate these realistic uncertainties by enhancing their education toward wisdom. People should prepare for retirement by uplifting their personal concerns:

> The years of old age may enable us to attain high values we failed to sense, the insights we have missed, the wisdom we ignored. They are indeed formative years, rich in possibilities to unlearn the follies of a lifetime, to see through inbred self-deceptions, to deepen understanding and compassion, to widen the horizon of honesty, to refine the sense of fairness.[31]

After developing his analysis of old age, he summarizes its preciousness in a striking aphorism:

> There is no human being who does not carry a treasure in his soul; a moment of insight, a memory of love, a dream of excellence, a call to worship. . . . It takes three things to attain a sense of significant being: God, A Soul, and a Moment.
> And the three are always there.
> Just to be is a blessing. Just to live is holy.[32]

Heschel's succinct formulation—if not reduced to a slogan—might imprint this faith within our own spirits. That is why his pronouncements, which suspicious readers might consider to be glib, should be pondered with reference to depth theology.

Reverence depends ultimately upon our ability—physically, viscerally—to perceive God's presence in each person. It must not remain an abstract deduction of theology, nor a moralistic platitude. Heschel's rhetoric becomes a discipline of the spirit, imbuing us with his almost mystical certainty that God treasures every human life.

Prayer and Political Courage

Prayer can train us to absorb prophetic values. Heschel envisages a harmony between what a person thinks and feels and the substance of ritual. Confluence of word and consciousness is the standard: "Prayer and prejudice cannot dwell in the same heart. Worship without compassion is worse than self-deception; it is an abomination."[33] Authentic worship culminates in our sometimes shattering, usually subtle loyalty to absolute truth. Prayer is our supreme test as it is our ultimate training: "While it is true that being human is verified in relations between man and man, depth and authenticity of existence are disclosed in moments of worship."[34]

Integrity is both a personal and public goal. A complete act of Jewish prayer, for example, harmonizes the three dimensions of being human: the self, the community, and the holy.[35] Such fullness can be achieved by discipline; shared ritual can educate our ability to scrutinize ourselves. That is why Heschel joins both poles of Jewish worship: the regularity of law (or *kevah*) and spontaneity or intention (*kavanah*). Inwardness and collectivity form one act of worship.

Yet, to define his standards, Heschel probes the qualities of the individual prayer consciousness. He goes beyond theological principles in order to locate the churning of emotion and judgment when the worshiper focuses his or her substance into the words:

> To pray is to pull ourselves together, to pour our perception, volition, memory, thought, hope, feeling, dreams, all that is moving in us, into one tone. Not the words that we utter, the service of the lips, but the way in which the devotion of the heart corresponds to what the words contain, the consciousness of speaking under His eyes, is the pith of prayer.[36]

Heschel's musical metaphor of "tone" captures the polyvalent and semantic complexity of spiritual insight. When prayer succeeds, we surrender our ego to the divine Subject, God's awareness of us.

Theocentric prayer also challenges the integrity of our institutions. Religious services cannot remain simply recurrent gatherings during which, if not too bored, we mumble phrases, visit neighbors, and listen to sermons. Ideally, we can personally enter the dramas contained in the prayerbook: "Prayer is a perspective from which to behold, from which to respond to, the challenges we face. Man in prayer does not seek to impose his will on God; he seeks to impose God's will and mercy upon himself. . . . To pray is to open a door, where both God and the soul may enter."[37]

The ideal of holiness challenges worshippers to emulate divine compassion and prophetic demands. That is why Heschel would not compromise with symbolism or religion shrunk to ethics. God is real, not a fiction. Heschel's persistent pointing to ultimate reality warns us not to reduce righteousness to nearsighted expediency, be it sentimental, scientific, or political.

His view of human beings as divine image has international as well as community applications. Sacred ethics requires us to exercise our democratic responsibility by defending truth. From 1965 on, Heschel's outspoken opposition to the Vietnam War shocked cautious people who let politics inhibit their revulsion at American injustice and governmental lying (which Heschel called "mendacity"). Many Jews, believing that they were shielding Israel at a vulnerable moment, also feared an outbreak of anti-Semitism as backlash for liberal religious action. Depth theology, which includes audacious prophetic thinking, drives beyond such calculations.

The Vietnam emergency became the religious imperative of Heschel's final years of life. At a worship meeting in Washington, D.C., in 1967, in which I participated, he explained how the divine image brought him to oppose the war:

> The encounter of man and God is an encounter within the world. We meet within a situation of shared suffering, of shared responsibility.
>
> This is implied in believing in One God in whose eyes there is no dichotomy of here and there, of me and them. . . . Oceans divide us, God's presence unites us, and God is present wherever man is afflicted, and all of humanity is embroiled in every agony wherever it may be.
>
> Though I am not a native of Vietnam, ignorant of its language and traditions, I am involved in the plight of the Vietnamese.[38]

Heschel was speaking as a religious educator asserting the holiness of all human life. Even in our age of God's silence, we can learn to view events from the perspective of the Eternal. The breakdown of trust during that turbulent period made all the more urgent our commitment to biblical standards of personal integrity and civic responsibility.

Heschel represented Jewish tradition even more dramatically at that same interfaith protest against the Vietnam war. He shared the experience of "a child of seven who was reading in school the chapter [of Genesis] which tells of the sacrifice of Isaac."[39] As he continued the story of a childhood empathy with the text, he discreetly introduced the first person pronoun:

> Isaac was on the way to Mount Moriah with his father;
> then he lay on the altar, bound, waiting to be sacri-
> ficed. My heart began to beat even faster; it actually
> sobbed with pity for Isaac. Behold, Abraham now lifted
> the knife. And now my heart froze within me in fright.
> Suddenly, the voice of the angel was heard: "Abraham,
> lay not thine hand upon the lad, for now I know that
> thou fearest God."
>
> And here I broke out in tears and wept aloud. "Why
> are you crying?" asked the Rabbi. "You know that Isaac
> was not killed."
>
> And I said to him, still weeping, "But Rabbi, suppos-
> ing the angel had come a second too late?"
>
> The Rabbi comforted me and calmed me by telling
> me that an angel cannot come late.
>
> An angel cannot be late, but man, made of flesh and
> blood, may be.

We can almost see the Hasidic boy in Warsaw questioning the harrowing contingency of human conscience. This sensibility is a model of prayer, meaningful to Jews, Christians, and Muslims alike. Observant Jews read of the Akedah every day in the morning preparatory service, in the Torah twice a year, on Sabbath *Parashat Vayera* (Genesis 17–22), and on the second day of Rosh Hashanah, the Jewish New Year. Even relatively nonobservant or "three-day Jews"—those who attend synagogue only during the "high holy days"—might seriously ponder the *fear of God,* a powerful, troubling compound of awe and reverence before the Creator and humankind's ultimate responsibility.[40]

Heschel was convinced, from experience, that true prayer could save our religious institutions. Prayer can create commitments, strengthening the self and its militant independence. Addressing an interreligious convocation held in Milwaukee, Wisconsin, Heschel upheld liturgical inwardness (not abstract ethics or theology) as the measure of democracy:

> Religion as an establishment must remain separated
> from the government. Yet prayer as a voice of mercy,
> as a cry for justice, as a plea for gentleness, must not be
> kept apart. Let the spirit of prayer dominate the world.
> Let the spirit of prayer interfere in the affairs of man.
> Prayer is private, a service of the heart; but let concern

and compassion, born out of prayer, dominate public
life. . . .

Prayer is meaningless unless it is subversive, unless
it seeks to overthrow and ruin pyramids of callousness,
hatred, opportunism, falsehoods. The liturgical movement must become a revolutionary movement, seek-
ing to overthrow the forces that continue to destroy
the promise, the hope, the vision.[41]

Prayer is subversive because it requires an absolute commitment
to truth and to recasting society according to God's values. The
divine presence validates Heschel's ethical stands, in much the
same way as his rhetoric is energized by an ardor for the holy.

God as Touchstone

Have these biblical ideals been irremediably perverted by funda-
mentalists, political and religious? It is a painful historical irony
that for centuries, and even now, lethal conflicts have been fostered by "peoples of the Book." The Old and New Testaments—
and the Koran—seem to have engendered viciously self-righteous
progeny, poised to devour each other. Universal justice and compassion have too often been forgotten, as we have silenced the
One God speaking in those pages. We can only speculate how
Heschel might have judged the prospering fanaticisms of our
times.

Within Jewish self-reflection, Heschel's universal application of
biblical ethics challenges a narrow destiny for the State of Israel.[42]
While nationalism and the struggle for ethnic autonomy seem to
be sundering humanity, Heschel warned Israeli Jews not to confuse
religious responsibilities with political rights: "It would be a fatal
distortion to reduce Judaism to individualism. . . . At the same
time, it would be suicidal to reduce Judaism to collectivism or
nationalism. Jewish existence is a personal situation."[43] The
notion of polarity—or a confluence of opposing elements—preserves both individual and group identity. Again, inwardness and
community cannot be separated.

We can apply Heschel's critique of Jewish ideologies to all
nations and traditions that, inevitably, combine politics and
prayer. Depth theology, which presupposes the person's total situation before God and humankind, would impede authoritarian
religion that deprives the individual of freedom (while it may
alleviate some uncertainty). Today's Jews, Christians, and Mus-

lims—in the Holy Land and in our various Diasporas—might emulate the prophets who defended God's vision of oneness against self-interest. Heschel accepted the "insecurity of freedom."

In the United States, developments of the last three decades, it is sad to say, have made Heschel's message all the more compelling. Since the breakdown of trust in our government during the Vietnam war, American politics, with the complicity of some advertising media, has institutionalized mendacity (or deception). Cynicism is the norm, as Heschel recognized, "Distrust thy neighbor as thyself."[44] Hedonism, tolerance or even admiration of greed, and the quest for stimulation have trivialized reverence for the individual.

Spiritual radicalism emboldens us to seek truth, justice, and compassion, in our politics as well as in our hearts. The prophetic model helps us judge the civil and ethnic wars that now threaten the "new world order." There is only one human race. Religious and educational institutions—as well as governments—also submit to judgment. Insight, Heschel reminds us, occurs within consciousness; but God meets the person equally in prayer and in the jungles of the world.[45]

CONFRONTING THE HOLOCAUST
God in Exile

> There are times when defeat is all we face, when horror
> is all that faith must bear. And yet, in spite of anguish,
> in spite of terror . . . we are never overcome with
> ultimate dismay. . . . Wells gush forth in the deserts of
> despair. This is the guidance of faith: "Lie in the dust
> and gorge on faith."
>
> —Heschel, 1951[1]

Heschel's loyalty to the divine image appears to contradict his
recognition of radical evil within history. Yet he does acknowledge dismay, ultimate abandonment, while continuing to address the living God. His itinerary toward faith and observance
(the fulfillment of which is piety) includes ethical anguish. As
seen in chapter 4, his phenomenology of religious insight places
despair at the threshold of revelation: "We must first peer into the
darkness, feel strangled and entombed in the hopelessness of living without God, before we are ready to feel the presence of His
living light."[2]

Heschel extends this cognitive process into a theology of history, as he points to a "meaning beyond absurdity." The principle
of God's pathos—the divine concern—does not exclude a
premise of raw alienation. His Jewish theological summa, *God in
Search of Man*, published in 1955 before the trend of "Holocaust
theology," starkly asks the basic question, "Where is God?"

> This essential predicament of man has assumed a pecu-
> liar urgency in our time, living as we do in a civiliza-
> tion where factories were established in order to exter-
> minate millions of men, women, and children; where
> soap was made of human flesh. What have we done to
> make such crimes possible? What are we doing to
> make such crimes impossible?[3]

How could the author reconcile this evidence of God's indifference with his certainty that God cares for humankind? The short answer is that he separates perplexities about God from the scope of human responsibility. His exposition, however, is more subtle, more compassionate than this rational distinction.

As a witness rooted in the legacy of Sinai, Heschel absorbs the greatest disaster of the twentieth century, known as the Holocaust or the Shoah. Within a nuanced confidence, Heschel answers theologians who have indicted the Almighty for the destruction of European Jewry. To begin reconceiving faith, he carefully differentiates religious doubt from ethics. He maintained his part of the covenant because he believed that the Bible, as a vehicle of God's presence—not secular philosophy or physical science—could provide answers.

Yet Heschel's writings do not focus deliberately on the Holocaust, nor did he write about his life in Europe. He did not share the details of his private losses and his several emigrations. But twenty-five years after his arrival on our shores, in his inaugural lecture as Harry Emerson Fosdick Visiting Professor at the Union Theological Seminary, he defined himself as a refugee:

> I speak as a member of a congregation whose founder was Abraham, and the name of my rabbi is Moses.
>
> I speak as a person who was able to leave Warsaw, the city in which I was born, just six weeks before the disaster began. My destination was New York, it would have been Auschwitz or Treblinka. I am a brand plucked from the fire, in which my people was burned to death. I am a brand plucked from the fire of an altar of Satan on which millions of human lives were exterminated to evil's greater glory, and on which so much else was consumed: the divine image of so many human beings, many people's faith in the God of justice and compassion, and much of the secret and power of attachment to the Bible bred and cherished in the hearts of men for nearly two thousand years.[4]

Addressing Christian theologians and divinity students, Heschel identifies with their common ancestors, Abraham and Moses, who heeded God's call and fathered the Hebrew people. More significant, I believe, is his attempt to penetrate the spiritual consequences of Hitler's intended genocide. The death and torture—physical and psychological—of multitudes of Jews and non-Jews points to a peril from which we increasingly suffer: namely, our diminished image of ourselves.

The biblical thinker answers the most insidious danger of our age. Echoing the prophet Zechariah (3:2) two decades after the allied victory in Europe, Heschel, as "a brand plucked from the fire," asserts human sanctity and the potential of biblical religion to rescue civilization. Repudiating racism that sunders the human family, he calls the next generation to revive "the divine image of so many human beings, many people's faith in the God of justice and compassion, and much of the secret and power of attachment to the Bible."

Before examining the vein of Holocaust theology scattered throughout Heschel's writings, I quote another rare self-description. Responding to a question about a citizen's responsibilities during the Vietnam war, he justified his democratic protest against immoral government policies:

> I am really a person who lives in anguish. I cannot forget what I have seen and have been through. Auschwitz and Hiroshima never leave my mind. Nothing can be the same after that. After all, we are convinced that we must take history seriously and that in history signs of the future are given to us. I see signs of a deterioration that has already begun. The war in Vietnam is a sign that we don't know how to live or how to respond. God is trying us very seriously. I wonder if we will pass the test? I am not a pessimist, because I believe that God loves us. But I also believe that we should not rely on God alone; *we* have to respond.[5]

Heschel speaks here with the authority of a refugee who had witnessed, in Poland and Germany, the War's brutal inception. This faith of a naturalized citizen alludes to the excruciating period—from 1938 when Heschel was expelled from Germany, through his return to Warsaw, nine months of transit in London, until his emigration in 1940 to the United States—which had nurtured a prophetic theology committed to the sanctification of humanity and the redemption of the Holy Name from exile.

Language was his only instrument. Safe in the United States, Heschel became a writer for whom translation, in more than its literal sense, became his only means of rescuing the soul (human and divine) in agony. Within two years of his arrival, by dint of effort and his linguistic gifts, he had mastered the English idiom.

From Yiddish and Hebrew through German and finally in English, he became an activist author in another adopted homeland.

"The Mountain of History"

During his first decade in the United States, Heschel consolidated his theology under the pall of events that became symbolized as Auschwitz and Hiroshima. He defied the destruction of Jewish lives, religion, and cultures by translating his mystical intimacy and Judaic knowledge into terms speakers of English might fathom. He began by revising papers already prepared in Germany and Poland. Two essays on prayer, one written in German, the other in Hebrew, condense his European spiritual legacy.[6]

Heschel drew his first American writings from these formulations, remarkable for their insight but still groping for a systematic vocabulary. While at Hebrew Union College in Cincinnati, he began to construct an academic reputation with essays on the dynamics of inwardness.[7] His first major book in English, *Man Is Not Alone*—published in 1951 after he had moved to New York— includes and extends these reflections of the 1940s.

In light of the Holocaust, the theological category of the "ineffable" reveals its ethical meaning: implicitly, Heschel's writings on prayer and piety burn with an awareness that he was an escapee whose family, friends, colleagues, holy texts, and cultures were decimated. Yet why did his first writings in English focus almost exclusively upon spirituality?

Was the immigrant simply a writer, an "artist" who avoided direct action? Not at all. During the early 1940s, Heschel made several unsuccessful attempts to persuade American Jewish leaders to aid their European brethren. His relative silence about the Holocaust is only apparent, and it disguises a valiant discretion. We find a hint in a little-known interview, published in Yiddish in 1963, in which he recalls the grief of his first years of freedom:

> I was an immigrant, a refugee. No one listened to me. Let me mention three examples: In 1941 I met with a prominent Jewish communal leader, a devoted Zionist. I told him that the Jews of Warsaw endure in the belief that American Jewry is working ceaselessly on their behalf. Were they to know of our indifference, Jews in Warsaw would perish from shock. My words fell on deaf ears. [Another incident in 1942.] In 1943 I attended the

American Jewish Conference of all Jewish organiza-
tions, to appeal that they act to extinguish the flames
that had engulfed East European Jewry. The "conference" had a long agenda—Eretz Yisrael, fascism,
finances, etc.—the last item of which was Jews under
the Germans. By the time they reached this issue,
almost all the representatives had left. I went away bro-
kenhearted.

[Interviewer: "What then, in fact, did you do?"]

I went to Rabbi Eliezer Silver's synagogue in Cincinnati [where Heschel resided], recited Psalms, fasted, and
cried myself out. I was a stranger in this country. My
word had no power. When I did speak, they shouted me
down. They called me a mystic, unrealistic. I had no
influence on leaders of American Jewry.[8]

My purpose in citing these encounters is not to condemn, with
historical hindsight, Heschel's judgment (spoken only in Yiddish) of these narrow, though well-meaning representatives.
Blaming is irrelevant. Their failure to respond to the refugee's
pleas was at the very least a symptom of institutional inertia.
(There were also strict quotas and a general unwillingess of the
American governmental bureaucracy to help Jews.)

However, one prejudice is particularly symptomatic of Heschel's
handicap with regard to the Jewish establishment: a suspicion of
his so-called mysticism. A narrow secularism had closed their
hearts as well as their minds to his authority. As a writer, teacher,
and activist, Heschel would be dogged by this bias against spirituality during his entire career.

The interview describes how Heschel confronted the Holocaust *personally,* after his initial failures to help European Jews
materially. First, he sought solace in the Orthodox synagogue of
Rabbi Eliezer Silver, an activist who rescued many European Jews.
Heschel defied the Destruction through halakhically established
ritual: he prayed, recited psalms and lamentations, fasted, and
wept. The Tradition had provided a context for meaning, if not
the meaning itself.[9] Second, he spoke of his inability to help only
much later—and in his native Yiddish. He thus maintained his
privacy and separated his intimate distress from the confident
persona of his publications in English.

Still the immediate problem remained. How could he save
lives? The dilemma was brutally simple: as an immigrant, he had
no status. Realizing that his influence depended only upon his

writings, in 1943 he published in the *Hebrew Union College Bulletin* an English revision of a speech he had first given in 1938 in Frankfurt, Germany.* Rendered all the more grave by the raging conflicts, the essay now entitled "The Meaning of This War" opened thus:

> Emblazoned over the gates of the world in which we live is the escutcheon of the demons. The mark of Cain in the face of man has come to overshadow the likeness of God. There has never been so much guilt and distress, agony and terror. At no time has the earth been so soaked with blood. Fellow men turned out to be evil ghosts, monstrous and weird. Ashamed and dismayed to live in such a world, we ask: Who is responsible?[10]

This "translation" tragically confirms his European theology of God's exile, even after learning of Germany's most hideous atrocities. Heschel maintained the theology of his 1938 German speech, which he transformed by mastering English syntax, enlivening his previous abstractions through imagery. Again he acknowledged that two dimensions of being human clashed. It took a world war to separate the demonic from the divine.

Settled in the United States, as before in Europe, Heschel judged all humanity to be responsible. A historical—and not a transcendent—process was at work. By 1943 when he published this essay, people could recognize that Hitler was attempting to exterminate Jewish life. For Heschel, genocide was not a recent mutation:

> Our world seems not unlike a pit of snakes. We did not sink into the pit in 1939, or even in 1933. We had descended into it generations ago, and the snakes have sent their venom into the bloodstream of humanity, gradually paralyzing us, numbing nerve after nerve, dulling our minds, darkening our vision. Good and evil, that were once as real as day and night, have become a blurred mist. In our everyday life we worshiped force, despised compassion, and obeyed no law but our unappeasable appetite. The vision of the sacred has all but died in the soul of man. . . .

---

*See Appendix B, "Heschel in Germany."

The outbreak of war was no surprise. It came as a long expected sequel to a spiritual disaster. Instilled with the gospel that truth is mere advantage and reverence weakness, people succumbed to the bigger advantage of a lie—"the Jew is our misfortune"—and the power of arrogance—"tomorrow the whole world shall be ours," "the peoples' democracies must depend upon force." The roar of bombers over Rotterdam, Warsaw, London, was but the echo of thoughts bred for years by individual brains, and later applauded by entire nations. It was through our failure that people started to suspect that science is a device for exploitation; parliaments pulpits for hypocrisy, and religion a pretext for a bad conscience.

He judged that expediency had supplanted the prophetic demand for truth. Human conscience was calloused. God was segregated from thinking, and so our sacred foundation was eclipsed. It did not enter our hearts that images of God were led to slaughter.

That is why, as a writer and teacher, Heschel in America struggled to enhance our spiritual sensitivity. God was present to history. As he had proclaimed in 1938, humanity was not alone in exile. The Divine itself, repudiated, was still crying for redemption. His wartime essay ends with this challenge:

The greatest task of our time is to take the souls of men out of the pit. The world has experienced that [sic] God is involved. Let us forever remember that the sense for the sacred is as vital to us as the light of the sun. There can be no nature without spirit, no world without the Torah, no brotherhood without a father, no humanity without attachment to God. . . .

The martyrdom of millions [in this very hour[11]] demands that we consecrate ourselves to the fulfillment of God's dream of salvation. Israel did not accept the Torah of their own free will. When Israel approached Sinai, God lifted up the mountain and held it over their heads, saying: "Either you accept the Torah or be crushed beneath the mountain."

The mountain of history is over our heads again. Shall we renew the covenant with God?[12]

History had forced Heschel to become a prophetic witness. He had decided that he would represent, for the post-Holocaust world, a model of observant East European Jewry and the continuing covenant. He defended authentic religion—which includes a real God Who demands everything—and its terrifying imperative: "The mountain of history."

The year 1945 marked a decisive turning point in Heschel's translation of the Spirit. He had reaffirmed his loyalty to God in Germany, in 1938; now in New York City, on 7 January 1945, four days before his thirty-eighth birthday, he spoke in his native Yiddish before the YIVO (Jewish Scientific Institute) on the piety of East European Jewry.[13] Then in May of that year, during his last semester of teaching at Hebrew Union College, he became a naturalized American citizen.[14] The following academic year he joined the faculty of The Jewish Theological Seminary of America, where he remained for the rest of his life.

Heschel's first American book, *The Earth Is the Lord's: The Inner Life of the Jew in East Europe* (1950), a translated expansion of his 1945 YIVO speech,[15] completes his metamorphosis from European to American witness. *Earth* is more than a *kaddish* (prayer for the dead) and a lamentation; it summons us to action. The chapter entitled "Kabbalah" recalls the evil that haunted Jews in seventeenth- and eighteenth-century Eastern Europe, echoing his 1938 response to the expulsion of Jews from Germany.

> Man's good deeds are single acts in the long drama of redemption, and not only the people of Israel, but the whole universe must be redeemed. Even the *Shekhinah* itself, the Divine Indwelling, is in exile. God is involved, so to speak, in the tragic state of this world; the *Shekhinah* "lies in the dust." The feeling of the presence of the *Shekhinah* in human suffering became indelibly engraved in the consciousness of the East European Jews. To bring about the restitution of the universe was the goal of all efforts.[16]

We are responsible for God's exile. This is not a metaphor of a human conception, such as "the eclipse of God." It represents a theological insight from God's perspective. At the same time, Heschel could also interpret banishment as a potential source of energy—painful, unforeseeable, but not defeating.

Heschel's theology of the *Shekhinah*, his visceral empathy with the Indwelling, envigorates his ethics.[17] To be a Jew was to share both dispersion and consolation. We can help fulfill God's messianic dreams. A painful and yet elevating "feeling for the presence of the *Shekhinah* in human suffering" should lead to activism—not to cynicism or despair.

Exile and redemption were the systole and diastole of his prophetic faith: "Judaism is the track of God in the wilderness of oblivion. By being what we are, namely Jews; by attuning our own yearning to the lonely holiness of this world, we will aid humanity more than by any particular service we may render."[18] We must not forget, despite our comforts, whose exile we still share: "We are God's stake in human history. We are the dawn and the dusk, the challenge and the test."[19] Jewish tradition is a universal beacon.

Writing and Unspeakable Evil

Heschel's American writings, therefore, respond to his experience of persecution and murder—and express, with discretion, his personal agony. *Man Is Not Alone*, his foundational philosophy of religion, does in fact respond *theologically* to the Destruction. This book, emphasizing God's presence, appeared in 1951, well before "the commanding voice of Auschwitz" (in Emil Fackenheim's phrase) entered public discourse.[20] Chapter 16, "The Hiding God," outlines a post-Holocaust theology Heschel would never presume to elaborate.

These six pages (*Not Alone*, pp. 151–57) compose a narrative—with a prologue, development, and coda. Put another way, "The Hiding God" is a prose poem comparable in richness with the evocation of mystical insight developed earlier in chapter 9 (*Not Alone*, "In the Presence of God"). It is a text of depth theology, evoking ineffable insights and refusing to devise conclusions.[21] "The Hiding God" summarizes, in miniature, a pious thinker's challenge to the living God—Whom, at the same time, he embraces with prayerful intimacy.

The first paragraph introduces the article he had published in the 1943 *HUC Bulletin*, "The Meaning of This War," which comprises the second paragraph.[22] He retains the powerful rhetoric of his original article (without citing the source), while repudiating the accusation of God it seems to imply:

> For us, contemporaries and survivors of history's most terrible horrors, it is impossible to meditate about the compassion of God without asking: Where is God?

> Emblazoned over the gates of the world in which we
> live is the escutcheon of the demons. The mark of Cain
> on the face of man has come to overshadow the like-
> ness of God. There has never been so much distress,
> agony and terror. It is often sinful for the sun to
> shine. . . .
> The major folly of this view seems to lie in its shift-
> ing the responsibility for man's plight from man to
> God, in accusing the Invisible though iniquity is ours.
> Rather than admit our own guilt, we seek, like Adam,
> to shift the blame upon someone else. For generations
> we have been investing life with ugliness and now we
> wonder why we do not succeed.

Responding implicitly to some negative thinkers, Heschel seeks
to discredit the so-called death-of-God conceptions of the time.
Even the phrase was anathema to his Jewish devotion. He insists
that our fellow human beings—not God—chose to annihilate
European Jewry. We do not and cannot adequately understand
the nature of God to justify reproaching the Almighty with mali-
cious neglect.

Applying theocentric thinking, he accuses humankind of projecting onto "God" its own crimes. He focuses, rather, upon
symptoms of human insensitivity—that which we can do something about. He rejects a naive theology of "the ultimate Scape-
goat" in favor of a prophetic imperative:

> We live in an age when most of us have ceased to be
> shocked by the increasing breakdown in moral inhibi-
> tions. The decay of conscience fills the air with a pun-
> gent smell. Good and evil, which were once as distin-
> guishable as night and day, have become a blurred
> mist. But that mist is manmade. God is not silent. He
> has been silenced.

If God is to blame, it is only for giving us freedom. We have the
power to increase God's distance. The interpretation continues:
"Instead of being taught to answer the direct commands of God
with a conscience open to His will, men are fed on the sweetness
of mythology, on promises of salvation and immortality as a des-
sert to the pleasant repast on earth." Theology cannot view history from the vantage point of selfish wish fulfillment.

Modern religion is largely at fault for misreading the Bible and reducing God to symbols. Perfunctory observance of "customs and ceremonies" had supplanted a courageous loyalty to the Ultimate: "God is known from hearsay, a rumor fostered by dogmas, and even nondogmatic thinkers offer hackneyed, solemn concepts without daring to cry out the startling vision of the sublime on the margin of which indecisions, doubts, are almost vile." Again citing (still without reference) his 1943 *HUC* essay, he denounces the institutionalization of religion's ineffable Source: "We have trifled with the Name of God. . . . How skillfully it was trapped and imprisoned in the temples! How thoroughly distorted!"

Two more movements at the end of "The Hiding God" complete Heschel's "theological" response to unspeakable evil. First, he recognizes a sort of objective hinterland in which God allows depravity to flourish. (This view might correspond to an atheistic position. What the faithful interpret as God's silence may be judged to be nonexistence.)

> We have witnessed in history how often a man, a group or a nation, lost from the sight of God, acts and succeeds, strives and achieves, but is given up by Him. . . . God has withdrawn from their life, even while they are heaping wickedness upon cruelty and malice upon evil. The dismissal of man, the abrogation of Providence, inaugurates eventual calamity.
>
> They are left alone, neither molested by punishment nor assured by indication of help. The divine does not interfere with their actions nor intervene in their conscience.[23]

Heschel thus advances his exegesis of history from God's perspective. A strange dialectic defines the modern condition—not without precedent in ancient times. His depth theology of the hiding God recognizes the demonic potential of human callousness.[24]

The narrative's second stage asserts a sacred ethics derived from the Kabbalistic principle that God needs persons to hasten the world's redemption. God responds to human behavior with more than "pathos," reactive emotions. Biblical prooftexts (which he cites in footnotes) validate this mystical exegesis of contemporary events:

> Man was the first to hide himself from God, [Genesis 3:8] after having eaten of the forbidden fruit, and is

still hiding. [Job 13:20–24] The will of God is to be here, manifest and near; but when the doors of this world are slammed on Him, His truth betrayed, His will defied, He withdraws, leaving man to himself. God did not depart of His own volition; He was expelled. *God is in exile.*[25]

God may actively imitate Adam's original withdrawal from responsibility. Theocentric thinking confirms, simultaneously, a transcendent process beyond human control and humankind's accountability to God. Silence with regard to disaster is but a radical form of divine nonintervention—itself provoked by human evil.

Heschel then constructs his sacred ethics, defining a pre-messianic goal: How can we redeem the *Shekhinah,* the divine Presence? Theocentric thinking has reversed the usual ego-centered, subject-object relationship. God is not the problem, we are. A reciprocal process is at work. Refusing to conclude prematurely either that God does not exist or that God had some specific motive in mind for the Holocaust, he elucidates our task:

> More grave than Adam's eating the forbidden fruit was his hiding from God after he had eaten it. "Where art thou?" Where is man? is the first question that occurs in the Bible. It is man's alibi that is our problem. It is man who hides, who flees, who has an alibi. God is less rare than we think; when we long for Him, His distance crumbles away.
>
> The prophets do not speak of the *hidden God* but of the *hiding God.* His hiding is a function not His essence, an act not a permanent state. It is when the people forsake Him, breaking the Covenant that He has made with them, that He forsakes them and hides His face from them. [Deuteronomy 31:16–17] It is not God who is obscure. It is man who conceals Him. His hiding from us is not in His essence: "Verily Thou art a God that hidest Thyself, O God of Israel, the Saviour!" (Isaiah 45:15). A hiding God, not a hidden God. He is waiting to be disclosed, to be admitted into our lives.

We can now explain Heschel's overwhelming emphasis on God's presence. Thirst for the Divine can liberate our passion for holiness. Since God, too, requires help. If we think only of our needs, we remain incapable of identifying with God's need for us. Above all, we must surpass self-concern.

What about those of us who cannot believe? Most of us are more overwhelmed by God's silence than by the divine Presence. For some, the "hiding God" fosters agnosticism or skeptical disbelief; for Heschel, this absence points to the "meaning beyond the mystery":

> Our task is to open our souls to Him, to let Him again enter our deeds. We have been taught the grammar of contact with God; we have been taught by the Baal Shem that His remoteness is an illusion capable of being dispelled by our faith. There are many doors through which we have to pass in order to enter the palace, and none of them is locked.
>
> As the hiding of man is known to God and seen through, so is God's hiding seen through. In sensing the fact of His hiding we have disclosed Him. Life is a hiding place for God. We are never asunder from Him who is in need of us. Nations roam and rave—but all this is only ruffling the deep, unnoticed and uncherished stillness.[26]

Heschel's acknowledgment of diverse, contradictory paths to ultimate value speaks directly to modern and postmodern experiences of fragmentation and infinite slippage of meaning. He invokes the Baal Shem Tov, the founder of Hasidism, to translate his own "grammar of contact" with the Divine beyond language, beyond thought—beyond belief. Tradition again validates his personal insight. Paradoxical thinking is required to grasp it.

The paragraph closes with a rhythmical sentence whose alliterations signal a deeply held conviction. The writer encourages us to "ruffle the stillness" of our own resistance to God's call.

As the narrative ends, the author abruptly switches his tone to evoke despair—for that is where today's faith, especially Jewish faith—must seek rebirth. In order to erect moral agony as its authentic precursor, he cites the Book of Job and a bitter paraphrase of Psalm 37:3 by the Kotzker rebbe:

> There are times when defeat is all we face, when horror is all that faith must bear. And yet, in spite of anguish, in spite of terror, we are never overcome with ultimate dismay. "Even that it would please God to destroy me;

that he would let loose His hand and cut me off, then should I yet have comfort, yea, I would exult even in my pain; let Him not spare me, for I have not denied the words of the holy One" (Job 6:9–10). Wells gush forth in the deserts of despair. This is the guidance of faith: "Lie in the dust and gorge on faith."[27]

Is Job's absurd confidence pertinent—or even possible—in our age? Can we actualize Heschel's paradoxical approach to faith: that in "sensing the fact of [God's] hiding we have disclosed [God]"? To resolve the contradiction, Heschel does not develop a philosophical argument. He responds with a prayer.

A liturgical text is Heschel's most substantial defiance of the Holocaust. The two final pages of "The Hiding God" quote in its entirety Psalm 44, a direct address to the Divine traditionally used to commemorate martyrs.[28] It begins by juxtaposing the people Israel's past intimacy with the Protector with their present abandonment. The incantatory, conventionally poetic style anchors the emotion more deeply than mere reasoning:

> We have heard with our ears, O God, our fathers have told us, what work Thou didst in their days, in the times of old.
> How Thou didst drive out the heathen with Thy hand, and plantedst them; how Thou didst afflict the people, and cast them out.

The middle lines reverberate into the present. Heschel clearly rejects the conventional notion that past disasters—such as the destruction of the Temple by the Romans, the Babylonian exile, and the expulsion of the Jews from Spain—were God's punishment for Jewish sins and lack of faith:

> All this has come upon us; yet have we not forgotten Thee: neither have we dealt falsely in Thy convenant.
> Our heart is not turned back, neither have our steps declined from Thy way. . . .
> If we have forgotten the name of our God, or stretched out our hands to a strange god:
> Shall not God search this out? for He knoweth the secrets of the heart.

And the chapter closes with the Psalm's final words of hope and supplication:

> Wherefore hidest Thou Thy face? and for-
> gettest our affliction, and our oppression?
>   For our soul is bowed down to the dust; our
> belly cleaveth unto the earth.
>   Arise for our help, and redeem us for Thy
> mercies sake.[29]

Heschel's written recital of Psalm 44 does not itself comprise an interpretation. For the general reader, it is a bold prayer, an original act of depth theology that focuses the worshipper's struggle with meaning into a *tone*. And that tone is polyphonic, manifold, perplexing: pained and rebellious—loyal and loving. What is the Psalmist's attitude toward the Almighty? For the traditional reader, it reinforces loyalty to God's law.

Is Heschel bitter, angry—or submissive? Does he challenge God, or place himself, as it were, under God's protective wings? Each time we read printed prayers, each time we worship, the words can become alive with our anguish, with our love, with our spirit—with our endless yearning. Such are the ambiguities, the openendedness of Tradition.

No Post-Holocaust Theology

Heschel's final two books written in English—*Israel: An Echo of Eternity* (1969) and *A Passion for Truth* (1973)—face even more directly the irreducible contradictions of twentieth-century history. His fullest ethical response to the Holocaust remains *The Prophets* (1962), which he dedicated "To the martyrs of 1940–45." Quite significantly, the dedication page again cites Psalm 44, but this time, he selected passages that question *God's* responsibility. Highlighting human pain, the biblical scholar challenges God by repeating the Psalmist's supplication. That selection from the prayer magnifies the author's defiant trust.

For Heschel, Jewish spiritual vitality is the only enduring answer to the Holocaust. That message, stated passionately at the end of *The Earth Is the Lord's* (see our chapter 2), lies at the heart of *Israel: An Echo of Eternity*. Heschel wrote this book after the June 1967 war, in the wake of fears of annihilation provoked by Arab attacks. Reflections on the Holocaust provide the context for explaining to Christians the Jewish attachment to the State of Israel:

> What should have been our answer to Auschwitz? Should this people, called to be a witness to the God of mercy and compassion, persist in its witness and cling to Job's words: "Even if He slay me yet will I trust in Him" (Job 13:15), or should this people follow the advice of Job's wife, "Curse God and die!" (Job 2:9), immerse itself into the anonymity of a hundred nations all over the world, and disappear once and for all?
>
> Our people's faith in God at this moment in history did not falter. At this moment in history Isaac was indeed sacrificed, his blood shed. We all died in Auschwitz, yet our faith survived. We knew that to repudiate God would be to continue the holocaust. . . .
>
> What would be the face of Western history today if the end of twentieth-century Jewish life would have been Bergen-Belsen, Dachau, Auschwitz? The State of Israel is not an atonement. It would be blasphemy to regard it as a compensation. However, the existence of Israel reborn makes life in the West less unendurable. It is a slight hinderer of hindrances to believing in God.[30]

Heschel does not rationalize the Holocaust theologically. He verifies the fact that the Jewish people, as a collective personality, has overcome despair, and that the creation of the State of Israel is a concrete repudiation of Hitler's blasphemy, the racist defilement of the divine image. Israel represents a possible answer to the question of faith after Auschwitz, but the answer is *not* definitive; it is a task.

Heschel refuses to systematize the unspeakable—whether it be the divine Presence, God's silence at our agony, or massive evil. As is faith itself, trust in God is not static, like a formulated creed, but an unending challenge, a way of thinking about nothing less than redemption: "And yet, there is no answer to Auschwitz. . . . [Heschel's ellipses] To try to answer is to commit a supreme blasphemy. Israel enables us to bear the agony of Auschwitz without radical despair, to sense a ray of God's radiance in the jungles of history."[31]

This is no reassuring conclusion. Although his "theology of pathos" trains us to view events from the perspective of the Eternal, he offers no dutiful explanations for suffering and injustice. Depth theology asserts that no position taken by the mind is final. Ultimate meaning remains a mystery, unknown.

What faith can be realistic at the end of our present century? The world in which we live is a post-Auschwitz, post-Hiroshima world. Does our responsibility for these abominations contradict Heschel's trust that God remains involved in a continuing human process of redemption? Heschel does not provide slogans to lighten our charge, insisting that we face the Creator—our helplessness and our powers—directly. This view implies that Jewish identity must come from the living God of the Bible, not primarily from Auschwitz nor from the State of Israel.

Yet antitheses or logical aporia cannot encompass the reality of evil. Heschel's prophetic ethics introduces a further distinction. Beyond the duality of good and evil, existence comprises a mixture, an inseparable *amalgam*. Radical evil is part and parcel of radical goodness:

> Even more frustrating than the fact that evil is real, mighty, and tempting is the fact that it thrives so well in disguise of the good, that it can draw its nutriment from the life of the holy. In this world, it seems, the holy and the unholy do not exist apart, but are mixed, interrelated and confounded. It is a world where idols may be rich in beauty, and where the worship of God may be tinged with wickedness.[32]

Even faith cannot untie the Gordian knot. Only piety can: truly religious action. Depth theology keeps unanswerable questions alive, and in such a way that our courage in face of God's remoteness is strengthened. Whatever we believe, Heschel calls us to repudiate evil (within us and outside) and to redeem the world. We remain vigilant.

METAPHOR AND MIRACLE
Modern Judaism and the Holy Spirit

> A fiery blast seems to issue from his mouth when he
> speaks of the prophetic vision. He describes this state in
> the fiery colors that only a man who has undergone the
> experience could invoke. . . . Just as the individual
> perishes if he ceases breathing for one instant, so will
> he perish if the holy spirit, or prophecy, abandons him.
> —Heschel, 1945[1]

Our literary analysis, if successful, has elucidated how Heschel's style pulses with the holy. Reading his multilayered narrative is itself an existential process leading to a "turning" to God. Readers learn the art of depth theology, intuitions preceding statements of creed. Surrendering ego-centered thought, we become ready to receive the commanding incursion of the Divine. Briefly put, Heschel's metaphors, which reflect human experience, prepare us for the miracle of revelation.

His narrative dramatizes one modern Jew's confidence in God's covenant. But rhetoric alone cannot explain why Heschel's writings (and the Bible) have inspired religious commitment in readers of all backgrounds. He believed that, beyond the verbal experience, God, the ultimate Source of sanctification, energizes us. He hoped that readers would meditate his words thoughtfully and prayerfully and so identify with his part in *ruah ha-Kodesh*—a term rendered in English by "Holy Spirit."

Yet he concealed from English-speaking readers this esoteric source of his own power. He unveiled his secret only indirectly, in two abundantly documented monographs written in Hebrew, "Prophetic Inspiration in the Middle Ages" and "Did Maimonides Believe He Had Attained the Rank of Prophet?"[2] Two to three hundred carefully footnoted references in each paper cite rabbinic scholars (and other authorities) who claim that postbiblical Judaism may include prophetic inspiration—also referred to as *ruah ha-Kodesh.* Remarks imbedded in his analysis of other people's testimonies suggest that Heschel himself participated in divine inspiration.

As a Hasidic child in Warsaw, Heschel lived among the devout leaders of his parents' generation. He told some of his closest students that his first American article, "An Analysis of Piety" (1942), was a portrait of his uncle, the rebbe of Novominsk, Rabbi Alter Israel Shimon Perlow (1874–1933), his mother's twin brother:[3] "Awareness of God is as close to him as the throbbing of his own heart, often deep and calm, but at times overwhelming, intoxicating, setting the soul afire."[4] Our chapter 5 describes how Heschel transported this ideal into his writings in English. We now consider how his academic scholarship (written mostly in German, Hebrew, and Yiddish) implies his own uplifting by the Presence.[5]

The Historicity of Divine Inspiration

The European prehistory of Heschel's American writings demonstrates an esoteric foundation, God's continuing voice. On a cultural level, his ideal of "piety" (in Hebrew, *hasidut*) flows directly from his ancestry as scion of the noble Hasidic dynasties of Apt, Ruzhin, Novominsk, and Berditchev. Yet beyond lies a mystical claim. As early as 1933, Heschel began to insert his personal conviction into his academic research. His Berlin doctoral dissertation, *Die Prophetie* (On Prophecy), inaugurates a lifetime commitment to a theocentric vision.[6]

Even this highly technical, objective study suggests that contemporaries can in some way partake of the Spirit. Its two concluding chapters—"Theology of Pathos" and "Religion of Sympathy"[7]—define humankind's relation to God in terms of "prophetic sympathy," active identification with the "divine pathos," the emotions that God conveys in reaction to historical and personal events.

A detail in *Die Prophetie* introduces Heschel's own hypothesis (which he shared with medieval philosophers) that normal consciousness includes a cognitive faculty analogous to God's *ruah ha-Kodesh.* Referring to a (then and still) unpublished paper he wrote on "The Word *Ruah* in the Bible" (*Das Wort Ruah in der Bibel*), Heschel defends his use of "human" emotions as metaphorical approximations of the prophet's understanding of God: "We find in the Bible a theomorphic anthropology. The spiritual construction of mankind is comprised of divine elements. The biblical person considers the soul, thought, feeling, even the passions, as inspired by God."[8]

Readers of his German thesis can sense the author's devotion to his subject. Amidst the sometimes strained, scrupulous analysis there emerges a compelling confession of his own calling:

> We understand the person impassioned with prophetic zeal, who knows himself to be in emotional agreement and harmony with God. We understand the power of Him impassioned with anger and who turns away from his people.
>
> That overwhelming knowledge [*erschütterndes Wissen*] of the concern and suffering that God experiences for the world, and the prophet's sharing of that lived predicament and suffering, is of such power, of such obvious value, and so unique, that even today this idea acts as a summons carrying distinct shapes and possibilities. Perhaps this is the final meaning, value, and dignity of an emotional religion. The depths of the individual soul thus become the place where the comprehension of God [*Verständnis für Gott*] flowers, the harmony of agreement [*Einverständnis*] with the transcendent pathos.[9]

Heschel's next work in German (published the year before his dissertation went to press) brings prophetic inspiration closer to modernity. It is a biography of Moses Maimonides (1135–1204), the medieval philosopher, Talmudic genius and sage, codifier and physician, admired particularly for his rational theology. This was Heschel's first book written for a wide public, based upon the latest scholarly resources; it appeared in Berlin in 1935 to commemorate the eight hundredth anniversary of the Rambam's birth. In retrospect, Heschel's *Maimonides* emerges as an anticipatory autobiography, shaping his ideal of the Jewish mind, spiritual personality, and ethical commitments.

Maimonides's life and writings demonstrate the mystical foundation of reason and obedience to *halakhah* (revealed law). Significantly, Heschel highlights the Rambam's inward development and his search for unmediated divine communication—opposing the prevailing view that Maimonides himself refused to claim prophetic inspiration.[10] The chapter on "Prophecy" describes how the philosopher's entire life was absorbed by a desire to encounter God:

> His family preserved a tradition that was handed down
> from father to son since the Destruction of the Temple:
> as of the year 1216, the spirit of prophetic illumination
> would return to the world. Could not Maimonides's
> intense yearning for prophecy have helped him partic-
> ipate in this precious gift? . . . Only this personal moti-
> vation can explain the central place held by the prob-
> lem of prophecy in Maimonides's philosophy.[11]

Maimonides, like Heschel, "quite early in life" decided to write a
book on the prophets. The Rambam did not fulfill this ambition;
Heschel succeeded.

The last chapter of Part 1, "Meditation on God," stresses the
mystical or prophetic elements in Maimonides's philosophy.
There Heschel insists that the thinker from his youth was possessed by "an urge to know God." His rationalistic metaphysics
was fueled by mystical aspiration:

> His thought, his reflections, his concentration on that
> problem determined his spiritual attitude for his entire
> life. His passion of the intellect, his almost naive desire
> to understand, his quest and his research to achieve an
> understanding of that secret never ended; for in his
> mind, which ceaselessly throbbed with emotion, the
> longing for God came not only from a vague, dark feel-
> ing, but more from an intellectual necessity: that
> yearning thought is what provoked his research into a
> metaphysical system.[12]

Maimonides's spiritual passion explains how an intellectual process allowed him to reach God. Heschel's scholarship followed
the same path.

During his first five years in the United States, Heschel's writings
return to this preoccupation. He published several articles in
English on prayer and inward piety. He also communicated more
directly to Judaic scholars in two monographs written in Hebrew,[13]
both of which counter "the unanimous belief of the sages of the
Talmudic era (may their memory be for a blessing) and also in the
Middle Ages, that with the death of Haggai, Zechariah and Mala-
chi, prophetic inspiration ceased in Israel."[14]

Again Maimonides, mentor for modern Orthodox defenders of
the halakhic mind, becomes the model. Heschel's 1945 monograph in Hebrew, "Did Maimonides Believe that He Had Attained

the Rank of Prophet?" complements the less formal essays in English on piety, faith, and prayer written during the same period. Now he unequivocally claims what the 1935 biography had suggested: The consummate rationalist had not only yearned for prophecy since youth, but his descriptions of the lightning flash, fiery colors, and other signs of divine illumination, were autobiographical: "In this book [*Chapters Concerning Felicity*] Maimonides does not hesitate to admit that he has reached the 'ultimate felicity,' that is, prophecy. This admission is clear and explicit. He sets up the principle that the man who has attained such perfection is in duty bound to influence other persons as he has been influenced by the divine efflux."[15]

Heschel's next paragraph further proves that the Rambam admitted that he was inspired by God. We can interpret the scholar's lyricism as a veiled confession: "A fiery blast seems to issue from his [Maimonides's] mouth when he speaks of the prophetic vision. He describes this state in fiery colors that only a man who has undergone the experience could invoke."

Let me formulate a bold hypothesis: Heschel saw himself, like Maimonides, as a philosopher inspired by the Holy Spirit. His 1945 monograph "makes public" what the medieval apologist had kept secret. One further detail must suffice: Maimonides seems to anticipate the expository technique of *Man Is Not Alone* and Heschel's other books: "[Maimonides] openly asserted in the introduction to the *Guide to the Perplexed* that he would not reveal any 'secrets' beyond the citation of 'chapter headings' alone." Heschel's expository format—with its dramatic chapter subtitles—strikes a note of extraordinary confidence. Heschel too, like Maimonides, felt compelled to "influence other persons as he [had] been influenced by the divine efflux."

Heschel's monograph continues by comparing Maimonides with a major predecessor, Saadia Gaon (882–942), the Egyptian philosopher, Talmudist, and translator of the Bible into Arabic: "[Maimonides] does not ask, as Saadia does, What is the purpose of prophecy? He asks rather: What is the nature of prophecy? What happens when a man receives the divine efflux? What are the preconditions that ready the soul for prophecy? The object of inquiry is the place of the Holy Spirit in the life of the prophet and not its function in the life of the people."[16]

Heschel's phenomenology of religious cognition answers both questions. Taken together, these medieval thinkers justify the link in Heschel's apologetics between "philosophical thought" and "mystical insight." (Heschel, in another monograph, written in pellucid English, *The Quest for Certainty in Saadia's Philosophy*, grounds his refutation of contemporary skepticism on a technical analysis of this early metaphysician.[17])

Heschel's Hebrew monograph on Maimonides, as Moshe Idel points out in his preface to the English translation, "illustrates Heschel's effort to detect an organic link between what are, prima facie, distinct spiritual phenomena: Jewish philosophy and Kabbalah." Heschel indeed points out (in the final section VI) that Maimonides's son, Rabbi Abraham, who represented his father's thought, greatly influenced the Sufi mystics of his day. Rabbi Abraham Maimonides, for his part, considered these Islamic luminaries as the true inheritors of Hebrew prophecy.

Heschel further confirms this link between philosophy and Kabbalah in remarks about Rabbi Abraham ben Samuel Abulafia (b. 1240), the great ecstatic mystic.[18] The study of Maimonides concludes with these challenging lines about Abulafia: "He too claimed doctrinal derivation and descent from Maimonides. Was he being completely arbitrary when he declared that the *Guide* and the *Sefer Yetzirah* [Book of Creation] were the sole guides to esoteric wisdom? Perhaps such a statement is not without special significance. Or perhaps a secret was revealed to him that is hidden from our view. The answer is the Lord's." Heschel does not invoke God in vain. At the very end of his monograph, crafted with the rigor of *Wissenschaft des Judentums*, he gently flutters the veil of his own spirit. He too, like Abulafia, would guide readers across the bridge from reason to revelation.

Heschel's complementary Hebrew monograph, "Prophetic Inspiration in the Middle Ages" (1950) further demonstrates the continuity of divine revelation, prophecy, and Jewish mysticism: "The attainment of the rung of the Holy Spirit and prophecy was the strongest wish of the great Kabbalists [note 89]. It was a traditional belief among those esoterics that the secrets were revealed to the Kabbalists by Elijah himself. This opinion, which contributed mightily to the diffusion of the Kabbalah, was already prevalent in Kabbalistic circles in the thirteenth century [note 90]."[19] In addition, Heschel cites authorities who were convinced that Rashi [Rabbi Shlomo Yitzhaki, 1040–1105, author of the standard commentaries on Bible and Talmud], among others, had regularly received insights of textual interpretation directly from the Holy Spirit.

Space limitations preclude even a hint of Heschel's copious documentation. Again, I point only to the author's guarded confessions of faith. The monograph's final paragraph, in fact, asserts that *ruah ha-Kodesh* remains current. After citing plausible instances among the Babylonian sages, he carefully summarizes *their* positions:

> One cannot grasp the innermost thought of the holy men of Israel without remembering that in their eyes, prophetic inspiration hovered over human reason, and, at times, heaven and earth would meet and kiss. They believed that the divine voice that issued from Horeb was not stilled thereafter. "These commandments the Lord spoke in a great voice to your whole assembly on the mountain out of the fire, the cloud and the thick mist, then he said no more" (Deuteronomy 5:19). Onkelos translated (and also Targum Jonathan), "it—the great voice—has not ceased from speaking." [note 196: Rashi adds: "for His voice is mighty and exists forever." This interpretation is found also in the Babylonian Talmud, *Sanhedrin* 17b and *Sotah* 10b.]

In such passages, the "esoteric Heschel" and the "exoteric Heschel" are one. He would transport this entire text, with its precise references, into *God in Search of Man* (chapter thirteen). There his voice subsumes the interpretative Targum translations and Rashi, maintaining the contradiction: God has spoken in a definitive way and yet God's power to inspire minds continues. For all practical purposes, Heschel is confident that twentieth-century readers can still receive the Voice.[20]

Contemporary Judaism and God's Presence

We have surveyed the strategy of *Man Is Not Alone* and *God in Search of Man*, both of which begin by evoking emotions of awe and wonder, eventually provoking "radical amazement," which leads to the brink. (Chapters 3 to 5 of the present book describe how the depth theologian recenters consciousness from the person to God.) Readers are introduced to *ruah ha-Kodesh* through a philosophical argumentation aimed at provoking a "profound awareness of the incongruity of all categories with the nameless unfathomable omnipresence of the mystery."[21] Yet we ultimately depend upon God's initiative. Heschel makes a literal claim.

Heschel's Hebrew monographs name as *ruah ha-Kodesh* what he calls "radical insight" in his books in English. *Man Is Not Alone,* chapter 9, "In the Presence of God" (pp. 67–79) dramatizes the goal to harmonize piety and prophetic activism. As a pedagogical model, that episode traces how God's self-disclosure inspires the person to lead a moral and holy life (see chapter 5).

The author documents the same revelation (which we can also call "mystical illumination") in *God in Search of Man*, its sequel. Revelation should complete Heschel's frequent assertions of *certainty*—not only that God exists but that God has "spoken" and still speaks to the children of Abraham. The footnote references to rabbinic and rare Jewish prooftexts certify how tradition recognizes the probability of revelation after the time of the prophets. His intricate defense adduces Jewish historical testimonies to claim universal validity to God's original covenant at Mount Sinai (*In Search*, "Revelation," pp. 167–278). Much is at stake in this additional framing of the Holy Spirit.

The central chapter of *God in Search of Man*—also entitled "God in Search of Man," epitomizing the book's goal—reiterates the divine encounter previously examined. For the sake of brevity, I emphasize the text's general organization without dwelling on details.

To begin, Heschel introduces the miraculous moment with a theological assertion, supported by rabbinic authority. Even as the author conveys his certainty in resplendent prose, he hallows his predecessors:

> For God is not always silent, and man is not always blind. His glory fills the world; His spirit hovers above the waters. There are moments in which, to use a Talmudic phrase, heaven and earth kiss each other; in which there is a lifting of the veil at the horizon of the known, opening a vision of what is eternal in time. Some of us have at least once experienced the momentous realness of God. Some of us have at least caught a glimpse of the beauty, peace, and power that flow through the souls of those who are devoted to Him. There may come a moment like a thunder in the soul, when man is not only aided, not only guided by God's mysterious hand, but also taught how to aid, how to guide other beings. The voice of Sinai goes on forever: "These words the Lord spoke unto all your assembly in the mount out of the midst of the fire, of the cloud, and of the thick darkness, with *a great voice that goes on for ever*" [Heschel's emphasis].[22]

Integrating private intuition and sacred history, Heschel claims that revelation is still available. He duplicates prooftexts cited more succinctly in his 1950 Hebrew monograph on medieval manifestations of *ruah ha-Kodesh* and pledges to "guide other beings." As a modern philosopher of religion, Heschel recognizes that his readers demand both reasoned and experiential verification.

To that end, Heschel again rallies the aid of Maimonides. He cites a long passage from *Guide of the Perplexed* (also included in his 1945 Hebrew monograph) that defines different degrees of contact with God's presence. Heschel thus lends to his own insights the authority of the revered rationalist and codifier. This strategy confirms suggestions in his 1935 biography and 1945 monograph that, since the Rambam had claimed (even covertly) prophetic illumination, others could do so. Here is what Heschel highlights from Maimonides:

> "Some of us experience such flashes of illumination frequently, until they are in almost perpetual brightness, so that the night turns for them into daylight. . . . With others again there are long or short intermissions between the flashes of illumination, and lastly there are those who are not granted that their darkness be illuminated by a flash of lightning, but only, as it were, by the gleam of some polished object or the like of it, such as the stones and [phosphorescent] substances that shine in the dark night; and even that sparse light that illumines us is not continuous but flashes and disappears as if it were the *gleam of the ever-turning sword* (Genesis 3:24)."[23]

Significantly, Heschel's footnote to this quotation (p. 143, n. 6) adduces an analogous passage from the *Zohar*, suggesting that there is no intrinsic antagonism among the mystical, the rational, and the prophetic perspectives. The passage from Maimonides continues by stating that "the great mass of mankind" possesses no inkling of divine Truth. Heschel, for his part, rejects the Rambam's harsh judgment of the multitudes.

In the United States, Heschel directed his writings primarily to those who have experienced either vague moments of religious insight or none at all—that is, to most of us. For he recognized that, in the twentieth century, Maimonides is right: Spiritual blindness is our normal state. Each type of discernment—from the atheist or agnostic, who receives no light, to the mystic, habitually charged with splendor—deserves a distinct appeal from the apologist.

That is why Heschel's literary style emphasizes intuitions of the sacred as conveyed by "reflected objects," not by God directly. His lyrical expositions usually dwell upon the phosphorescent aura of sublime nature, the majestic accomplishments of music, literature, or art, and the tender beauties of personal kindness. Refractions of the supernal are within reach: "Music, poetry, religion—they all [originate] in the soul's encounter with an aspect of reality for which reason has no concepts and language has no names."[24]

Yet, a harsher, negative process is ultimately needed. Heschel's discourse can be poetically seductive, but he recognizes finally that darkness can be overcome only by demolishing intellectual arrogance. He applies Maimonides's hierarchy of insights as he evokes the same moment of illumination already developed in *Man Is Not Alone*. This time, as well, Heschel insists that despair is necessary to unshackle the mind:

> Only those who have gone through days on which words were of no avail, on which the most brilliant theories jarred the ear like mere slang; only those who have experienced ultimate not-knowing, the voicelessness of a soul struck by wonder, total muteness, are able to enter the meaning of God, a meaning greater than the mind.
>
> There is a loneliness in us that hears. When the soul parts from the company of the ego and its retinue of petty conceits; when we cease to exploit all things but instead pray the world's cry, the world's sigh, our loneliness may hear the living grace beyond all power.[25]

Heschel's peroration—his rhythmical prose, internal rhymes, repetitions, and powerful images—arouse within readers the forceful pull of emptiness and yearning for God. Yet immediately after the potentially lethal moment, he reassures us: "our loneliness may hear the living grace" of God. He wants us to ask: What within us attends to the Divine?

The answer awaits us. The next two paragraphs repeat the moment of crisis while adding quotations to interpret the essentially formless, wordless event. This expository method mixes literature and testimony, demonstrating that alienation is not final.

The person receiving revelation participates, by that very fact, in Jewish spiritual and communal history:

> We must first peer into the darkness, feel strangled and entombed in the hopelessness of living without God, before we are ready to feel the presence of His living light.
>
> "And it shall come to pass, when I bring a cloud over the earth, that the bow shall be seen in the cloud" (Genesis 9:14). When ignorance and confusion blot out all thoughts, the light of God may suddenly burst forth in the mind like a rainbow in the sky. Our understanding of the greatness of God comes about as an act of illumination. As the Baal Shem said, "like a lightning that all of a sudden illumines the world, God illumines the mind of man, enabling him to understand the greatness of our Creator." This is what is meant by the words of the Psalmist: "He sent out His arrows and scattered [the clouds]; He shot forth lightnings and discomfited them." The darkness retreats, "The channels of water appeared, the foundations of the world were laid bare" (Psalms 18:15–16).

In the end, Heschel's recapitulation of terrifying despair advances his retrieval of Tradition. He assumes that contemporary Judaism, as well, can provide a home for the Holy Spirit. His rhetoric demonstrates pragmatically that the *mitzvot* (divine commandments), regular prayer, and Torah study are necessary means of cleaving to God: "Jewish law is sacred prosody. The Divine sings in our deeds, the Divine is disclosed in our deeds. . . . In exposing our lives to God we discover the Divine within ourselves and its accord with the Divine beyond ourselves."[26]

Heschel considers Judaism—ancient and present—as a repository of the Holy Spirit, envigorated by a supernatural Presence both beyond and within our texts, systems of beliefs, and practices. All his works direct our minds and hearts to the eternal Source: "The essence of Jewish religious thinking does not lie in entertaining a concept of God but in the ability to articulate a memory of moments of illumination by His presence."[27]

The force of Heschel's writings thus derives from both classical Jewish prooftexts and spiritual conviction—confirmed by contact with God. He asserts, with normative Judaism, that all Jews can bear witness to the *original* event: "There is no one who has no faith. Every one of us stood at the foot of Sinai and beheld the voice that proclaimed, *I am the Lord thy God*. Every one of us participated in saying, *We shall do and we shall hear*. However, it is the evil in man and the evil in society silencing the depth of the soul that block and hamper our faith."

Then, surpassing parochial inference, he cites the Midrashic interpretation of this passage to validate his universality: "*Tanhuma, Yitro*, I. The words, according to the Rabbis, were not heard by Israel alone, but by the inhabitants of all the earth. The divine voice divided itself into 'the seventy tongues' of man, so that all might understand it. *Exodus Rabba*, 5,9."[28]

At the borders of orthodoxy and liberalism, Heschel's writings call to the Holy Spirit within all readers. For he assumes that sensitivity to holiness—a gift emanating from the Divine—is intrinsic to all people: "Recondite is the dimension where God and man meet, and yet not entirely impenetrable. He placed within man something of His spirit (see Isaiah 63:10), and 'it is the spirit in a man, the breath of the Almighty, that makes him understand' (Job 32:8)."[29] Condensing in an aphorism the theology of *God in Search of Man*, the final sentence of *The Prophets* reaffirms *ruah ha-Kodesh* within intuition: "There is no self-understanding without God-understanding."[30]

Toward the Future

Heschel hoped thus to nurture the Holy Spirit of today's Judaism. Yet he did not depend entirely upon miracles. *Ruah ha-Kodesh* can ring the bells, but we do not have to wait for God to pull the cords. In the end, for all his deft rhetoric, bold textual exegesis, and mystical testimony, Heschel's route to illumination is relatively modest:

> Inspirations are brief, sporadic and rare. In the long interims the mind is often dull, bare and vapid. There is hardly a soul that can radiate more light than it receives. To perform a *mitzvah* is to meet the spirit. But the spirit is not something we can acquire once and for all but something we must constantly live with and pray for. For this reason the Jewish way of life is to reiterate the ritual, to meet the spirit again and again, the spirit in oneself and the spirit that hovers over all beings.[31]

He urges us to practice Judaism as best we can. Although he strives to bring readers to the divine threshold, to help us shatter our banal consciousness, he understands that religious living is a practical matter. His suggestions are elementary.

Heschel patiently introduces those traditions he considers to be nearest to holiness. The Sabbath—consistent observance of the Seventh Day—provides a regular entrance to the Holy of Holies.[32] Yet he respected our shortcomings and proposed a "ladder of observance," a "pedagogy of return" to Judaism.[33] The norm is traditional, the teaching liberal: "The highest peak of spiritual living is not necessarily reached in rare moments of ecstasy; the highest peak lies wherever we are and may be ascended in a common deed. There can be as sublime a holiness in fulfilling friendship, in observing dietary laws, day by day, as in uttering a prayer on the Day of Atonement."[34]

There is mystery but no secret. The exoteric Heschel opens the window to the Holy Spirit. God's presence lies waiting in our primal Jewish texts: the Bible and the prayerbook. These are the foundation of Sabbath observance—eventually, they may become guides to our daily prayer and study, thinking and feeling. It is true that we need teachers, flesh-and-blood examples. Yet we may find that books maintain the vision more authentically than do most people. That remains our drama: Rising to the standards God has defined. Whatever the yearning is that throbs within us—whether or not we call it the Holy Spirit—it is our responsibility to make it live.

HESCHEL'S UNFINISHED SYMPHONY
Reverence, Dismay, and Exaltation

> To Jewish tradition, too, paradox is an essential way of understanding the world, history, and nature. Tension, contrast, contradiction characterize all of reality. . . . However, there is a polarity in everything except God. For all tension ends in God.
>
> —Heschel, 1955–56[1]

Our expedition began with the question, "How do we rise from saying (or reading) the word *God* to sensing God's realness?" Heschel's testimony, both scholarly and personal, insists that God still speaks: "The words of the Bible are sources of spirit. They carry fire to the soul and evoke our lost dignity out of our hidden origins. Illumined, we suddenly remember, we suddenly recover the strength of endless longing to sense eternity in time."[2] His polyphonic narrative appeals to our entire awareness—emotional and intellectual—integrating our being. His "indicative" language moves us into the presence of the divine Subject, God.

Reading Heschel can become a propaedeutic of the spirit. We study him for the fearful purpose of transforming our very consciousness of reality—not only for learning and edification. Linguistic awareness prevents us from "imprisoning God's voice in the temples,"[3] from replacing the Transcendent with creed or ideology. His poetics of faith and piety advances our engagement with the Bible, the prayerbook, traditional commentaries, and contemporary interpretations. By construing the religious idiom as "more than literal," we can surpass "symbols" and retrieve the living fountain of all spiritual traditions.

Religious thinking rediscovers the common foundation. As Heschel often repeated: "Theologies divide us, depth theology unites us."[4] All the religions of the Book—Judaism, Christianity, Islam, the progeny of Abraham—struggle with the same God.

Depth theology deconstructs concepts and dogmas, often used to justify war and hatred. At the same time, theologies can give structure and meaning to our lives and define communities. Doctrines lend shape to the ineffable.

Theocentric thinking provides an evaluative standard for contemporary religion. God cannot be avoided nor subordinated to narrow aims. To those Jews who secularize the tradition (some Reform and Reconstructionist), to those who obey the law without reference to inward authenticity (some Orthodox and Conservative), Heschel insists that the *mitzvot* (commandments) are true expressions of God's will—and that God wants both soul and body. Adherents to Orthodoxy, Reform, Conservative, Reconstructionist, or alternative communities can thus share this common source of energy, and ultimate validation, beyond institutional self-definitions.

Yet Heschel addresses a vaster audience, translating the Spirit into the vernacular for all people, Jew, Gentile, or nonbeliever. Of course his vision derives from Judaism as revealed to the people Israel at Mount Sinai and elucidated over the generations. But he insists that "all people stood at Sinai" and that the "great voice goes on for ever."[5] For traditional Jews, the Hebrew language provides "hyphens between heaven and earth."

Heschel also addresses those who do not or cannot believe that God cares, or that God speaks through the Torah. For readers with little or no knowledge of Hebrew, he echoes the foundational texts: Bible, Talmud, medieval Jewish philosophy and poetry, Kabbalah, and other mystical and Hasidic commentaries. For some readers, Heschel is a palimpsest of ancient and eternal voices. For others, Heschel's own words are enough. Even considered as "fictional" narratives, his writings convey "holiness in words."

Heschel's most enduring legacy, perhaps, is *a sacred humanism*: every person—regardless of mind, race, gender, and social status—is an image of the Divine. The Bible refutes definitions of human beings as animals, objects, instruments, or consumers. There is no essential separation of sacred and profane, and Heschel also noted that secular Jews refine the Spirit in the crucible of their prophetic ideals.[6] Reverence is a universal value.

Heschel's sacred humanism may speak to atheists and agnostics—if they strive with passion toward integrity and truth.[7] His challenge may resemble an exhilarating Nietzschean call: "We must first peer into the darkness, feel strangled and entombed in the hopelessness of living without God, before we are ready to feel the presence of His living light."[8] For Heschel, the shattering of ego can become a positive intuition of God as the ultimate Subject.

The ideal of piety—living in a manner compatible with God's presence—strengthens our resolve in face of divine silence and contends with today's dangers: nationalism and racism; fundamentalism and authoritarian thinking; the amoral pursuit of self-gratification; greed; and the trivilization of morality, politics, and religion. For Heschel, mysticism and the moral life are one and the same.

A Scholarly Goldmine

We can further this legacy at many levels. First and foremost, return to Heschel's own writings, which reveal treasures far richer than I have been able to suggest. We enter the visible narrative and meet the Spirit; or we can penetrate the palimpsest, illuminating and lifting to the surface its tacit or documented sources. Heschel is both a primary and secondary source for scholars, original insight with immense learning.

Elucidate Heschel's references and allusions. For example, he documented the rabbinic foundation of his thought in *Torah min ha-shamayim be-ispaklaryah shel ha-dorat* (Torah from heaven in light of the generations).[9] Talmudic rabbis also debated a theology of pathos, an ethics of the *Shekhinah*, and interpreted revelation in radically divergent ways. A historical hermeneutics would find in Heschel's German, English, Hebrew, and Yiddish works allusions to classical as well as recondite texts that his memory had absorbed since childhood—confirming his contention that traditional Judaism is, in today's parlance, pluralistic.

Translate Heschel's English terminology into Hebrew or Yiddish; in that way one can discover his starting point for both conceptualization and literary expression.[10] Most fundamental are his Hasidic sources—oral, written, lived—in Yiddish and Hebrew. *Man Is Not Alone, God in Search of Man,* and *Quest for God* might then appear more clearly as paraphrases and encyclopedic echoes of several Jewish traditions. Beyond texts, however, is *ruah ha-Kodesh*. The lens of Hasidic mysticism can highlight Heschel's interpretation of Judaism, vitalized by the Holy Spirit. His mystical and prophetic hermeneutics would enrich the fields of Bible, *halakhah* and *aggadah*, and Kabbalah.

In the end, however, Heschel teaches us to recover a second simplicity, an uncomplicated intimacy with God. His ability to

make known the holiness *within* words—God's vital presence—
confutes secular reductions of Judaism to an intricate web of texts
and intertexts or symbols of social processes. As passionate readers, as seekers, we entrust ourselves to his language, to his thinking, to his prayers. There is no essential conflict between study,
critical analysis, and "the kiss of God."[11]

A Personality for Our Times

In our present postmodernity, where knowledge appears as frag-
ments, and faith in nothingness is our fairest dogma, Heschel
honestly confronts our contradictions. He urged all religions to
comprehend life from a divine perspective, fortifying a "passion
for truth." His faith includes irreconcilable tensions: moral courage versus (or along with) loyalty to a caring God Who, creating
free human beings, allows us the power to destroy ourselves.
Depth theology points to "meaning beyond the mystery."[12]

Heschel's alarm at our calloused conscience recognizes the
inextricable "mixture of good and evil." Yet acquiescence to
moral relativity can be overcome by treating every injustice as an
emergency, as did the Hebrew prophets. Heschel trusts that God
cares. His revulsion at malice and deceit shames the timid conscience. The emotions shared are almost overwhelming in their
intensity.

Heschel's complex personality speaks directly to our doubts.
There is a phrase he first wrote in 1951 that reverberates throughout his work, echoing the absolute tensions of a realistic religion:

> Dark is the world to me, for all its cities and stars. If not
> for my faith that God in His silence still listens to my
> cry, who could stand such agony?[13]

Can those of us who do not share his confidence bear the conflict?

Heschel revealed his own internal battle only in his final book,
A Passion for Truth (1973), delivered to the publisher weeks before
his death. His exposure to triviality and evil collides with prayer-
like ecstasy. Two Hasidic extremists, "two teachers," as he called
them—the uncompromising Rabbi Mendl of Kotzk and the compassionate Baal Shem Tov—compose his dynamic sensibility:

> One may look upon the world with enthusiasm and
> absorb its wonder and radiant glory; one may also see

and be shocked by its ugliness and evil. The Prophet Isaiah heard the seraphim proclaim, "The whole earth is full of His glory" (Isaiah 6:3); Job, however, maintained that "the earth is given over to the power of the wicked" (9:24). Reb Mendl drew closer to Job than to the seraphim.

The Baal Shem adopted the perspective of the seraphim; the world was filled with glory, evil being but an instrument of the good, capable of conversion to good. The Kotzker did not want to listen to angels; what he heard and saw was a world dominated by falsehood.[14]

Heschel conjoins opposing but equally authentic perspectives: dismay at the pervasiveness of self-deception and evil—versus awe at the persistence of divine concern and human compassion: "In a very strange way, I found my soul at home with the Baal Shem Tov but driven by the Kotzker. Was it good to live with one's heart torn between the joy of Mezbizh [the town of the Baal Shem Tov] and the anxiety of Kotzk? To live both in awe and consternation, in fervor and horror, with my conscience on mercy and my eyes on Auschwitz, wavering between exaltation and dismay? I had no choice: my heart was in Mezbizh, my mind in Kotzk."[15]

Heschel safeguards human holiness while confronting our resolute barbarism. But he does not promote a "golden mean," a compromise with sacred values, a safe middle ground. He is a spiritual radical who absorbs the outmost limits of each. His notion of polarity, a dynamic coexistence of contraries, attempts to maintain the absolute. That is why extremist proclamations such as these abound in Heschel's discourses: "Prayer is of no importance unless it is of supreme importance."[16] "If God is unable to listen to us, then we are insane in talking to Him."[17]

God does not compromise. And only absurd faith can redeem civilizations built upon the ashes of Auschwitz and Hiroshima, fed on the abuse of nature, and the heritage of dictatorship and colonialism. Heschel's insistence upon a divine standard preserves both contradiction and unity:

> Since each of the two principles moves in the opposite direction, equilibrium can only be maintained if both are of equal force. But such a condition is rarely attained. Polarity is an essential trait of all things. Tension, contrast, and contradiction characterize all of

reality. In the language of the *Zohar*, this world is called *alma deperuda*, "the world of separation." Discrepancy, contention, ambiguity, and ambivalence afflict all of life, including the study of the Torah; even the sages of the Talmud disagree on many details of the law.[18]

Heschel remains our contemporary in his refusal to deny the stubborn paradoxes of existence. He embraces absurdity—the human perspective—but thrusts us beyond. The mind is our cage, gilded or foul. So his narrative helps us imagine the human condition from the perspective of absolute compassion, absolute concern. Religious faith, which engages "the world of separation," requires passionate commitment. The solution lies in our angle of vision.

Transcendence in Disguise

Heschel's sacred humanism assumes that we are morally autonomous, responsible for our deeds, and needed by God and by all humanity. A divine-image anthropology disputes today's view of persons as the pawns of fate or instruments of political and economic appetites, refuting the implicit ideology of our age—nihilism, a disbelief in freedom and virtue. This perverse faith appears as cynicism, or a skeptical disposition, whose antidote is self-interest, hedonism, and contempt for others and for oneself. Groups, as well as individuals, proclaim themselves supreme while the "other" is perceived, and treated, as less than human.

Heschel's narrative of a soul in search of its divine Self forces us behind the mind, revealing, perhaps, an angelic being within. Before God can enter consciousness, we must extirpate vanity. Who is a human being? Or as Heschel, with his timebound pronouns, asked, "Who is man?" His phenomenology of reflective thought unveils the eternal Mind: "Once we discover that the self in itself is a monstrous deceit, that the self is something transcendent in disguise, we begin to feel the pressure that keeps us down to a mere self."[19]

The abyss of Heschel's voyage toward piety is a mystical death, in which the ego surrenders before the Mystery: not a self-indulgent emotion, but a terrifying intuition of our fragility without God. Heschel expects the Almighty to appear on the other side. The result, to which he repeatedly testifies, is a cosmic embrace: "There are moments in which, to use a Talmudic phrase, heaven and earth kiss each other. . . . Some of us have at least caught a glimpse of the beauty, peace, and power that flow through the souls of those who are devoted to Him."[20]

Reading Heschel teaches us the art of exaltation, living at the margins of true holiness. That is why his rhetoric of devotion appeals to people bored with conventional religion: "Man cannot live without moments of rapture. When moral efforts end in frustration and religious instruction abounds in pious platitudes, they turn to drugs that expand illusion and slowly but surely exterminate the soul."[21] (Writing in the 1960s, he understood that "drugs" included compulsive entertainment as well as pharmaceutical substitutes for authentic ecstasy.)

He taught Jews the sacred potential of Sabbath that integrates study and worship, inwardness and community, sensuous pleasure and the holy. Through regular observance, as individuals and with companions or family, we devote one day a week to prayer, reflection on Torah and serious subjects, eating, relaxation—and adults whose love is consecrated can bless God through sexual intercourse "under the wings of the *Shekhinah.*"

Heschel's poetics of piety helps us repossess traditional texts and rituals, and make them personally ours. It frees our imagination from bland or simplistic justifications. Observance for the sake of the Divine gives metaphysical substance to acts considered to be "symbolic." The vexed problem of belief becomes secondary to performance, which claims nothing more than celebrating life and facing its demands and mysteries. By *doing*, we may *understand* what Heschel means by "living in a manner compatible with God's presence."

Interfaith Activism

Heschel affirms the plurality of beliefs while subsuming systems under divine unity. He asserted that "[i]n this aeon diversity of religions is the will of God," so that the restricted needs of groups need not remain our measure.[22] Prophetic activism subsumes apparently antagonistic ideas into a universal mission: "The goal of all efforts is to bring about the restitution of the unity of God and world. The restoration of unity is a constant process and its accomplishment will be the essence of Messianic redemption."[23]

Depth theology establishes community at a fundamental level. Humankind can aspire toward holiness by sharing its vehement dissatisfaction. A long sentence summarizes the process:

> I suggest that the most significant basis for meeting of
> men of different religious traditions is the level of fear
> and trembling, of humility and contrition, where our
> individual moments of faith are mere waves in the
> endless ocean of mankind's reaching out for God,
> where all formulations and articulations appear as
> understatements, where our souls are swept away by
> the awareness of the urgency of answering God's com-
> mandment, while stripped of pretension and conceit
> we sense the tragic insufficiency of human faith.[24]

Modern faith thrives within the tensions between its negative
and positive poles. "Fear of God" (in Hebrew, *yirat Elohim*) places
self-interest into its true light. This can include an intimation of
the mystery of existence in addition to biblical examples of
divine punishment. Heschel envisages a sophisticated humility.
"Fear of God" (like Kierkegaard's "fear and trembling") stands as
a cognitive nakedness before the Creator.

True piety combines fear and love. Spirit and moral courage
meet in this complex insight. "Fear of God" helps subdue the passions that divert us from the core.[25] Its complementary force,
"love of God" (*ahavat Elohim*), then gains influence. Perhaps the
term *reverence*—in the context of depth theology—can summarize its fulfillment. What we might call "radical reverence" surpasses the moral cliché (anathema to authentic religion) as it
combines transcendent love, sacred terror, and veneration of
each and every human being.

I believe, with Heschel, that religious thinking is indispensable. Religions are among the highest cultural translations of our
dedication—often unto death—to ultimate truth, to ultimate justice. So I have tried to explain what he can say to those who do
not, or cannot, respond fullheartedly to religious language. God,
then, is more than just a metaphor for a universal ideal—and a
power—both transcending thought and making human striving
possible.[26]

Not everyone can emulate Heschel's closeness to God. But
there are values we affirm as absolute: values for which we are
willing, and courageous enough, to devote our soul. In our age of
competing notions of reality, reading Heschel helps us recover
the Sabbath consciousness: "Faith does not spring out of nothing. It comes with the discovery of the holy dimension of our
existence. Suddenly we become aware that our lips touch the veil
of the Holy of Holies. Our face is lit up for a time with the light

from behind the veil. Faith opens our hearts for the entrance of the Holy. It is almost as if God were thinking for us."[27]

However we understand it, Heschel's confidence braces our lives, our decisions. Awe, wonder, radical amazement—and its fulfillment in piety and prophetic action—dislocate our mental habits and nourish our receptivity to the sacred. As individuals we may then forge commmunities, sharing the Holy Spirit both beyond and within beliefs and institutions—beyond and within personal, ethnic, or national self-interest.[28] Under Heschel's guidance, our intuition of life's essential sanctity might energize the future. At the very least, his writings brighten the threshold of the Holy of Holies.

 Appendix A

Study Guide

What follows is a list of readings related to each chapter of *Holiness in Words*. It is not necessary to consult all the sources indicated. More specialized information appears in the notes and bibliography. The basic reference work about Judaism is the *Encyclopaedia Judaica*, 16 volumes (Jerusalem: Keter, 1972).

Chapter One:
"Abraham Joshua Heschel in America"

Goals: An overview of Heschel's life in Europe and his career and writings in the United States. Introduction to the author's background and standards of religious authenticity.

Heschel, *The Earth Is the Lord's*, chapters 1–4 (pp. 13–44).
Heschel, *Quest for God*, chapters 3–4: "Spontaneity is the Goal," and "Continuity is the Way" (pp. 47–114).
Heschel, *The Prophets*, Introduction, and chapter 1, "What Manner of Man Is the Prophet?" (pp. 3–26).
Heschel, *A Passion for Truth*, Introduction (pp. xiii–xv).
Steven T. Katz (ed.), *Interpreters of Judaism in the Late Twentieth Century* (Washington, D.C., 1993). The chapter on Heschel (pp. 131–50) can be studied with the essays on Emil Fackenheim, Will Herberg, Gershom Scholem, Joseph Soloveitchik, and others.
Hillel Goldberg, *Between Berlin and Slobodka: Jewish Transition Figures from Eastern Europe* (Hoboken: KTAV, 1989), provides suggestive biographical and cultural sketches of Heschel and other immigrants such as Harry Wolfson and Joseph Soloveitchik. Some interpretations open to question.
Robert M. Seltzer and Norman J. Cohen (eds.), *The Americanization of the Jews* (New York, 1995). The chapter on Heschel (pp. 355–71) can be studied with articles on American Jewish culture and history and essays on Will Herberg and Mordecai Kaplan.
Robert G. Goldy, *The Emergence of Jewish Theology in America* (Indiana University Press, 1990). Introduction to the field.
Awaiting the publication of an intellectual and cultural biography, readers can gain some insight into Heschel's European background from the following novels: Soma Morgenstern, *The Son of the Lost Son*; Sholom Asch, *Three Cities* (Petersburg, Warsaw, Moscow); and I. J. Singer, *The Brothers Carnovsky*.

Chapter Two:
A Reading Strategy

Goals: Initiation into slow reading of Heschel and familiarity with his style. Meditative study of his works can enrich our prayer life and critical self-understanding.

Heschel, *The Earth Is the Lord's* (finish the book): chapters 5–15 (pp. 45–109).
Heschel, *Man Is Not Alone*, chapters 1–5 (pp. 3–41).
Heschel, *The Sabbath* (136 pages).
Fritz A. Rothschild (ed.), *Between God and Man: An Interpretation of Judaism* (New York, 1959; 1975). Introduction to Heschel's philosophy of religion (pp. 7–32), selections, and bibliography.
Some other examples of meditative reflection and reading: Aryeh Kaplan, *Jewish Meditation: A Practical Guide* (New York, 1985); Howard Thurman, *The Centering Moment,* and Gaston Bachelard, *The Poetics of Reverie.* My original introduction to reading Heschel is still useful: Edward Kaplan, "Form and Content in A. J. Heschel's Poetic Style," *CCAR Journal* 18, 2 (April 1971): 28–39.

Chapter Three:
"The Divine Perspective"

Goals: To understand Heschel's manner of entering the spiritual dimension, leading to theocentric thinking and insights that precede verbal formulation, the ineffable.

Heschel, "Depth Theology," *Insecurity of Freedom* (pp. 115–26).
Heschel, *Man Is Not Alone*, chapter 26, "The Pious Man" (pp. 273–96).
Heschel, *God in Search of Man*, chapters 1–8 (pp. 3–87).
Compare with Paul Tillich's analysis of modern religious understanding, *The Dynamics of Faith.*

Chapter Four:
"Language and Reality"

Goals: Link Heschel's theological and his linguistic system. This "poetics of faith" should help readers appreciate religious discourse no matter what one's state of belief. Specialists can evaluate the author's putative anthropomorphism and his rhetoric.

Heschel, *Quest for God*, chapters 1–2, "The Inner World" and "The Person and the Word" (pp. 3–46).

Heschel, *In Search*, chapter 18, "The Prophetic Understatement" (pp. 176–83).

Heschel, "Prophetic Inspiration," reprinted in Neusner and Neusner, *To Grow in Wisdom* (pp. 53–69).

Begin reading *The Prophets*, a somewhat diffuse work which formulates Heschel's theology of divine pathos; read esp. chapter 15, "Anthropopathy" (pp. 268–78).

From the vast literature on rhetoric and metaphor, I recommend the book Heschel himself cites: Philip Wheelwright, *The Burning Fountain. A Study in the Language of Symbolism* (New York, 1954; 1968), chapters 5, 9, "Traits of Expressive Language" and "Expressive Statement and Truth."

Chapter Five:
"Mysticism and Despair"

Goals: Define the Kabbalistic or mystical foundation of Heschel's depth theology and ethics. To advance reading *Man Is Not Alone* and introduce the problem of revelation.

Heschel, "The Mystical Element in Judaism" (1949).

Heschel, *Earth Is the Lord's*, chapters 10–11, "Kabbalah," "Hasidism" (pp. 69–82).

Heschel, "Prayer as a Discipline," *Insecurity* (pp. 254–61).

Heschel, *Man Is Not Alone*, chapters 9–14 (pp. 67–133).

Heschel, *In Search*, chapter 20, "The Paradox of Sinai" (pp. 191–99).

The writings of Evelyn Underhill on mysticism are fundamental to the field; see also Howard Thurman, *Disciplines of the Spirit*, and Thomas Merton, *Dark Lightning*; Herbert Fingarette, *The Self in Transformation*, studies its personal aspects in detail. For cultural manifestations of mysticism in the United States (with a chapter on Heschel, Thurman, and Merton) see Hal Bridges, *American Mysticism, from William James to Zen* (New York: Harper & Row, 1970).

Advanced students can compare Heschel and the groundbreaking scholarship of Gershom Scholem, *Major Trends in Jewish Mysticism* (Schocken, 1941; 1967) and Moshe Idel, *Kabbalah: New Perspectives* (Yale University Press, 1988). The review essay of Hava Tirosh-Rothschild, "Continuity and Revision in the Study of Kabbalah," *AJS Review* 16 (1991): 161–92, presents a useful summary.

Chapter Six:
"Sacred versus Symbolic Religion"

Goals: Apply Heschel's linguistic criteria and depth theology to the *mitzvot* (commandments), ritual obligations, and ethics. The author refutes anthropological or sociological approaches to religious observance.

Heschel, *Quest for God*, chapter 5, "Symbolism" (pp. 117–44).
Heschel, *In Search*, chapters 28–34 (pp. 281–360).
Compare with Ernest Johnson (ed.), *Religious Symbolism* (New York: Harper and Brothers, 1954), in which Heschel's essay on symbolism first appeared; see esp. essays by Daniel Sullivan (on Catholic worship), Paul Tillich (a Protestant view), and Mordecai Kaplan (a Jewish naturalist view). One might also compare Heschel with Gershom Scholem, *On the Kabbalah and Its Symbolism* (New York: Schocken Books, 1960).
Compare with Martin Buber's *I and Thou* (1923), an epoch-making meditative philosophy that differs from Heschel's biblical perspective. Buber's clear exposition of his theory of "Dialogue" appears in *Between Man and Man*. Ernst Cassirer, *An Essay on Man*, gives an elegant overview of philosophical anthropology.

Chapter Seven:
"Prophetic Radicalism"

Goals: Specify Heschel's contribution to American politics and social action. His "sacred humanism" defines an all-inclusive ethics energized by the living God and interpreted through the Hebrew Bible.

Heschel, *Insecurity*, chapters 1–7 on the moral obligations of institutional religion, medicine, youth, aging, problems of race (pp. 3–114); chapter 10, "Sacred Image of Man" (pp. 150–67).
Heschel, *The Prophets*, Introduction and chapters on individual prophets. Readers can skip the scholarly debates (chapters 13, 19–24) and trace Heschel's own theology in the following: "What Manner of Man is the Prophet?" (chapter 1), "Chastisement," "Justice," "The Theology of Pathos" (chapters 10–12), and "Anthropopathy," "Religion of Sympathy," "Event and Experience," and "Conclusions" (chapters 15, 18, 25, 28).
Heschel, "The Moral Outrage of Vietnam," in *Vietnam: Crisis of Conscience*, with Robert McAfee Brown and Michael Novak (New York, 1967), pp. 48–61.
Heschel, *Who Is Man?* (119 pages).
Heschel opposes philosophical anthropology and other sociological approaches, as valuable as they are. Compare with Martin Buber, "What is Man?" in *Between Man and Man* and other essays in that important collection.
For a broader comparative study see Heschel, "The Concept of Man in Jewish Thought," reprinted in Neusner and Neusner (eds.), *To Grow*

in Wisdom (pp. 97–145). The original publication in S. Radhakrishnan and P. T. Raju (eds.), *The Concept of Man: A Study in Comparative
Philosophy* (Lincoln, Nebraska: Johnsen Publishing Company,
1960), contains illuminating essays on Greek, Indian, and Chinese
conceptions, in addition to Heschel's.

Chapter Eight:
"Confronting the Holocaust"

Goals: Provide theological and logical criteria for evaluating
attempts to give meaning to the destruction of European Jewry.
Heschel's personal responses to radical evil.

Heschel, *Quest for God*, chapter 6, "The Meaning of this Hour" (pp. 145–
51).
Heschel, *Not Alone*, chapter 16, "The Hiding God" (pp. 150–58).
Heschel, *In Search*, chapters 35–36, "Mitsvah and Sin," "The Problem of
Evil" (pp. 361–81); compare with "Confusion of Good and Evil," in
Insecurity (pp. 127–49).
Heschel, "No Religion Is an Island" (1965).
Heschel, *Israel: An Echo of Eternity:* chapter 3, "Between Hope and Dis-
tress" (pp. 93–122).
Heschel, *A Passion for Truth*, chapter 1, "The Two Teachers" (pp. 3–82);
chapters 9, 10, "The Kotzker and Job," "The Kotzker Today" (pp.
263–323).
Heschel, *The Prophets*, chapter 10, "Chastisement" (pp. 187–94), chapter
12, "The Theology of Pathos" (pp. 221–31).
As a guide to the vast literature, primary and reflective, on the Holocaust,
see Eva Fleischner (ed.), *Auschwitz: The Beginning of a New Era* (New
York, 1977), and Steven T. Katz, *Post-Holocaust Dialogues: Critical
Studies in Modern Jewish Thought* (New York, 1983). A wise historical
perspective is provided by Jacob Neusner, "How the Extermination
of European Jewry Became 'The Holocaust,'" in *Stranger at Home*
(Chicago, 1981), pp. 82–96. See also Lawrence L. Langer, *Admitting
the Holocaust: Collected Essays* (New York: Oxford University Press,
1995).

Chapter Nine:
"Metaphor and Miracle"

Goals: Introduce the "esoteric Heschel," the erudite scholar, writing in Hebrew, who implicitly justifies the availability of divine
inspiration through rabbinic and other authoritative sources.
God in Search of Man, with its copious footnotes, exemplifies how
the author transmutes classical texts.

Heschel, *In Search*, chapters 13–16, on the mystic insight (pp. 136–66); chapters 17–27, on the doctrine of revelation (pp. 167–280).
Heschel, *The Prophets*, chapter 18, "Religion of Sympathy" (pp. 307–23).
Heschel, *Insecurity*, chapters 13–15, "The Individual Jew and His Obligations," "Israel and the Diaspora," "Jewish Education" (pp. 187–241).
Heschel, *Maimonides: A Biography*.
Specialists can study the original Hebrew monographs comprising Heschel, *Prophetic Inspiration After the Prophets* (New Jersey: KTAV,1995); Heschel's three-volume compendium of rabbinic theology in Hebrew, *Torah min ha-shamayim*.

Chapter Ten:
"Heschel's Unfinished Symphony"

Goals: Suggest four main directions of studying Heschel's writings and applying his depth theology and sacred humanism: (1) scholarly research and interpretation; (2) personal theology and ethics; (3) interfaith cooperation; (4) institutional reform.

Heschel, "On Prayer" (1971).
Heschel, "Teaching Jewish Theology at the Solomon Schechter Day School" (1969).
Heschel, *In Search* (finish the book), esp. chapters 33–34, "The Problem of Polarity," "The Meaning of Observance" (pp. 336–60).
Heschel, *Insecurity*, chapters 11–12, "Protestant Renewal," "The Ecumenical Movement" (pp. 168–86); chapter 14, "Israel and the Diaspora" (pp. 212–22).
Heschel, *A Passion for Truth* (finish the book).

For the Future

Heschel's depth theology—his insistence that God is real, and that the *mitzvot* (the commandments) and our ethical actions affect God—provides criteria for evaluating contemporary religion. For example, feminist theology can benefit from a poetics of faith that subverts anthropomorphism and fosters openness to the ineffable. Perhaps the closest to Heschel's starting point, though diverging radically from it, is Arthur Green, *Seek My Face, Speak My Name* (Jason Aronson, 1993); see also Michael Lerner, *Jewish Renewal* (Grosset/Putnam, 1994). The work of Michael Fishbane, *The Kiss of God: Spiritual and Mystical Death in Judaism* (University of Washington, 1994), exemplifies a historical hermeneutics compatible with sacred values. Heschel's standards help us restore our religious institutions to their holy mission and ethical obligations.

Heschel in Germany[1]

Living under Hitler, Heschel's interpretation of Nazism and its tyrannies underlies the theology and ethics he developed in the United States.[2] In 1937, hired by Martin Buber, Abraham Heschel (as he called himself) had left Berlin for Frankfurt-am-Main to become the codirector of the Central Organization for Adult Jewish Education and the Jüdisches Lehrhaus. The following year, in February 1938, Heschel defined his position as a modern religious philosopher in a speech entitled "Versuch einer Deutung" (Inquiry into a Meaning).[3]

The circumstances are instructive. Buber had been invited by Rudolf Schlosser, a German Quaker and pacifist, to address a group of Quaker leaders. But Buber was suffering from influenza and that evening he designated Heschel to address the group, among whom were the Schlossers and the widow of Franz Rosenzweig.[4] A participant describes "Buber's assistant" as "a very serious young man, with strong inner concentration, [who] attempted to fathom the meaning of this new persecution of the Jewish people."[5]

Heschel's speech (which we translate from the German) is at once eloquent, prophetic in its bold questioning of divine purpose, and somewhat abstract. His theological mind interpreted the rapidly increasing attacks against Jews, and it opens dramatically with a symbolic scene:

> Carried over the gates of the world in which we live are the weapons of the demons. It is happening in our time that the peoples are forging their sickles into swords and their scythes into spears. And by inverting the prophetic words entirely, the peoples turn away from the words that come from Zion. It is our lot that we must face that world. We learn how the vision of the prophets is fulfilled in the distortion of the two characteristics of the human face, the likeness to the Creator and the mark of Cain, of which the latter shows more and more clearly and threatens to wipe out the former more and more thoroughly.[6]

Heschel formulates devastating judgments. Somewhat reminiscent of Buber, who also spoke in solemn, abstruse, and biblical terms, he probes the theological implications of the terror against the Jews that would subsequently expand into the intended genocide known as "the Holocaust."

Heschel declares that God speaks through historical events. Religious people are ultimately responsible for exposing the emergency's true meaning. He is well aware of his audience: Jews and Quakers who heroically saved Jews, and others, from the ravages of disease, poverty, and persecution. They would certainly understand his view that major conflicts can bespeak divine meaning: "The prophets gained their wisdom either through the event of revelation or through [humankind's] desecration of the world. And the people either received the words from the mouths of the prophets or they received punishment from the 'weapons of divine fury.'" In either case, we remain responsible.

Nazi hatred serves a verdict on both Christians and Jews. Even more ironically, the people victimized by German persecutions was the best prepared morally to fathom its significance: "No human community among our contemporaries has observed the true face of the present time as closely as those who remain faithful to HIM. The events of this hour, as God's action, affect primarily and immediately the people of this belief." He cites a dictum from "Rabbi Baal Shem, the founder of Hasidism": "If a person sees something evil, he should know that it is shown to him so that he may realize his own guilt—repent for what he has seen."

Heschel's allusion to the Baal Shem Tov is difficult to unpack. He does not suggest that victims are responsible for producing the evil. Rather, he avers that the oppressed, with courageous conscience and faith in God, can "repent"—that is, the faithful can reexamine their own spiritual integrity. Here Heschel suggests that evil is *radical*, at the foundation of all human nature, whatever the person's relation to power and injustice. Religious people, relatively liberated by their biblical faith, have greater responsibility to rescue civilization.

Heschel's speech of 1938 interprets recent history. The German terror—whose full intent the world could begin to recognize only four or five years later—passes judgment on Western culture as such. Some consequences of the eighteenth-century "emancipation" from religious thinking may have begun the process. The moral failures of religion are connected with an increased trivialization of ethics:

At the beginning of this era there was blasphemy. The sanctuaries of this world—justice, peace, belief—were abused and desecrated. And then desecration degenerated to a level without precedence.

We have long neglected to consider the Name in earnest. We have trifled with the Name, using it lightly, bearing it lightly. Now judgment is upon us.

Through the millenia, His voice has wandered throughout the world. How it was trapped and imprisoned in the temples! How it was misunderstood and distorted, cheated and disfigured!—And now we behold how this voice gradually withdraws, grows faint and is muted.

For a believer, this was a grim diagnosis. God is in exile! Emulating the prophets, Heschel announces that the Transcendent remains imprisoned even "in the temples." People had lost interest in ultimate truth and replaced "His Name"—the ineffable divine Presence—with idols. Modern Europe was not different from Bible times, when God hid the Face and withdrew compassion from the people.

Nevertheless, Heschel ends his speech with a hopeful vision, as he highlights the paradoxical dynamics of religious consciousness. He trusts that mindful people may recover their ability to address God. Prayer can awaken within us acts of resistance:

In view of the unprecedented profanation of the holiest of all values we are often moved by the question as to whether and how we can or may utter the Name.

It occurs sometimes that the Name erupts from our heart like a cry. Then this happens not just as an event within us but as a miracle before us: that this word is there, mighty and holy, the Name of One who is more than cosmos and eternity, and we cannot grasp it, and we know that this word is infinitely more than our life and our heart from which it has erupted. In such tension our prayer matures, and the right to call Him by His name.

A people with faith is a strong people. Miracles are possible. Spontaneous prayer might "erupt" from this fragile dialectic of confidence and anguish.[7] If we face reality courageously, prayer might release us from immobilizing despair. The very tension between our horror and our yearning for deliverance can awaken God's immanent prayer, which can save us.

At the same time, Heschel's historical assessment was thoroughly realistic. The speech ends by recognizing that the Jews must leave Germany. Yet even when facing the abyss, in 1938, he trusted God. His theology of the exiled *Shekhinah* (the divine Indwelling) throws a ray of consolation on his people's forced emigration:

> Perhaps we are all now going into exile. It is our fate to live in exile, but HE has said to those suffering: "I am with him in his oppression." The Jewish teachers tell us: Wherever Israel had to go into exile, the Eternal went with them. The divine consequence of human fate is for us a warning and a hope.

These words of faith illumine the wilderness. Heschel's ethical imperative, derived from the *Zohar* and rabbinic theology, that "the *Shekhinah* lies in the dust,"[8] justifies his commitment—then and for the rest of his life—to redeem God's presence from worldly corruption. God, too, was suffering. By stressing divine exile as immanent to human events, Heschel had unified mystical theology and prophetic ethics.

After this speech, Schlosser was so captured by Heschel's message that, at great personal risk, he distributed hundreds of mimeographed copies in Germany. Heschel revised and translated it in 1943, after his emigration. He published "The Meaning of this War" in the *Bulletin* of the Hebrew Union College in Cincinnati.

 NOTES

Introduction

1. *In Search*, p. 244.
2. Ibid., p. 3.
3. See below chapter 9, "Metaphor and Miracle: Modern Judaism and the Holy Spirit."
4. *In Search*, p. 8.

Chapter One.
Abraham Joshua Heschel in America

1. *Prophets*, p. 5.
2. *Newsweek* (31 January 1966).
3. *New York Herald Tribune* (1 April 1951).
4. *Passion*, p. xiii.
5. For the best summary of Heschel's Hasidic background, see the introduction of Samuel H. Dresner (ed.), Abraham Joshua Heschel, *The Circle of the Baal Shem Tov: Studies in Hasidism* (Chicago and London: The University of Chicago Press, 1985), pp. vii–xlv. Much biographical and bibliographical information is due to the research of Fritz A. Rothschild (ed.), A. J. Heschel, *Between God and Man* (New York: Free Press, 1959; bibliography revised most recently in 1975 edition).
6. *Die Prophetie* was published in Cracow by the Polska Akademja Umiejetnosci (Polish Academy of Sciences) in 1936 and distributed in Berlin by the Erich Reiss Verlag. The same text also appears with a different title page carrying the title of his dissertation, *Das prophetische Bewusstsein*, with the dates of his oral examination (23 February 1933) and final "Promotion" (11 December 1935).
7. Heschel's first poem had appeared in the anthology *Varshever shriftn* (1926/27), published by the Literarn-klub baym farayn fun yidishe literatn un zhurnalistn in Varshe (Warsaw Writers and Journalists Club, which later became the PEN Club). His first significant sequences of verse appeared in the New York Yiddish periodical *Zukunft* (Future): December 1929 and November 1930. See Jeffrey Shandler, "Heschel and Yiddish: A Struggle with Signification," *Journal of Jewish Thought and Philosophy* 2 (1993): 245–99. Heschel's collection was published by Verlag Indzel in Warsaw in 1933.
8. Translation by Zalman Schachter (distributed privately). This poem first appeared in *Zukunft* in December 1929. See below chapter 6, "Sacred versus Symbolic Religion," for a discussion of Heschel and Buber; also Appendix B.

9. See Ernst Simon, "Jewish Adult Education in Nazi Germany as Spiritual Resistance," *LBIY* 1 (1956): 68–104, for one basic study of the phenomenon.

10. *Maimonides: Eine Biographie* (Berlin: Erich Reiss Verlag, 1935); *Maimonide*, French translation by Germaine Bernard (Paris: Payot, 1936). The English translation, *Maimonides: A Biography*, trans. by Joachim Neugroschel, was published in 1982 by Farrar, Straus & Giroux. *Don Jizchak Abravanel* (Berlin: Erich Reiss Verlag, 1937), 32 pages; Polish translation, Lwow, 1938, sponsored by the Friends of the Hebrew University, Jerusalem. An abridged translation into English by William Silverman appeared in *Intermountain Jewish News—Literary Supplement* (19 December 1986), pp. 5–13.

11. The author signed "Dr. Abraham Heschel." It would have been misunderstood, in Western Europe, to state his full Hasidic name, Abraham Joshua Heschel Heschel—or the abridgment that later became famous in the United States.

12. Interview with Fritz A. Rothschild. Heschel would help Rothschild, a penniless immigrant, enter The Jewish Theological Seminary, and Rothschild, after joining the faculty, would publish an anthology of Heschel's writings, *Between God and Man* (1959), with a lucid systematization of his philosophy, making Heschel accessible to a wide readership.

13. Letter dated 6 April 1939. Preserved at the Jewish Archives, Cincinnati, Ohio. See the important article by Michael Meyer, "The Refugee Scholars Project of the Hebrew Union College," in Bertram W. Korn (ed.), *A Bicentennial Festschrift for Jacob R. Marcus* (Waltham: American Jewish Historical Society; New York: KTAV Publishing Company, 1976), pp. 359–75.

14. Heschel's essay, "Das Gebet als Äusserung und Einfülung" (Prayer as expression and empathy), took its place among the more academic monographs by leading German-speaking Jewish scholars, appearing in the famous swan-song issue of the *Monatsschrift*, vol. 82 (1939). The Hebrew essay, "ʿAl mahut ha-tefillah" (On the essence of prayer), was originally written for the *Meir Balaban Jubilee Volume* (to be published in Warsaw in 1939, but confiscated and destroyed by the Nazis); it was published in the Hebrew monthly *Bitzaron* 3, 5 (February 1941): 346–53. These exploratory papers begin to define the categories that readers of *Quest* (1954) will recognize.

15. "No Religion Is an Island," p. 3.

16. I agree with Jacob Neusner that American Jewish institutions tend to validate themselves in relation to Israel or to the Holocaust—to the exclusion of knowledge of the multifarious Jewish worlds before World War II, and to the exclusion of religious imperatives. See Jacob Neusner, *Stranger at Home: "The Holocaust," Zionism, and American Judaism* (Chicago: University of Chicago Press, 1981); also Jacob Neusner, *American Judaism: Adventure in Modernity* (Engelwood Cliffs, N.J.: Prentice-Hall, 1972).

17. See A. J. Heschel, "God, Torah, and Israel" (translated by Byron

Sherwin), in Edward Long, Jr., and Robert Handy (eds.), *Theology and Church in Times of Change: Essays in Honor of John Coleman Bennett* (Philadelphia: Westminster Press, 1970), pp. 71–90. See note 18 below.

18. *In Search*, p. 246. The sentence that follows underlines the gravity of his endeavor: "In this problem lies the dilemma of our fate, and in the answer lies the dawn or the doom" (loc. cit.); cf. ibid., pp. 252–53. See below chapters 3 and 4.

19. In 1949 Heschel published *Pikuach Neshamah* (New York: Baronial Press), a broadside (15 pp.) calling for Jewish spiritual survival. This little-known (and important) essay, written in rich allusive Hebrew, was first given as a talk to the Union of Principals of Day Schools and Yeshivas in the New York Metropolitan Area.

20. Heschel did not confine himself to writing. In 1941, 1942, 1943, he unsuccessfully attempted to get American Jews to send food and other help to Jews under German control. See his interview in Yiddish with Gershon Jacobson, *Day-Morning Journal* (13 June 1963), quoted in translation by Samuel Dresner (ed.), Heschel, *The Circle of the Baal Shem Tov* (op. cit.), p. xxv, note 30; see below chapter 8, "Confronting the Holocaust."

21. Interview with Thena Heshel Kendall, daughter of Heschel's brother Jacob who emigrated to London.

22. He expressed his private agony only through dedications to his Hebrew books on rabbinic theology and his Yiddish study of Reb Mendl of Kotzk, completed just before his death. He dedicated *Torah min hashamayim be-ispaklaryah shel ha-dorot* (translated on the cover as *Theology of Ancient Judaism*) (New York and London: Soncino Press, vol. 1, 1962) to his mother and three sisters; and his two-volume Yiddish book, *Kotzk: In gerangl far emesdikeyt* (*Kotzk: The Struggle for Integrity*) (Tel Aviv: Hamenora Books, 1974) to people who had helped him in Europe before his emigration.

23. The original English essay, "The Meaning of this War," first published in the *HUC Bulletin* of March 1943 (pp. 1–2, 8), was revised slightly and reprinted in February 1944 in *Liberal Judaism*, pp. 18–21; I quote from the version published as the final chapter of *Quest*, pp. 147–51. For the original German version, entitled "Versuch einer Deutung," see Margarethe Lachmund (ed.), *Begegbung mit dem Judentum: Ein Gedenkbuch. (Stimmen der Freunde [Quäker] in Deutschland)* Heft 2 (Bad Pyrmont: 1962), pp. 11–13, chapter 8, and Appendix B of this book.

24. *Quest*, p. 149; this part was added in the 1944 version.

25. "An Analysis of Piety," *The Review of Religion* 6, 3 (March 1942): 293–307—published by Columbia University; "The Holy Dimension," *The Journal of Religion* 23, 2 (April 1943): 117–24—published by the University of Chicago; and "Faith," *The Reconstructionist* 10, 13 (November 3, 1944): 10–14; no. 14 (November 17, 1944): 12–16—edited by Mordecai Kaplan, who soon became his colleague at The Jewish Theological Seminary.

26. *The Review of Religion* 9, 2 (January 1945): 153–68.

27. "The Mystical Element in Judaism." The essence of Heschel's article, based exclusively on references to the Zohar, can be found in chapters 10 and 11 of *Earth*, "Kabbalah" and "Hasidism."

28. Heschel also completed his studies of medieval Jewish philosophy with a monograph combining rigorous historical and philological research and theological reflections on faith, "The Quest for Certainty in Saadia's Philosophy," first published in the distinguished *Jewish Quarterly Review* 33, nos. 2–3 (1943): 263–313, and vol. 34, no. 4 (1944): 391–408. These two papers were combined in a broadside published as *The Quest for Certainty in Saadia's Philosophy* (New York: Philip Feldheim, 1944).

29. The original was published in the *Yivo Bleter* 25 (1945), and then in English translation (probably by Shlomo Noble) in the *Yivo Annual of Jewish Social Science* 1 (1946): 86–106. See the astute observations of Jacob Neusner, "How the Extermination of European Jewry Became 'The Holocaust,'" *Stranger at Home* (op. cit), pp. 82–96.

30. *Earth*, p. 109. See also the end of "The Mystical Element in Judaism."

31. Both published by the prestigious literary house, Farrar, Straus & Young—and the second jointly with The Jewish Publication Society of America.

32. "The Spirit of Jewish Prayer," *Proceedings of the Rabbinical Assembly of America* 17 (1953): 151–77; discussion, pp. 200–17; abbreviated here as RA; revised and reprinted in *Quest*, chapter 3, "Spontaneity is the Goal," pp. 49–89. It would be worthwhile to consult the original publication.

33. RA (1953), p. 152.

34. Ibid., p. 159.

35. Incidently, Heschel traces this "sociological fallacy" to the 1913 book by Josiah Royce, *The Problem of Christianity*, instead of citing Mordecai Kaplan's *Judaism as a Civilization*, which first appeared as a book in 1934; see RA, p. 156, note 3 on Royce. During the discussion, Heschel makes another covert reference to Mordecai Kaplan, whom he admired as a person and as a passionate Jew: "The strange thing about many of our contemporaries is that their life is nobler than their ideology, that their faith is deep and their views are shallow, that their souls are suppressed and their slogans proclaimed. We must not continue to cherish a theory just because we embraced it forty years ago" (ibid., p. 215)—which dates to 1913 and Royce!

36. RA, 158; from "Prayer," published in *The Review of Religion* in 1945.

37. For a more detailed analysis of Heschel's apologetic strategy see chapters 4 and 9 of this book.

38. RA, p. 163. Cf. *Quest*, p. 62, where this paragraph ends: "*The Shekhinah is in exile*, the world is corrupt, *the universe itself is not at home.*" Heschel reiterated this theology of divine exile throughout his life.

39. RA, p. 163.

40. "Toward an Understanding of Halacha," *CCAR Yearbook* 63

(1953): 386–409; abbreviated as CCAR; revised slightly as "Continuity is the Way," chapter 4 of *Quest*, pp. 93–114.

41. CCAR (1953), p. 386. Then follows the impressive passage about his student days in Berlin, which begins: "I came with great hunger to the University of Berlin to study philosophy . . ." (loc. cit.); cf. *Quest*, pp. 94–95. An important statement omitted in the version revised for *Quest* attributes the emptiness of rational religion, which inspired the ideology of classical Reform, to neo-Kantian professors who regarded "religion as a *fiction*, useful to society or to man's personal well being. Religion is not a relationship of man to God but a relationship of man to the symbol of his highest ideals. There is no God, but we must go on worshipping his symbol" (CCAR, p. 387). See below chapter 6, "Sacred versus Symbolic Religion."

42. CCAR, p. 390, quoted in Hebrew; *Quest*, p. 96.

43. CCAR, p. 391; *Quest*, p. 97.

44. CCAR, p. 399; *Quest*, p. 106.

45. CCAR, p. 409, these are the final sentences of his speech. Unfortunately, the discussion that followed was not preserved. Omitted in *Quest*, but see pp. 113–14.

46. *Not Alone*, p. 78. See below chapter 5, "Mysticism and Despair," for a detailed analysis of this passage.

Chapter Two.
Reading Heschel

1. *Earth*, p. 31.

2. For a definition of Rorty's edifying philosopher as applied to Martin Buber see Laurence J. Silberstein, *Martin Buber's Social and Religious Thought: Alienation and the Quest for Meaning* (New York: New York University Press, 1989), chapter 5, "Edification and the Meaning of Personhood." Silberstein's book would provide an excellent foundation for an in-depth comparative study of Heschel and Buber.

3. I stress the dynamic term *thinking* as opposed to philosophical "thought," which may be more rigid and abstract. See Emil Fackenheim's reviews of *Not Alone* in *Judaism* I, 1 (January 1952): 85–89, and of *In Search* in *Conservative Judaism* XV, 1 (Fall 1960): 50–53. Fackenheim astutely distinguishes between Heschel's stated philosophical task to erect a system and Heschel as a phenomenologist of "religious thinking" more interested in its dynamics. I find that Fackenheim is mistaken to separate the different modes of Heschel's discourse and to reject the conceptual in favor of the expressive: see Edward K. Kaplan, "Form and Content in A. J. Heschel's Poetic Style," *Central Conference of American Rabbis Journal* (April 1971), pp. 28–39; Avraham Holtz, "Religion and the Arts in the Theology of A. J. Heschel," *Conservative Judaism* (Fall 1973): 27–39; cf. David Hartman, *The Breakdown of Tradition and the Quest for Renewal* (Montreal: The Gate Press, 1980), pp. 40–54 on Heschel. For one theoret-

ical context see Frank B. Brown, "Transfiguration: Poetic Metaphor and Theological Reflection," *The Journal of Religion* 62, 1 (January 1982): 39–56, which integrates propositional theology and the study of metaphor—and includes a useful bibliography.

4. See *In Search*, chapter 1, sections "Philosophy and Theology," "Situational Thinking," "Depth Theology," pp. 4–8; see "Depth Theology," in *Insecurity*, pp. 115–26, and *Who Is Man?* The quotation that follows is from "Depth Theology," *Insecurity*, p. 119.

5. See below chapter 9, "Metaphor and Miracle: Modern Judaism and the Holy Spirit."

6. *In Search*, p. 244.

7. *Prophets*, p. 274.

8. See Fritz A. Rothschild, "Varieties of Heschelian Thought," in John Merkle (ed.), *AJH: Exploring His Life and Thought*, pp. 87–102; see Rothschild's earlier article, "The Religious Thought of A. J. Heschel," *Conservative Judaism* 23, 1 (Fall 1968): 12–24. See especially chapters 3 and 4 of this book.

9. For examples of this process see Howard Thurman, *Meditations of the Heart* (New York: Harper and Row, 1953), *The Centering Moment* (Harper and Row, 1969), and *Disciplines of the Spirit* (Harper and Brothers, 1954). See Edward Kaplan, "Howard Thurman: Meditation, Mysticism and Life's Contradictions," *Debate and Understanding* (Boston University, Spring 1982), pp. 19–26. Also, Gaston Bachelard, *The Poetics of Reverie*, translated by Daniel Russell (Boston: Beacon Press, 1969).

10. *Earth*, p. 9.

11. Ibid., pp. 23–38. This chapter was originally published as "The Two Great Traditions" in *Commentary* 5, 5 (May 1948): 416–22.

12. Ibid., p. 55.

13. Ibid., p. 64.

14. Ibid., p. 71.

15. Ibid., p. 75.

16. Ibid., pp. 103–4.

17. Ibid., p. 106.

18. Ibid., p. 107.

19. *Not Alone*, p. 61. The next quotation is from ibid., p. 60.

20. Ibid., p. 68.

21. See the partially quoted passage from *Not Alone*, chapter 9, p. 75; and p. 78: "But, then, a moment comes like a thunderbolt, in which a flash of the undisclosed rends our dark apathy asunder." See below chapter 5, "Mysticism and Despair," for an analysis of this process.

22. Ibid., p. 94; see also *In Search*, chapters 4 and 5, "Wonder" and "The Sense of Mystery" (pp. 43–72).

23. See *Not Alone*: "Some men go on a hunger strike in the prison of the mind, starving for God. There is a joy, ancient and sudden, in this starving. There is a reward, a grasp of the intangible, in the flaming reverie breaking through bars of thought" (p. 90); also ibid., p. 94: "God's existence can never be tested by human thought. All proofs are mere

demonstrations of our thirst for Him. Does the thirsty one need proof of his thirst?" Cf. Howard Thurman: "'the givenness of God' in the hunger of the heart. This is native to personality, and when it becomes part of a man's conscious focus it is prayer at its best and highest. It is the movement of the heart toward God; a movement that in some sense is with God . . ." (*Disciplines of the Spirit*, op. cit., p. 87).

Chapter Three.
The Divine Perspective

1. *In Search*, p. 246; cf. ibid., pp. 252–53.
2. Ibid., p. 8. Cf. *Not Alone*: "We have to press the soul with questions, compelling it to understand and unravel the meaning of what is taking place at the ultimate horizon. While penetrating the consciousness of the ineffable, we may conceive the reality behind it" (pp. 60–61).
3. Two scholars in particular have paved the way. Fritz A. Rothschild (ed.), *Between God and Man* (New York, 1959), was the first to organize Heschel's system in his important introduction (pp. 3–32); and John C. Merkle, *The Genesis of Faith: The Depth Theology of Abraham Joshua Heschel* (New York, 1985). See bibliography for other sources.
4. Herbert Fingarette, *The Self in Transformation: Psychoanalysis, Philosophy, and the Life of the Spirit* (New York: Harper & Row, Torchbooks, 1965), p. 305. I have found this to be the best study of the relationship of religious experience to personal growth. It is not at all reductionistic.
5. *Not Alone*, p. 129. See especially *In Search*, chapter 13, "God in Search of Man" (pp. 136–44).
6. "Depth Theology," *Insecurity*, p. 119; *In Search* elaborates the project: "The theme of theology is the content of believing. The theme of the present study is the act of believing. Its purpose is to explore the depth of faith, the substratum out of which belief arises, and its method may be called *depth theology*" (p. 7); cf. Merkle, *Genesis of Faith*, chapter 2, "Depth Theology," pp. 27–52.
7. *Prophets*, p. xviii. Over the years I have refined this notion (originally called the "*displacement* of subjectivity") in my articles (1973, 1977, 1983) and in the present book's chapters 3, 4, and 5; see also, Maurice Friedman, "Divine Need and Human Wonder: The Philosophy of Abraham J. Heschel," *Judaism* 25, 1 (Winter 1976), esp. pp. 72–74. From among numerous references implying the recentering of subjectivity, see especially *Not Alone*: pp. 48, 64, 109, 120, 126, 215, 281–82.
8. *Not Alone*, p. 129; the next quotation is from the same page; see also *In Search*, pp. 252–53.
9. Ibid., p. 37.
10. *Quest*, p. 7.
11. Cf. *Not Alone*: "Life is tridimensional, every act can be evaluated by two coordinate axes, the abscissa is man, the ordinate God.

Whatever man does to man, he also does to God" (p. 225); see also ibid., pp. 47, 137.

12. *Not Alone*, p. 4. In my opinion, from a philosophical perspective, Heschel's dependence upon a priori reasoning weakens his demonstration: e.g., p. 19: "a universal insight into an objective aspect of reality, of which all men are at all times capable . . ."; see also ibid., pp. 62, 84, 89, 98, 104, 199, 222, 247, for other explicitly stated a prioris. See Lawrence Perlman, "Heschel's Critique of Kant," in Jacob Neusner (ed.), *From Ancient Israel to Modern Judaism*, vol. 3 (Atlanta: Scholars Press, 1989), pp. 213–26 and Perlman's important book, *Abraham Heschel's Idea of Revelation* (Atlanta, 1989).

13. *Not Alone*, p. 4.

14. Ibid., p. 11.

15. This and the next quotation are from ibid., p. 22.

16. Ibid., p. 35.

17. Ibid., p. 37, cited above.

18. Ibid., p. 38.

19. This and the next quotation from ibid., p. 39.

20. Ibid., p. 45.

21. Ibid., p. 47.

22. Ibid., p. 48. The footnote refers to *Not Alone*, p. 128, part of chapter 4, "God Is the Subject" (pp. 125–33).

23. At this decisive point in the book, Heschel interrupts the itinerary and steps backward. In chapter 7 he attempts to refute "The God of the Philosophers." In the following chapter, he returns to the notion of God's subjectivity (chapter 8, "The Ultimate Question").

24. Ibid., pp. 67–79. For a complete analysis of this passage in context see below chapter 5, "Mysticism and Despair: The Threshold of Revelation." Heschel evokes a similar moment of illumination in *In Search*, chapter 13 (esp. pp. 140–41), which holds an equally decisive place in the book's rhetorical strategy; see below chapter 9, "Metaphor and Miracle."

25. *Not Alone*, p. 78.

26. Ibid., pp. 68–69.

Chapter Four:
Language and Reality

1. *Quest*, p. 30. The original English version of this text appeared as "Prayer," *The Review of Religion* 9, 2 (January 1945): 153–68; Heschel first used the image of prayer as a plumb line in the final paragraph of his programmatic essay, "Das Gebet als Äusserung und Einfühlung" (Prayer as expression and empathy), in *Monatsschrift für die Geschichte und Wissenschaft des Judentums* 83 (1939): 562–67. These bibliographical facts demonstrate that Heschel had begun formulating his fundamental ideas before he entered the United States in 1940.

2. *In Search*, p. 115. Heschel considers that tension between expression and the Ultimate to be the source of all culture: "Music, poetry, religion—they all [originate] in the soul's encounter with an aspect of reality for which reason has no concepts and language no names" (*Not Alone*, p. 36). This important sentence contains a misprint, the only one I have found in Heschel's works; I have replaced the word *initiate* with *originate*. One might also read: "they all initiate the soul's encounter with."

3. *In Search*, pp. 178–79.

4. Ibid., p. 265; see note 22, p. 277 for classical Jewish prooftexts.

5. Ibid., p. 258. Heschel uses biblical and Kabbalistic thought to support the difference between human and divine "speech:" "Surely man would flash into blaze, if he were exposed to the word in itself. Therefore, the word became clothed before it entered the world of creation" (ibid., p. 265); also, ibid., p. 181.

6. Ibid., p. 259. The entire chapter 27, "The Principle of Revelation" (pp. 257–78), is of utmost importance for defining Heschel's biblical hermeneutics.

7. *In Search*, p. 274–75. The book's entire section II (pp. 167–278) elaborates Heschel's apologia for divine revelation and is fundamental to his theology.

8. *In Search*, p. 274.

9. *Quest*, p. 41.

10. *In Search*, p. 116.

11. Ibid., p. 187. Heschel's religious philosophy develops a basic opposition between space and time, which may be considered in this context as a distinction between mediated or symbolic knowledge versus immediate or intuitive insight. Space is the dimension of external experience, whereas time is felt inwardly and more directly. Religious thinking requires inward purity: "The primitive mind [and conceptual thought] finds it hard to realize an idea without the aid of imagination, and it is in the realm of space where imagination wields its sway" (*Sabbath*, p. 4).

12. *Not Alone*, p. 98.

13. Ibid., p. 97.

14. *In Search*, p. 123; on pp. 122–23, Heschel cites Maimonides on the limits of our verbal understanding of God. Cf. *Quest*, pp. 41–44 on silence as a component of worship.

15. *Not Alone*, p. 167.

16. *Prophets*, p. 276.

17. *Not Alone*, p. 16. The passage continues by linking language as representation (sign) of the phenomenal world to the world itself as mere appearance: "The world of things we perceive is but a veil. Its flutter is music, its ornament science, but what it conceals is inscrutable." It is not that physical life is pure illusion (for example, the *Maya* of Hinduism). Rather, music and science are not to be considered as ends in themselves, but as two appropriate reactions to an intuition of the unknown. Heschel interprets the world as an *allusion* to God (see ibid., chapter 3, pp. 19–23).

18. *In Search*, p. 116.

19. Through ignorance of how poetic language works, Heschel has been mistakenly accused of anthropomorphism: "The boldness of Dr. Heschel's thought consists, first, in taking literally all biblical expressions that ascribe to God emotions of love and hatred . . . ," (Eliezer Berkovits, "Dr. A. J. Heschel's Theology of Pathos," *Tradition: A Journal of Orthodox Thought*, 6, No. 2 [Spring–Summer, 1964], 70). Firmly grounded on this astounding misunderstanding of Heschel's use and theory of language, Berkovits refutes its validity: "No matter how much we might magnify or purify [our concepts] in trying to apply them to God, we either associate some positive meaning with them, in which case we shall be describing something finite that will have no relevance to God, or else we shall be using words without any meaningful positive contents" (p. 72; also p. 73). By using the phrase "meaningful positive contents," Berkovits reduces all linguistic validity to its purely denotative, empirically referential function. Compare Philip Wheelwright, *The Burning Fountain: A Study in the Language of Symbolism* (1954; rev. 1968), esp. chapters 5, "Traits of Expressive Language," and 9, "Expressive Statement and Truth"; Heschel refers to Wheelwright's book in *In Search*, p. 124.

20. *Not Alone*, p. 37.

21. *In Search*, p. 240.

22. *Not Alone*, p. 218.

23. *Quest*, p. 26.

24. *In Search*, pp. 181–82; the next quotation from ibid., p. 183.

25. *Not Alone*, p. 64.

26. *Quest*, p. 26.

27. Ibid., p. 28.

28. Ibid., p. 27.

29. Ibid, p. 25.

30. *Prophets*, p. 274.

31. *In Search*, p. 122.

32. *Prophets*, p. 277.

33. *Quest*, pp. 39–40.

34. Ibid., p. 40.

35. *Not Alone*, p. 75.

36. *In Search*, p. 74.

37. *Quest*, p. 13.

38. *In Search*, p. 244.

39. Ibid., p. 252.

40. The terminology that follows was introduced by I. A. Richards in *The Philosophy of Rhetoric* (London, 1936), and examined by Max Black, *Models and Metaphors* (Ithaca, N.Y.: Cornell University Press, 1962), p. 47, note 23. See anthology edited by Sheldon Sacks, *On Metaphor* (University of Chicago Press, 1979), containing essays by Paul de Man, Wayne Booth, David Tracy, Paul Ricoeur, and others.

41. *Prophets*, p. 270.

42. Cf. *Prophets*, chapter 15, "Anthropopathy," pp. 268–78; *In*

Search, chapter 18, "The Prophetic Understatement," pp. 176–83, and note 19 above.

43. This and the next two quotations from *Prophets*, p. 271.

44. This and the next two quotations from ibid., p. 389. See ibid., chapter 22, "Prophecy and Prophetic Inspiration," pp. 367–89.

45. *In Search*, p. 180; also: "And yet, 'God spoke' is not a symbol. A symbol does not raise a world out of nothing. Nor does a symbol call a Bible into being. The speech of God is not less but more than literally real" (loc. cit.).

46. *Not Alone*, p. 225. Heschel thus makes his own the Kabbalistic doctrine of God's involvement; the sentence continues: "God's relation to the world is an actuality, an absolute implication of being, the ultimate in reality, obtaining even if at this moment it is not perceived or acknowledged by anybody; those who reject or betray it do not diminish its validity" (pp. 225–226). This conviction far surpasses any so-called religious existentialism, in which human awareness bestows ontological validity.

47. *In Search*, p. 180.

48. *Quest*, p. 139.

49. Ibid., p. 142.

50. This and the next quotation from *Not Alone*, p. 139. See my personal, exploratory essay, "Three Dimensions of Human Fullness: Poetry, Love, and Prayer," *Judaism* 22, 3 (Summer 1973): 309–21.

Chapter Five.
Mysticism and Despair

1. *In Search*, p. 140.

2. Briefly, here are the essay's sections and the books that elaborate them: (1) The Meaning of Jewish Mysticism: *Not Alone, In Search*; (2) The Exaltation of Man: *Earth, Who Is Man?*; (3) The *En Sof* and His Manifestations: *Quest, Sabbath*; (4) The Doctrine of the *Shekhinah*: *Prophets*; (5) Mystic Experience: *Quest, Not Alone*, etc.; (6) The Torah—A Mystic Reality: *Torah min ha-shamayim* (three vols. in Hebrew, 1962, 1965, 1990); (7) The Mystic Way of Life; (8) The Concern for God: *Insecurity, Israel, Passion*, etc.

3. "The Mystical Element in Judaism," p. 602.

4. See chapter 3 of this book, "The Divine Perspective," for a brief account of gaps (or leaps) in Heschel's logical argumentation. Cf. Gershom Scholem, "Jewish Theology Today," *Center Magazine* 7, no. 2 (March/April 1974): 58–71; reprinted in G. Scholem, *On Jews and Judaism in Crisis* (New York, 1976), pp. 261–97; Scholem mentions in passing Heschel and Martin Buber as "existential theologians" who have evaded the real issues of revelation. See also Emil Fackenheim's reviews of *Not Alone* in *Judaism* (January 1952) and *In Search* in *Conservative Judaism* (Fall 1960). Important suggestions have been made by Fritz A. Rothschild,

"The Religious Thought of Abraham J. Heschel," *Conservative Judaism* 23, no. 1 (Fall 1968): 12–24; Edmond LaB. Cherbonnier, "Heschel's Time Bomb," *Conservative Judaism* 28, no. 1 (Fall 1973): 10–18; Saul Tanenzapf, "Abraham Heschel and his Critics," *Judaism* 23, 3 (Summer 1974): 276–86; and Maurice Friedman, "Divine Need and Human Wonder: The Philosophy of Abraham J. Heschel," *Judaism* 25, no. 1 (Winter 1976): 65–78.

5. *In Search*, p. 140.

6. Loc. cit.

7. The Trappist monk Thomas Merton has defined a similar basis for dialogue between believers and people without faith: see "The Contemplative and the Atheist," in *Contemplation in a World of Action* (New York: Doubleday, Image Books, 1973), pp. 180–94; also Henry Corbin, "De la théologie apophatique comme antidote du nihilisme," in *Le Paradoxe du monothéisme* (Paris, 1981): 177–216, and below for other parallels.

8. *In Search*, p. 45.

9. See *Not Alone*, p. 12.

10. *In Search*, p. 98.

11. *Not Alone*, p. 35. Analyzed in the preceding chapter.

12. Some confusion arises concerning Heschel's terminology. He insists upon an excluding distinction between revelation and mysticism in *In Search*, chapter 20, "The Paradox of Sinai": "The mystic experience is an ecstasy of man; revelation is *an ecstasy of God*" (p. 199). Heschel repeats this exclusion in chapter 21 of *The Prophets*, "An Examination of the Theory of Ecstasy." In both instances "mysticism" gets short shrift. It is clear to me that Heschel conveniently limits his definition of mysticism for the immediate needs of his exposition, as he did with the doubt/wonder dichotomy examined above. His purpose was to illuminate the dynamics of revelation as opposed to the common (and overly restrictive) conception of mysticism as a human striving to absorb the personality into the Godhead. This chapter amply demonstrates how broad Heschel's characterization of mystical experience actually is.

13. *Not Alone*, p. 44.

14. This and the following quotation from ibid., pp. 77–79. My original analysis profited from the sensitive paper written by Janet Allen (Smith College '75) for my course at Amherst College, Mysticism and Moral Life, May 1973. Compare chapter 13 of *In Search* (pp. 136–44), which also describes a mystical breakthrough, analyzed in chapter 9, "Metaphor and Miracle: Modern Judaism and the Holy Spirit."

15. It is worth stressing a self-evident fact: in teaching such material one should appropriately emphasize the risks of involuntary self-surrender. The mystic writer, unlike most of us, *knows* after the fact that this loss of personality is temporary.

16. Compare with the chapter of Thomas Merton's *Bread in the Wilderness* (Collegeville, Minn.: Liturgical Press, 1971) entitled "Dark Lightning" (pp. 101–108), which describes the modalities of mystical experience in a way that parallels Heschel; compare also *The Seven Storey*

Mountain (New York: Doubleday, Image Books, 1948), pp. 341–45, for a presentation of Merton's own illumination. I hope that scholars will explore in detail the parallels between these contemporary mystics. For a suggestive beginning see Hal Bridges, *American Mysticism, from William James to Zen* (New York: Harper & Row, 1970), chapter 4, "The Varieties of Mysticism" (pp. 51–74), devoted to Heschel, Merton, and Howard Thurman. Cf. Arthur Green, "Three Warsaw Mystics" (On Rabbi Judah Leib Alter of Gur, Hillel Zeitlin, Abraham Heschel), in Rachel Elior (ed.), *Rivka Schatz Memorial Volume* (Jerusalem: Magnus, in press).

17. Some consequences of this notion are related to Heschel's treatment of anthropomorphism, prophetic inspiration, prayer; see above chapter 4, "Language and Reality: Toward a Poetics of Faith."

18. This manner of construing the word *God* as a verb has particular relevance for feminist theology; see Judith Plaskow, *Standing Again at Sinai*, chapter 4, "God: Reimaging the Unimaginable" (San Francisco: Harper, 1990), pp. 121–69, and notes.

19. *Not Alone*, p. 78.

20. It is beyond the scope of this book to examine Heschel's pervasive opposition to Martin Buber's philosophy of dialogue, to Buber's interpretation of prophetic experience in these human terms. See below chapter 6, "Sacred versus Symbolic Religion" and its bibliographical references. Cf. Heschel, "Prayer as Discipline": "Prayer begins as an 'it-He' relationship. I am not ready to accept the ancient concept of prayer as dialogue. The better metaphor would be to describe prayer as an act of immersion, comparable to the ancient Hebrew custom of immersing oneself completely in the waters as a way of self-purification to be done over and over again" (*Insecurity*, p. 255).

21. Heschel repeats this observation in several books and articles, but in *Earth* he extends it to a central issue of Jewish identity and self-definition: "There is a price to paid by the Jew. He has to be exalted in order to be normal. In order to be a man, he has to be more than a man. To be a people, the Jews have to be more than a people" (p. 64). See Heschel, "The Individual Jew and His Obligations" and "Israel and the Diaspora," *Insecurity*, pp. 187–222. Also below, note 35 on the universality of mystical Judaism.

22. Here I paraphrase a subtitle ("The Solution Is in the Problem") in Heschel's highly relevant essay, "The Kotzker and Job," in *A Passion for Truth*, p. 289.

23. *Not Alone*, p. 281.

24. "The Mystical Element in Judaism," p. 610; also *Earth*, "Kabbalah," p. 72: "God is involved, so to speak, in the tragic state of the world; the *Shekhinah* 'lies in the dust.'" Also *In Search*, the final words of chapter 15: "The *Shekhinah*, the presence of God, is in exile. To worship is to expand the presence of God in the world. To have faith in God is to reveal what is concealed" (pp. 156–57).

25. "The Mystical Element in Judaism," pp. 610, 611. This view does not focus upon ecstatic mysticism or the Jewish mystic's halakhi-

cally organized cleaving to God, within the boundaries of the Jewish community and prayerhouse.

26. *Not Alone*, p. 282.

27. See Kasimow and Sherwin, *No Religion is an Island* (op. cit.); Edward Kaplan, "Contemplative Inwardness and Prophetic Action," in Donald Grayston and Michael Higgins (eds.), *Thomas Merton: Pilgrim in Progress* (Toronto, 1983), pp. 98–105, with correspondence between Heschel and Merton. Also Hal Bridges, *American Mysticism* (op. cit.), pp. 51–74.

28. In Rome, on 31 January 1973, Pope Paul VI alluded to Heschel in a speech to Catholic pilgrims: "Even before we have moved in search of God, God has come in search of us." A Vatican press release later explained the reference to the French translation of *God in Search of Man*; Eva Fleischner, "Heschel's Significance for Christian-Jewish Relations," in John Merkle (ed.), *Abraham Joshua Heschel* (op. cit.), p. 159, and note 71. See Kasimow and Sherwin, *No Religion Is an Island* and its bibliography.

29. Thomas Merton, *The Waters of Siloe* (New York: Harcourt Brace, 1949), p. 364, glossary, article "Mysticism"; see also *Bread in the Wilderness*, p. 102, for a definition of "living faith" as an ardor of love that constitutes a kind of indirect experience of God. The later chapters of *The Seven Storey Mountain* on the Trappists eloquently evoke such contemplative consciousness.

30. Maurice Friedman defines the problem: "But the modern Jew's sense of the ineffable does not necessarily lead him to follow Heschel in prescriptions of the law as an objective order of divine will. . . . He does not see the dilemma enough from within to build a bridge to Jewish law for most liberal Jews . . ." ("Divine Need and Human Wonder," *Judaism* [Winter 1976], p. 78).

31. In *Not Alone* he asserts that awe is "a fundamental norm of human consciousness, a *categorical imperative*. Indeed, the validity and requiredness of awe enjoy a degree of certainty that is not even surpassed by the axiomatic certainty of geometry" (p. 27). "We do, indeed, claim that meanings, just as facts, are independent of the structure of the human mind and given with or within things and events" (p. 28). This innate sense of ineffable meaning has many synonyms: it is "a forgotten mother tongue" (p. 75), "a *dimension* of all existence" (p. 64); "our inner life [is] an anonymous quotation" (p. 43), and many more. See chapter 3, note 12.

32. *Prophets*, pp. 191–92. Compare with Heschel's 1938 speech in Frankfurt; see Appendix B, "Heschel in Germany."

33. Ibid., p. 193. On the same page Heschel writes: "When all pretensions are abandoned, one begins to feel the burden of guilt. It is easier to return from an extreme distance than from the complacency of a good conscience, from spurious proximity."

34. From a remarkable paper written by Mary Schenk (Mount Holyoke College '76) for my course, Mysticism and Moral Life (December 1975), Amherst College.

35. "According to the Kabbalah, redemption . . . is a continual process, taking place at every moment. Man's good deeds are single acts in the long drama of redemption, and not only the people of Israel, but the whole universe must be redeemed" (*Earth*, p. 72).

Chapter Six.
Sacred versus Symbolic Religion

1. *Quest*, p. 132. This final section of the essay, "Symbolism and Our Way of Living" (pp. 132–44), summarizes Heschel's views.

2. Ibid., p. xiii.

3. In his masterwork, *On the Kabbalah and Its Symbolism*, trans. Ralph Manheim (New York: Schocken Books, 1960; original German, 1960, Zurich), Gershom Scholem—the foremost interpreter of "symbolism" in Jewish mystical tradition—resolutely rejects Heschel's judgment: "For a discussion of symbolism in religion, see the symposium *Religious Symbolism*, ed. F. Ernest Johnson, New York, 1955. However, I cannot by any means support the view, here put forward by Professor Abraham Heschel, that Rabbinical Judaism is a religion constituted outside the categories of symbolism" (p. 22, note). See below note 5.

4. *Quest*, pp. 142–43.

5. See chapter 5 of *Quest*, pp. 115–44. Heschel's paper opposed many views expressed in the interreligious and interdisciplinary colloquium organized by Louis Finkelstein, Chancellor of the Jewish Theological Seminary (winter 1952–53 Institute for Religious and Social Studies). Heschel's paper, "Symbolism in Jewish Faith," was published in F. Ernest Johnson (ed.), *Religious Symbolism* (Institute for Religion and Social Studies and distributed by Harper and Brothers, 1955), pp. 53–79; compare with Mordecai Kaplan's paper, "The Future of Religious Symbolism—A Jewish View," ibid., pp. 203–17.

6. *Quest*, p. 128; from a speech originally published as "Toward an Understanding of Halacha," in *Central Conference of American Rabbis Yearbook* LXIII (1953), p. 387. Some detailed remarks on Kant and neo-Kantianism were removed from the revised version of this passage as reprinted in *Quest*, pp. 93–114; see below.

7. This and the following quotation from *Quest*, p. 131.

8. *Prophets*, pp. 273–74.

9. *Not Alone*, p. 108.

10. *Quest*, p. 118.

11. Ibid., p. 122.

12. Ibid., p. 123.

13. Ibid., p. 136.

14. Ibid., p. 114.

15. Ibid., p. 136.

16. *Quest*, p. 114.

17. "On Prayer," p. 4.

18. *Quest*, p. 121.
19. *The Prophets*, p. 486.
20. *In Search*, p. 320. See esp. chapter 32, "Religious Behaviorism," chapter 30, "The Art of Being."
21. Ibid., p. 306.
22. *Quest*, p. 137.
23. Ibid., p. 135.
24. Ibid., p. 68.
25. Chapters 28 to 34 of *In Search*—"A Science of Deeds," "More than Inwardness," "The Art of Being," "Kavanah," "Religious Behaviorism," "The Problem of Polarity," and "The Meaning of Observance." Scholars should note Heschel's abundant documentation: for example, chapter 31, note 3 (pp. 317–19) traces the debate about whether or not kavanah is necessary for a ritual act to be spiritually valid.
26. For more details see my paper, "Sacred versus Symbolic Religion: A. J. Heschel and Martin Buber," *Modern Judaism* 14, 3 (Fall 1994): 213–31, from which the following section is taken. (Since that publication I have modified my characterization of Buber.) For other letters from Heschel see Martin Buber, *Briefwechsel aus sieben Jahrzehnten* (Heidelberg: Verlag Lambert Schneider), Band II: 1918–1938, 1973; Band III: 1938–1965, 1975). The fuller context of these fundamental issues is studied with great care and ample documentation by Paul Mendes-Flohr, *Divided Passions: Jewish Intellectuals and the Experience of Modernity* (Detroit: Wayne State University Press, 1991). Compare with Maurice Friedman, *Martin Buber: The Life of Dialogue* (New York: Harper Torchbooks, 1960: chapter 19, "Buber's Theory of Knowledge"; chapter 24, "Symbol, Myth, and History."
27. "Sinnbildische und sakramentale Existenz in Judentum," in *Eranos-Jahrbuch* vol. 2, 1934 (Zurich: Rhein-Verlag, 1935), pp. 339–67; translated by Maurice Friedman in *The Origin and Meaning of Hasidism* (New York: Harper Torchbooks, 1960), pp. 152–81. Heschel's letter refers to pages in the original publication.

At that Eranos conference, Buber represented Judaism to a diverse community of experts, including Erwin Rouselle from Frankfurt-am-Main who presented a paper on Chinese mythology; J. W. Hauer of Tübingen on Indo-Arab symbolism of the self; Heinrich Zimmer of Heidelberg on Hindu mythology; C. G. Jung on archetypes of the collective unconscious; Mrs. C. A. F. Rhys Davids of London on mandala symbolism; Friedrich Heiler of Marburg on the Madonna as religious symbol; Swami Yatiswarananda of Madras on Hindu symbolism, and others.

28. Letter of 24 July 1935 published in Martin Buber, *Briefwechsel aus sieben Jahrzehnten* (op. cit.), vol. 2; letter no. 510, pp. 568–69. I have consulted the manuscript letter in the Buber Archive at the Jewish National and University Library, Jerusalem (Ms. Var. 350/290: 2); also published in English translation, which we modify, in Nahum Glatzer and Paul Mendes-Flohr (eds.), *The Letters of Martin Buber: A Life in Dialogue* (New York: Schocken, 1991), no. 463, pp. 430–31. See letter of Ernst

Michel, the progressive Catholic sociologist, to Buber, 26 March 1935, thanking him for the same paper, *Briefwechsel*, no. 503, p. 563. Heschel's letters to Buber (most of them as yet unpublished) are preserved at the Martin Buber Archive, Jerusalem, Ms.Var. 350/290: 1–59.

Heschel's letter continues by citing a much-debated interpretation: "You interpret the marriage of Hosea as a personified 'representation of an experience of God, of his experience with Israel,' (p. 349). The agreement of this reading with the fundamental reason of the 'sign' (p. 347) is not clear to me. Certainly the experience of God is in itself a reality. Where, then, is the advantage of incarnation in the sign as opposed to the reality of experience of the actual history? Does the prophet's private affair express the constituent facts 'more substantially, more perfectly' than the original events?"

Buber published his opposing view in *The Prophetic Faith*, trans. Carlyle Witton-Davies (New York: Harper Torchbooks, 1949): "And Hosea does as he is bidden. But this does not at all mean that he 'feels with God,' as some think; [footnote: Cf. especially Heschel, *Die Prophetie* (1936), 76ff.]" (p. 112, note).

29. See Harold Stern, "A. J. Heschel, Irenic Polemicist," *Proceedings of the Rabbinical Assembly* (1983), pp. 169–77.

30. Rosenzweig submitted the essay around 1914 to a volume of collected essays, *Von Judentum*, which Buber was collecting but was never published; Rosenzweig's contribution appeared only twenty-one years later: "Atheistische Theologie," in Franz Rosenzweig, *Kleinere Schriften* (Berlin: Schocken Verlag, 1937), pp. 287–90. Translations: "Atheistic Theology: From the Old to the New Way of Thinking," *Canadian Journal of Theology* XIV, 2 (1968): 79–88, translated by Robert G. Goldy and H. Frederick Holch; cf. French translation of "Théologie Athée," by Jean-Marie Schlegel, *Revue des sciences religieuses* 74, 4 (1986): 545–57. For the best discussion of the issues, see Paul Mendes-Flohr, *From Mysticism to Dialogue: Martin Buber's Transformation of German Social Thought* (Detroit: Wayne State University Press, 1989); also Ernst Simon, "Martin Buber and German Jewry," LBIY 3 (1958): 33–36.

31. To me and confirmed by others. Beyond the scope of the present discussion, but essential, is Mendes-Flohr's discussion of Buber's apparent "atheism" against which Rosenzweig reacted: see *From Mysticism to Dialogue*, esp. pp. 165–66, note 321; p. 180, n. 247 for the relevant sources; and Steven T. Katz, "Martin Buber's Epistemology," in *Post-Holocaust Dialogues: Critical Studies in Modern Jewish Thought* (New York: New York University Press, 1983), pp. 1–51.

32. *The Prophets*, p. 487.

33. *Quest*, p. 136.

34. *Sabbath*, p. 8.

35. Ibid., p. 59. See also ibid., pp. 273–74 for the "idea of God's betrothal to Israel;" ibid., p. 276 for "The Lord is my shepherd;" *In Search*, p. 9 "our Father in Heaven;" and *Insecurity*, p. 120, for an analysis of the imagery of Psalm 19.

36. *Sabbath*, p. 60.

37. Loc. cit.

38. Ibid., pp. 53–54.

39. Ibid., p. 119, note 5; see p. 6.

40. *In Search*, p. 213. See also *Quest*, p. 143. Much work on the phenomenological and ontological differences between esthetic and religious experience remains to be done. A significant contribution in neo-Thomist thought has been made by Marcel de Corte, "Ontologie de la Poésie" (in French), *Revue Thomiste*, XLIII, 3 (Nov.–Dec. 1937): 361–92, and ibid., XLIV (Jan. 1938): 99–125. Cf. Jacques Maritain's criticism, in *Situation de la Poésie*, with Raissa Maritain (Desclée de Brouwer, 1964), esp. pp. 121–40; trans. Suther, Marshall: *Situation of Poetry: Four Essays on the Relations between Poetry, Mysticism, Magic and Knowledge* (New York: Kraus reprints, 1959).

41. *Quest*, p. 143.

42. Ibid., p. 62; the footnote to this passage cites *Not Alone*, chapter 23.

43. This "sacred humanism" may become Heschel's enduring contribution to twentieth-century religious thought: see "The Mystical Element," section 2, "The Exaltation of Man," pp. 604–6; "The Sacred Image of Man," in *Insecurity*, pp. 150–67; "The Concept of Man in Jewish Thought," in S. Radhakrishnan and P.T. Raju (eds.), *The Concept of Man: A Study in Comparative Philosophy* (Lincoln, Nebraska: Johnsen Publishing, 1960): 108–57 (reprinted in Jacob Neusner and Noam M. M. Neusner [eds.], *To Grow in Wisdom* [Lanham, 1990]: 97–146); and *Who Is Man?*

44. This and the following quotation from *Quest for God*, p. 124.

45. Ibid., p. 126.

46. Ibid., pp. 126–27. Heschel quotes Leviticus 19:2: "You shall be holy, for I the Lord your God am holy."

47. Ibid., p. 132. Humanity functions in a manner parallel to God, though not on the same plane: "We worship Him not by employing figures of speech but by the actual shaping of our lives according to His pattern."

48. "Religion and Race," *Insecurity*, p. 94. Heschel continues, with this ironic comparison: "From the perspective of eternity our recognition of equality of all men seems as generous an act as the acknowledgment that stars and planets have a right to be."

Chapter Seven.
Prophetic Radicalism

1. "Religion and Race," in *Insecurity*, p. 88. See below notes 18, 20.

2. See Arnold Eisen, "Re-Reading Heschel and the Commandments," *Modern Judaism* 9 (February 1989): 1–33. *The Insecurity of Freedom* (1966) contains most of the speeches we discuss in this chapter. See Robert McAfee Brown, "'Some are Guilty, All are Responsible': Heschel's Social Ethics," and Eva Fleischner, "Heschel's Significance for Jewish-

Christian Relations," both in John C. Merkle (ed.), *AJH: Exploring His Life and Thought*, pp. 123–64.

3. *Prophets*, p. 6.

4. "Conversation with Dr. Abraham Joshua Heschel," p. 6, interview with Carl Stern, aired on 4 February 1973, National Broadcasting Company, 1973. All rights reserved.

5. See chapter 1 and notes 6, 7, 10 for details. For the background see Ernst Simon, "Jewish Adult Education in Nazi Germany as Spiritual Resistance," *Leo Baeck International Yearbook* 1 (1956): 68–104.

6. "The Last Days of Maimonides" (*Insecurity*, pp. 285–98) was the only chapter of the 1935 biography Heschel himself revised, translated, and published in the United States.

7. For practical purposes, readers can skip the scholarly debates (for example, chapters 13, 19–24) and trace Heschel's own theology in the following: "What Manner of Man Is the Prophet?" (chapter 1), "Chastisement," "Justice," "The Theology of Pathos" (chapters 10–12), and "Anthropopathy," "Religion of Sympathy," "Event and Experience," and "Conclusions" (chapters 15, 18, 25, 28).

8. See especially Heschel, "The Moral Outrage of Vietnam," in *Vietnam: Crisis of Conscience*, with Robert McAfee Brown and Michael Novak (New York: Association Press, Behrman House, Herder and Herder, 1967), and the essays and addresses responding to current events, collected in *Insecurity*.

9. *Prophets*, p. 5: "This is the secret of the prophet's style: his life and soul are at stake in what he says and in what is going to happen to what he says. It is an involvement that echoes on. . . . Not only the prophet and the people, but God Himself is involved in what the words convey" (p. 6).

10. See Fritz Rothschild (ed.), *Between God and Man*, p. 25; Merkle, *The Genesis of Faith*, p. 132.

11. *Prophets*, p. 24.

12. *Who Is Man?* Compare with Martin Buber's fundamental survey of philosophical anthropology, "What Is Man?" in *Between Man and Man* (New York: Macmillan, 1965), pp. 118–208.

13. *Who Is Man?* pp. 13–14.

14. "The awareness of divine dignity must determine even man's relation to his own self. His soul as well as his body constitutes an image of God," *Insecurity*, p. 155; see also "The Patient as a Person," "Religion and Race," and "Sacred Image of Man"; see above chapter 6, note 43. The following quotation is from "Religion and Race," *Insecurity*, p. 86.

15. This and the following quotation from "No Religion Is an Island," pp. 7–8.

16. We recall Heschel's paradigmatic Yiddish poem, "I and Thou," first published in 1929; see above chapter 1, note 8. See especially, "The Mystical Element in Judaism," the final section of which considers prophets and mystics to be almost identical. Specialists can push the hermeneutical task further by comparing Heschel's formulations with

the *Zohar*, Talmud, and other rabbinic and Hasidic sources, common or recondite. While this research and interpretation will trace a history of modern theology (as I indicate in my conclusion, below chapter 10), it does not explain Heschel's own commitment; for he forged his system in the "crucible of his [own] mind," in Jacob Neusner's formulation, and I would add, in his own "holy spirit" (see below chapter 9).

17. "Religion and Race," p. 85; the next quotation from p. 86.

18. Ibid., p. 88.

19. Ibid., p. 93.

20. See "Teaching Jewish Theology in the Solomon Schechter Day School," p. 26, note 39; see ibid., pp. 25–27 for Heschel's explanation of "the Negro problem."

21. This is a central principle of the Hasidic world view, the details of which Heschel analyzed in "The Mystical Element in Judaism"; compare with *Earth*, chapter 10 on Kabbalah.

22. "The Individual Jew and His Obligations," *Insecurity*, p. 202. The sources, not quoted in this essay, can be found in "Teaching Jewish Theology" (see next note).

23. Heschel, "Teaching Jewish Theology in the Solomon Schechter Day School," p. 17: "When I quoted this for the first time, I received letters from all parts of the country, 'Such a Midrash does not exist.' This is the Sifre: '*Atem Eydai N'um Hashem, V'ani El'* [Isaiah 43:12]. 'You are my witnesses (says God) and I am God.' Says Rabbi Shimon ben Yochai, the disciple of Rabbi Akiva: 'If you are my witnesses, I am God; if you are not my witnesses, I am not God.' Now this is perhaps one of the most powerful statements found in Rabbinic literature. It is paradoxical to be sure, in that it indicates what I mentioned to you before—the necessity of cooperation."

24. "The Patient as a Person," *Insecurity*, p. 25.

25. "Religion in a Free Society," ibid., p. 8.

26. *Vietnam: Crisis of Conscience*, p. 50: "We must continue to remind ourselves that, in a free society, all are involved in what some are doing. *Some are guilty, all are responsible.*" Cf. *Prophets*, pp. 14–16, the section entitled, "Few are guilty, all are responsible."

27. *Insecurity*, p. 18.

28. "The doctor may be a saint without knowing it and without pretending to be one," ibid., p. 38.

29. "Children and Youth," ibid., p. 39.

30. Ibid., pp. 39–40.

31. "To Grow in Wisdom," ibid., p. 78.

32. Ibid., p. 84.

33. Ibid., "Religion and Race," p. 87.

34. "On Prayer," *Conservative Judaism* 25, 1 (Fall 1970), pp. 7–8.

35. *Not Alone*, p. 139. See my first, youthful essay, "Poetry, Prayer, and Social Action," *CCAR Journal* (October 1969): 69–73; and "Three Dimensions of Human Fullness: Poetry, Love, and Prayer," *Judaism* (Summer 1973): 309–21.

36. *Quest*, p. 13. See "The Vocation of the Cantor" (originally presented in 1957), *Insecurity*, pp. 242–53.

37. "On Prayer," p. 3.

38. *Vietnam: Crisis of Conscience*, pp. 52, 53. See also Heschel, "The Reason for My Involvement in the Peace Movement," *Journal of Social Philosophy* 4 (January 1973): 7–8. Mitchell K. Hall, *Because of Their Faith: CALCAV and Religious Opposition to the Vietnam War* (New York: Columbia University Press, 1990), studies the antiwar movement that Heschel helped establish.

39. This and the next quotation from *Vietnam*, pp. 51–52. An anonymous reader of this manuscript pointed out that Heschel's apparently autobiographical story was quoted, without citing the source, from the Yiddish poet Halper Leivik's play, *The Golem*, in Joseph C. Landis (ed.), *The Dybbuk and Other Great Jewish Plays* (New York, 1977). My view is that although Heschel may be absorbing Yiddish and other sources into a personal vision, the first person retains its autobiographical pathos. Heschel would have been seven years of age in 1914, during the turmoil preceding World War I or at its beginning.

40. I take the expression "Three-Day Jews" from an article of that title by Leo Hirsch in the Berlin periodical, *Der Morgen* vol. X (1934/35): 295–98. For a preliminary analysis of the "fear of God" or "fear of Heaven" as a prerequisite for moral conscience and true interfaith dialogue, see chapter 10, "Heschel's Unfinished Symphony."

41. "On Prayer," pp. 5,7.

42. Heschel concludes *In Search* with an incomplete discussion of this vexed issue: "The Dignity of Israel," pp. 424–26. See Arnold Eisen, *Galut: Modern Reflection on Homelessness and Homecoming* (Bloomington and Indianapolis: Indiana University Press, 1986), pp. 169–72, for an insightful placing of Heschel's views on Israel into their American context.

43. "Yisrael: Am, Eretz, Medinah. Ideological Evaluation of Israel and the Diaspora," *Proceedings of the Rabbinical Assembly of America* 22 (1958): 122; see also "The Individual Jew and His Obligations" (1957); "Israel and the Diaspora" (1958)—both reprinted in *Insecurity*; and "The Theological Dimensions of Medinat Yisrael," *Proceedings of the Rabbinical Assembly* 32 (1968): 91–103; discussion, pp. 104–9. Compare with *Israel: An Echo of Eternity* (1969), written in response to Christian misunderstandings of the significance to Jews of the June 1967 war.

44. Interview with Carl Stern, December 1972.

45. A paraphrase of Heschel's expression, "the jungles of history," in *Israel*, p. 115. See next chapter.

Chapter Eight.
Confronting the Holocaust

1. *Not Alone*, pp. 154–55. The omitted passage is taken from Job 6:9–10; the source of the quotation is explained on p. 155, note: "Rabbi

Mendl of Kotzk in paraphrasing Psalm 37:3." Later quoted in *Passion for Truth*, see below note 27.

2. *In Search*, p. 140. In addition to chapter 4, "Mysticism and Despair," see chapter 9, "Metaphor and Miracle: Modern Judaism and the Holy Spirit," which explores the full context of this quotation.

3. Ibid., p. 369. The next quotation is from the same page. See the entire chapter 36, "The Problem of Evil," pp. 367–81, and Heschel's essay on Reinhold Niebuhr, "Confusion of Good and Evil," *Insecurity*, pp. 127–49.

4. "No Religion Is an Island," p. 3.

5. From an interview in Patrick Granfield, O.S.B., *Theologians at Work* (New York: Macmillan, 1967), p. 81.

6. See chapter 1, note 14.

7. "An Analysis of Piety" (1942) was followed by "The Holy Dimension" (1943), "Faith" (1944), and "Prayer" (1945). See chapter 1, notes 25, 26, 28.

8. From the Yiddish newspaper, *Day-Morning Journal*, 1 June 1963; cited in Samuel Dresner (ed.), Heschel, *The Circle of the Baal Shem Tov*, p. xxv, note 30. Rabbi Eliezer Silver (1882–1968), a man of remarkable Jewish erudition and personality, was one of Heschel's main sources of personal support in Cincinnati.

9. Heschel confronted these issues explicitly in the final section of *Passion*, "The Kotzker and Job": "Life in our times has been a nightmare for many of us, tranquillity an interlude, happiness a fake. Who could breathe at a time when man was engaged in murdering the holy witness to God six million times? And yet God does not need those who praise Him when in a state of euphoria. He needs whose who are in love with Him when in distress, both He and ourselves. This is the task: in the darkest night to be certain of the dawn, certain of the power to turn curse into a blessing, agony into a song" (pp. 300–301); cf. ibid., p. 283.

10. *Quest*, p. 147; the next quotation from p. 149. *Hebrew Union College Bulletin* 2, 3 (March 1943): 1–2, 18. The following year an expanded version appeared in the British periodical, *Liberal Judaism* XI, 10 (February 1944): 18–21, reprinted as the final chapter of *Quest*, pp. 147–51, from which the following quotations are taken. Expressions in square brackets are found in the 1944 version.

11. Deleted from the version reprinted in *Quest*.

12. *Quest*, pp. 150–51.

13. *Newsletter of the YIVO*, no. 7 (February 1945), p. 5. The paper was published in Yiddish in the *Yivo Bleter* (March–April 1945), and translated into English, probably by Shlomo Noble, for the *Yivo Annual of Jewish Social Science* (1946). See Jacob Neusner, *Stranger at Home: "The Holocaust," Zionism, and American Judaism* (Chicago: University of Chicago Press, 1981), pp. 82–85 on the significance of Heschel's speech. See especially Jeffrey Shandler, "Heschel and Yiddish" (op. cit.), pp. 268–84 for a detailed analysis of this transition in the texts. Heschel also *translated* the process into Hebrew: see *Pikuah Neshamah* (1949), a fifteen-page

broadside that calls to surviving Jews in his other native language.

14. Certificate of Naturalization, no. 6475263, dated 28 May 1945, U.S. District Court, Southern District, Cincinnati, Ohio.

15. Heschel published an expanded Yiddish version of the speech in 1946 with Schocken in New York (see Jeffrey Shandler, "Heschel and Yiddish" [op.cit.], pp. 276–78). The first edition of *Earth* contained a preface referring to the Holocaust by the publisher Henry Schuman, which was omitted from subsequent editions. *Earth* is now published by Farrar, Straus & Giroux, as is *The Sabbath*.

16. *Earth*, p. 72. "Inspired by the idea that not only is God necessary to man, but that man is also necessary to God, that man's actions are vital to all worlds and affect the course of transcendent events, the Kabbalistic preachers and popular writers sought to imbue all people with the consciousness of the supreme importance of all actions. It became a matter of popular conviction that what takes place 'above' in the upper sphere, depends upon man 'below.' By every holy action, by every pure thought, man intervenes in the 'supernal worlds'" (ibid., p. 71).

17. Scholars might consult the first volume of *Torah min ha-shamayim*, where Heschel documents exhaustively the rabbinic theology of the *Shekhinah*. "It permeates Rabbinic literature, post-Rabbinic thought in Judaism, and it is missing in our discussions, and in Maimonides's list of Dogmas. Actually, the idea of *Pathos*, which I consider to be *the* central idea in prophetic theology, contains the doctrine of the *Shekhinah*" (Heschel, "Teaching Jewish Theology," p. 12).

18. *Earth*, pp. 107–8. These final pages appear to be a translation of a passage from Heschel's Hebrew essay, *Pikuah Neshama* (1949).

19. Ibid., p. 109.

20. The quoted phrase refers to an essay of that name by Emil Fackenheim in *God's Presence in History: Jewish Affirmations and Philosophical Reflections* (New York: Harper Torchbooks, 1970), originally presented as a lecture in 1968. Cf. Robert G. Goldy, "The Question of Jewish Theology in Heschel, Fackenheim, and Soloveitchik," in *The Emergence of Jewish Theology in America* (Bloomington and Indianapolis: Indiana University Press, 1990), pp. 66–86.

21. The following quotations are found in *Not Alone*, pp. 151–57. Compare with chapter 9 of *Not Alone*, "In the Presence of God," analyzed in chapter 5 above.

22. Note how this paragraph migrated from the 1938 German speech, through the revisions of 1943 and 1944, eventually ending up in *Not Alone*, chapter 9, "The Hiding God." See above notes 10–13.

23. *Not Alone*, pp. 152–53.

24. See *Prophets*, chapter 10, "Chastisement," pp. 187–94 and chapter 16, "The Meaning and Mystery of Wrath," pp. 279–98.

25. This and the next quotation from *Not Alone*, pp. 153–54.

26. Ibid., p. 154.

27. Ibid., pp. 154–55. The passage from Job is later quoted in *Pas-*

sion in the chapter entitled, "The Battle for Faith"; see the footnote: "Yiddish lit. *Lig in der erd, un pashe dikh mit emune.* Reminiscent of this saying is Kierkegaard's statement that one must lie in the depths of over seventy fathoms of water and still preserve one's faith" (p. 190, n.1). Compare the Kotzker rebbe's bitter paraphrase with Psalm 37:3: "Trust in the Lord; and do good; so that you will dwell in the land, and enjoy security."

28. "The literary shaping of martyrological events serves a double purpose: it instructs the culture in models of spiritual resistance and provides dramatic examples of sanctification whereby these acts could be inscribed in cultural memory," Michael Fishbane, *The Kiss of God* (University of Washington, 1994), p. 71.

29. *Not Alone*, pp. 155–57, cited without quotation marks and without change of font.

30. Originally presented as an address entitled "Jewish-Christian Dialogue and the Meaning of the State of Israel" at the St. Louis Symposium on "Theology in the City of Man," October 1968; published in *Cross Currents* XIX, 4 (Fall 1969), 409–25. This and other statements are included in *Israel*, pp. 112–13; cf. *Cross Currents*, pp. 422–23.

31. *Israel*, p. 115; *Cross Currents*, p. 423.

32. *In Search*, p. 369. See also, "A Hebrew Evaluation of Reinhold Niebuhr," in Ch. W. Kegley and R. W. Bretall (eds.), *Reinhold Niebuhr: His Religious, Social, and Political Thought* (New York: Macmillan, 1956), pp. 391–410; reprinted as "Confusion of Good and Evil," *Insecurity*, pp. 127–49.

Chapter Nine.
Metaphor and Miracle

1. A. J. Heschel, "Did Maimonides Believe that He Had Attained the Rank of Prophet?" p. 1 of galley proofs; translation of Heschel, "Haheemin ha-rambam shezakhah lanevuah," in *Louis Ginzburg Jubilee Volume* (Hebrew Section) (New York: The American Academy for Jewish Research, 1945), pp. 159–88. I quote from the English translation by David Silverman, and edited by Morris Faierstein, with an important preface by Moshe Idel: A. J. Heschel, *Prophetic Inspiration After the Prophets: Maimonides and Others* (New Jersey: KTAV, 1995).

2. A. J. Heschel, "Ha-heemin ha-rambam shezakhah lanevuah," in *Louis Ginzburg Jubilee Volume* (see note 1); and "'Al ruach ha-kodesh biymey ha-benayim," in *Alexander Marx Jubilee Volume* (Hebrew Section) (New York: The Jewish Theological Seminary of America, 1950), pp. 175–208. The latter paper, which covers the period from Talmudic times up until the time of Maimonides, further substantiates the Rambam's discreet claim that he had in fact been inspired by God. Heschel suggests the crucial importance of these two articles: *In Search*, chapter 14, "Insight" (p. 150, n. 1).

3. Samuel Dresner (ed.), Heschel, *The Circle of the Baal Shem*, pp. xxix–xxx.

4. *The Review of Religion* 6, 3 (March 1942), 299; the entire essay was transported verbatim to comprise the final chapter of *Not Alone*. In *Earth*, he wrote of the Hasidim of the eighteenth century: "Miracles no longer startled anyone, and it was no surprise to discover among one's contemporaries men who attained the holy spirit, men whose ear perceived the voice of heaven. . . . On the contrary, the Hasidim believed that it was easier to attain inspiration by the Holy Spirit in their own day then it had been in the early days of the Talmud. For such inspiration flows from two sources—from the Temple in Jerusalem and from the Complete Redemption in the time of the Messiah. And we are closer to the time of redemption than the Talmudic sages were to the era of the Temple" (pp. 91–92).

5. See in Hebrew, *Torah min ha-shamayim*, 3 volumes; monographs on Hasidic masters in Hebrew and Yiddish (collected in Samuel Dresner [ed.], *The Circle of the Baal Shem Tov*), and the following.

6. See chapter 1, note 6. Heschel's Yiddish poetry parallels his doctoral dissertation: both were completed by 1933.

7. *Die Prophetie*, pp. 127–83; cf. *The Prophets*, chapter 12, "The Theology of Pathos," and 18, "Religion of Sympathy." The conclusion to "The Mystical Element in Judaism" conflates prophetic inspiration and mystical contact with the Divine. This is the only statement in which Heschel does not insist upon their differences.

8. *Die Prophetie*, p. 147. Heschel probably integrated his unpublished paper on "Ruah" in the important section of *Prophets*, "Spirit as Pathos" (pp. 315–17), which makes a philological claim associating compassion, empathy, and the Holy Spirit.

9. Ibid., p. 171.

10. See *Guide to the Perplexed*, Introduction, Book III. Cf. Moshe Idel, "Maimonides and Kabbalah," in Isadore Twersky (ed.), *Studies in Maimonides* (Cambridge: Harvard University Press, 1990), pp. 312–79.

11. A. J. Heschel, *Maimonides: A Biography*, translation by Joachim Neugroschel (New York, 1982). I cite the English version, which I have sometimes modified, followed by the original German edition, *Maimonides: Eine Biographie* (Berlin: Erich Reiss Verlag, 1935): pp. 25–26; orig., pp. 28–29.

12. *Maimonides*, Eng., p. 157; orig., p. 175.

13. See above notes 1–2.

14. "Prophetic Inspiration in the Middle Ages," opening paragraph.

15. This and the next quotation from "Did Maimonides Believe that He Had Attained the Rank of Prophet?" Section III.

16. Ibid., beginning of Section IV.

17. See chapter 1, note 28: Heschel's erudite monograph on Saadia, after the reasoned arguments, explicitly hands the initiative to God: "Formulated belief is an attempt to translate into words an unutterable spiritual reality" (p. 408). I suggested in my introduction that Heschel's apologetics follows in the tradition that includes Saadia Gaon's, *The Book of Beliefs and Opinions*, trans. Samuel Rosenblatt (Yale University Press, 1948.)

18. See Moshe Idel, *The Mystical Experience in Abraham Abulafia* (Albany: State University of New York Press, 1988); Heschel published a text of Abulafia's in Hebrew, "A Cabbalistic Commentary on the Prayerbook," in Louis Ginzberg and Abraham Weiss (eds.), *Studies in Memory of Moses Schorr* (New York: The Professor Moses Schorr Memorial Committee, 1944): pp. 113–26. See Moshe Idel's groundbreaking work, *Kabbalah: New Perspectives* (New Haven: Yale University Press, 1988).

19. See "Prophetic Inspiration," section IV, and section V, "Divine Illumination" (and notes 105–10), for citations from Rashi. Footnotes 89–90 contain enough references for a book on biblical prophecy and Jewish mystical tradition.

20. See A. J. Heschel, "The Relevance of Prophecy" (pp. 13–19), in *Proceedings Fifth Annual Pedagogical Conference: Cleveland Bureau of Jewish Studies* (9 February 1958): "I am very excited about the fact that we have both interpretations. If we had only one interpretation, a great voice that never ceases, we would have slippery Jews, relativists. How marvelous that we have both interpretations. They supplement each other" (p. 19). This discussion typifies Heschel's conception of classical Judaism as pluralistic.

21. *Not Alone*, p. 44.

22. *In Search*, p. 138; see the note to this passage: "Deuteronomy 5:19, according to the Aramaic translation of Onkelos and Jonathan ben Uzziel and to the interpretation of *Sanhedrin*, 17b; *Sotah*, 10b; and to the first interpretation of Rashi" (p. 143, note 5).

23. Ibid., p. 139.

24. *Not Alone*, p. 36.

25. *In Search*, pp. 140–41 for this and the following quotations.

26. *Quest*, p. 106. Cf. *Not Alone*: "The art of awareness of God, the art of sensing His presence in our daily lives cannot be learned off-hand. God's grace resounds like a staccato. Only by retaining the seemingly disconnected notes comes the ability to grasp the theme" (p. 88).

27. *In Search*, pp. 140–41 for this and the next quotation.

28. Ibid., p. 144, note 8.

29. Ibid., p. 137.

30. *Prophets*, p. 488.

31. *Quest*, p. 107.

32. His 1951 book, *The Sabbath*, explains its essence in terms of philosophy, parable, and prayer. See also: "It will be through the Sabbath that the Torah will come back to the Jewish home," from "Israel and the Diaspora," in *Insecurity*, p. 221; "Jewish Education," ibid., pp. 223–41; and especially the transcript of his presentation to educators: "Teaching Jewish Theology at the Solomon Schechter Day School," in *The Synagogue School* 28, 1 (Fall 1969): 4–18, followed by questions and answers, pp. 18–33.

33. See "The Individual Jew and His Obligations," *Insecurity*, pp. 205–209.

34. *Quest*, p. 111.

Chapter Ten.
Heschel's Unfinished Symphony

1. Heschel, "Confusion of Good and Evil," *Insecurity*, p. 136; originally published as "A Hebrew Evaluation of Reinhold Niebuhr," in Charles W. Kegley and Robert W. Bretall (eds.), *Reinhold Niebuhr* (New York: Macmillan, 1956). See also *Not Alone*, chapter 33, "The Problem of Polarity," pp. 341–42, p. 347, n. 10.

2. *In Search*, p. 253.

3. *Not Alone*, pp. 151–52. See also Appendix B.

4. "Depth Theology," *Insecurity*, p. 119. It would be worth rereading the entire essay at this point.

5. *In Search*, p. 138; see above, chapter 9, notes 20, 22.

6. "The zeal of the pious Jews was transferred to their emancipated sons and grandsons. The fervor and yearning of the Hasidim, the ascetic obstinacy of the Kabbalists, the inexorable logic of the Talmudists, were reincarnated in the supporters of modern Jewish movements. Their belief in new ideals was infused with age-old piety" (*Earth*, pp. 103–104).

7. "Only those who have gone through days in which words were of no avail, on which the most brilliant theories jarred the ear like mere slang; only those who have experienced ultimate not-knowing, the voicelessness of a soul struck by wonder, total muteness, are able to enter the meaning of God, a meaning greater than the mind" (*In Search*, p. 140). In *Passion*, Heschel insists that we must bash our heads against the wall of absurdity and let God enter: "Faith comes about in a collision of an ending passion for Truth and the failure to attain it by one's own means" (p. 302); see the entire essay, "The Kotzker and Job," pp. 263–303. See above, chapters 4 and 8.

8. *In Search*, p. 140.

9. English title: *Theology of Ancient Judaism* (London and New York: Soncino Press, vol. 1, 1962; vol. 2, 1965; vol. 3 [Jerusalem: Jewish Theological Seminary], 1990). See Arnold Eisen, "Re-Reading Heschel on the Commandments" (op. cit).

10. A formulation suggested by an anonymous reader of the manuscript.

11. "Awareness of God is as close to him as the throbbing of his own heart, often deep and calm but at times overwhelming, intoxicating, setting the soul afire" (*Not Alone*, p. 282). See chapter 9, "Metaphor and Miracle."

12. Heschel extends this recognition of human cognitive limits in the section, "Meaning Beyond Absurdity," *Passion*, pp. 294–97. See also, "Idols in the Temples," *Insecurity*, pp. 52–69; and "The Individual Jew and His Obligations," "Israel and Diaspora," and "Jewish Education," ibid., pp. 187–241.

13. "On Prayer," p. 7. This outcry spans his American career. Cf. the original version in *Not Alone*: "Dark is the world to me, for all its cities

and stars, if not for the breath of compassion that God blew in me when he formed me of dust and clay, more compassion than my nerves can bear. God, I am alone with my compassion within my limbs. Dark are my limbs to me; if not for Thee, who could stand such anguish, such disgrace?" (p. 147). See also ibid., chapter 16, "The Hiding God," examined in chapter 8. See also "Prayer as Discipline" (first presented at the Union Theological Seminary, 1959), reprinted in *Insecurity*, pp. 254–61.

14. *Passion*, p. 34. During that period, Heschel also completed a two-volume book in Yiddish, *Kotsk: in gerangl far emesdikeyt (Kotzk: The Struggle for Integrity)* (Tel Aviv: Hamenorah Publishing House, 1973), as yet to be translated.

15. *Passion*, p. xiv.

16. *Quest*, p. 70.

17. "The Spirit of Jewish Prayer," RA (1953), p. 163.

18. *In Search*, pp. 341–42, and the entire chapter 33, "The Problem of Polarity" (pp. 336–47). The essay on Niebuhr, cited above in note 1, is taken in large part from this chapter and chapter 36, "The Problem of Evil."

19. *Not Alone*, p. 47. His appeal to intuition seeks to liberate the image of God dwelling within our consciousness. Put another way, each person includes a number of empirical, worldly selves and a divine self capable of transforming them. Some of the following thoughts were clarified by the essay of Henry Corbin, "De la théologie apophatique comme antidote du nihilisme," in *Le Paradoxe du monothéisme* (Paris: Editions de l'Herne, 1981), esp. pp. 194–213; and Herbert Fingarette, *The Self in Transformation* (New York: Harper and Row, 1965). See also my essay, "Contemplative Inwardness and Prophetic Action: Thomas Merton's Dialogue with Judaism" (op. cit.).

20. *In Search*, p. 138. See above, chapter 8 for a fuller analysis; and the book of Michael Fishbane, *The Kiss of God: Spiritual and Mystical Death in Judaism* (University of Washington Press, 1994), which combines erudition, sensitivity, and spiritual insight.

21. Heschel, "Celebration and Exaltation," in *Jewish Heritage* (Summer 1972), p. 8; see also, "Hasidism as a New Approach to Torah," ibid. (Fall/Winter 1972): 14–21.

22. "No Religion Is an Island," p. 14. See John Merkle, "Heschel's Attitude Toward Religious Pluralism," in Kasimow and Sherwin (op. cit.) (pp. 97–109) and other essays in the collection.

23. *Not Alone*, p. 112. This is an important page.

24. "No Religion Is an Island," p. 9.

25. "Because of his immense power, man is potentially the most wicked of beings. He often has a passion for cruel deeds that only fear of God can soothe, suffocating flushes of envy that only holiness can ventilate" (*Not Alone*, p. 211).

26. Heschel, "The Ecumenical Movement" (a reply to Cardinal Bea, April 1963): "To quote from classic rabbinic literature: 'Pious men of all nations have a share in the world to come,' and are promised the

reward of eternal life. 'I call heaven and earth to witness that the Holy Spirit rests upon each person, Jew or gentile, man or woman, master or slave, in consonance with his deeds'" (*Insecurity*, p. 182).

27. Heschel, "Faith" (part 2), *The Reconstructionist* 10, 4 (17 November 1944), p. 16, the final paragraph.

28. Harold J. Berman, "Law and Logos," *DePaul Law Review* 44, 1 (Fall 1994), 164–65: "I have called the new age into which mankind is entering the age of the holy spirit; this is an ecumenical image, which not only corresponds to Christian tradition but is also congenial to adherents of other religions as well as to those humanists who disclaim religious affiliation but nevertheless hold some values to be sacred. I believe that only a shared faith in the common destiny of mankind gradually to form a world community will provide the vision and the emotional support necessary to the continued creation of a world order governed by law. / There is an intimate connection between the creation of such a world order and an integrative jurisprudence . . . ," and the notes.

Appendix B.
Heschel in Germany

1. For an expanded version of this essay see "God in Exile: Abraham Joshua Heschel, Translator of the Spirit," in Amy Colin and Elisabeth Strenger (eds.), *Bridging the Abyss: Essays in Honor of Harry Zohn; Brücken über dem Abgrund: Festschrift für Harry Zohn* (Munich: Wilhelm Fink Verlag, 1994), pp. 239–54.

2. Heschel's first public response to Nazism was a powerful Yiddish poem (*"In tog fun has"*—Day of Hate), published under the pseudonym of "Itzik," which appeared in the Warsaw Yiddish weekly *Haynt*, 10 May 1933. Heschel first claimed authorship when he republished this piece in a brochure with YIVO, commemorating the twenty-fifth anniversary of the founding of Yung Vilna, 12 March 1955, with this explanation: "Berlin, 1 April 1933; written when the Nazis in the Berlin Opern-Platz burned the works of Jewish philosophers." See the translation by Jeffrey Shandler, "Heschel and Yiddish," *The Journal of Jewish Thought and Philosphy* 2 (1993): 260–63.

3. The following quotations are taken from the original German text as printed in Margarethe Lachmund (ed.), *Begegnung mit dem Judentum. Ein Gedenkbuch*. Heft 2 (Bad Pyrmont, 1962), pp. 11–13.

4. Martin Buber to Ernst Simon, 2 March 1938, in *Briefwechsel* vol. 2 (op. cit.), letter no. 594, p. 658. See my article, "Sacred versus Symbolic Religion: A. J. Heschel and Martin Buber," *Modern Judaism* 14 (Fall 1994): 213–31.

5. Lachmund (op. cit.), p. 11.

6. Here are the opening lines: "Die Welt in der wir leben, trägt das Wappen der Dämonen an ihrem Eingang. Es geschieht in unseren Tagen, daß die Völker ihre Sicheln zu Schwertern umschmieden und ihre Win-

zerhippen zu Speeren. Und in voller Umkehrung der prophetischen Worte wenden sich die Völker ab von der Weisung, die von Zion ausgeht. In dieser Welt Antlitz schauen, ist unser Los. Wir erfahren, wie die Vision der Propheten in ihrer Verrzerung erfüllt wird. Von beiden Merkmalen des menschlichen Antlitzes, der Ebenbildlichkeit mit dem Schöpfer und dem Kainszeichen an der Stirn, tritt das zweite immer deutlicher hervor und droht das erste immer gründlicher zu verwischen."

7. Heschel develops this paradoxical doctrine of "punishment" or suffering as a goad to divine insight in *The Prophets*, chapter 10, entitled "Chastisement," pp. 187–94; for example: "Agony is the final test. When all hopes are dashed and all conceit is shattered, man begins to miss what he has long spurned. In darkness, God becomes near and clear," p. 193; cf. ibid., pp. 90, 93–95, 146–55.

8. *Earth*, p. 72; also "The Mystical Element in Judaism," p. 610. See also, *Torah min ha-shamayim*, volume 1 (see above, chapter 8, notes 17–19).

 ANNOTATED
BIBLIOGRAPHY
IN ENGLISH

For the most complete listing of primary and secondary works in all languages, see Fritz A. Rothschild (ed.), Heschel, *Between God and Man* (New York, 1959; most recent revision, 1975). The selected bibliographies in John C. Merkle, *The Genesis of Faith* (New York, 1983), and Harold Kasimow and Byron Sherwin (eds.), *No Religion Is an Island* (New York, 1991) are also quite useful.

Books in English by Abraham Joshua Heschel, Arranged Chronologically

Maimonides: A Biography. Translated by Joachim Neugroschel. New York, 1982. Originally published in Berlin in 1935, this lively narrative traces the spiritual development of Judaism's greatest (medieval) philosopher and theologian through history and biography. Heschel's precocious autobiography.

The Quest for Certainty in Saadia's Philosophy. New York, 1944. A sixty-seven-page broadside reprinting two major articles on Saadia Gaon (882–942), Talmudist, translator of the Bible into Arabic, and philosopher, whose *Book of Beliefs and Opinions* might have provided a model for Heschel's own philosophy of Judaism. See below for original articles.

The Earth Is the Lord's: The Inner Life of the Jew in East Europe. New York, 1950. Heschel's cultural autobiography. A graceful evocation of Hasidic spirituality and Kabbalistic ethics. An introduction to his work.

The Sabbath: Its Meaning for Modern Man. New York, 1951; expanded edition 1963. Philosophical and poetic meditations on Judaism as a religion of sanctified time. Sabbath is a foretaste of eternity. Another excellent introduction.

Man Is Not Alone: A Philosophy of Religion. New York, 1951. First volume of Heschel's depth theology and all the basic categories of his system, accompanied by profound, lyrical evocations and analyses of universal religious experience. Principles of Judaism also explained.

Man's Quest for God: Studies in Prayer and Symbolism. New York, 1954; reprinted as *Quest for God.* Lucid and inspiring analyses of language, Jewish prayer, ritual, spiritual insight, and Jewish observance as a polarity of law and spontaneity.

God in Search of Man: A Philosophy of Judaism. New York, 1955. Second
volume of Heschel's interpretation of religious experience, longer
and richly documented from classical Jewish and secular philosophical sources. This is Heschel's theological summa and it
includes sections relevant to all his subsequent books.

The Prophets. New York, 1962. A passionate introduction to the Hebrew
prophets that combines vivid insights, historical commentaries,
and detailed critiques of other scholarly approaches. The foundation of Heschel's moral and political commitments.

Who Is Man? Stanford, 1965. Lucid and concise exposition of Heschel's
theology of human being and responsibility. Systematic summary,
though somewhat abstract, of the sacred humanism of his two
philosophical volumes.

The Insecurity of Freedom: Essays on Human Existence. New York, 1966. Collected writings and addresses on civil rights, medical ethics, aging,
youth, Israel and the Diaspora, depth theology, prayer, Reinhold
Niebuhr, ecumenism, Soviet Jewry, and Maimonides. Heschel in
action.

A Passion for Truth. New York, 1973. Fascinating comparison of Kierkegaard with the Kotzker rebbe, two abrasive spiritual dissidents,
Christian and Jewish. Tremendous psychological as well as theological interest.

The Circle of the Baal Shem Tov. Edited by Samuel H. Dresner. Chicago,
1986. Translation of Heschel's scholarly monographs on Hasidic
masters previously published separately in Yiddish and in Hebrew.
Important biographical introduction by the editor.

Prophetic Inspiration After the Prophets: Maimonides and Others. Translated
by William Silverman, edited by Morris Faierstein. New Jersey,
1995. A richly documented study of God's unending Voice, implying that divine inspiration is still available. Crucial observations on
the historical relationship of prophecy and Jewish (and Islamic)
mysticism. Originally published as articles in Hebrew in 1945 and
1950.

Anthologies

Between God and Man: An Interpretation of Judaism, selected, edited, and
introduced by Fritz A. Rothschild. New York, 1959; revised 1976.
The best access to Heschel's varied writings with an authoritative
analysis of his philosophical and theological system. Most complete bibliography of Heschel's writings and those of his critics.
Still the best research tool.

I Asked for Wonder: A Spiritual Anthology, edited by Samuel H. Dresner.
New York, 1987. Brief selections organized by topics and subtitles.
Inspirational reading, reflection, and a handy introduction.

The Wisdom of Heschel, edited by Ruth Marcus Goodhill. New York, 1975.

A collection of striking aphorisms, useful for inspiration and brief meditation.

To Grow in Wisdom, edited by Jacob Neusner with Noam Neusner. Lanham, MD, 1990. Twelve papers including "The Concept of Man in Jewish Thought," essays on time, revelation, and interfaith dialogue. With Susannah Heschel's essay on her father, and the editor's incisive introduction to Heschel the man and the significance of his intellectual achievement.

Selected Articles by Heschel

"The Quest for Certainty in Saadia's Philosophy," *The Jewish Quarterly Review* 33 (1943): 263–313; ibid., 34 (1944): 391–408.

"The Mystical Element in Judaism," in Louis Finkelstein (ed.), *The Jews: Their History, Culture, and Religion* (New York: Harper & Brothers; Philadelphia, The Jewish Publication Society, 1949), pp. 602–23. Heschel's article appears in vol. 1 of the two-volume edition, and in vol. 2 of the four-volume edition. Based exclusively on quotations from the *Zohar*, this is Heschel's own system in miniature.

"The Spirit of Jewish Education," *Jewish Education* 24, 2 (Fall 1953): 9–20.

"Toward an Understanding of Halacha," *Yearbook, Central Conference of American Rabbis* 63 (1953): 386–409.

"The Spirit of Jewish Prayer," *Proceedings of the Rabbinical Assembly of America* 17 (1953): 151–215.

"Yisrael: *Am, Eretz, Medinah*: Ideological Evaluation of Israel and the Diaspora." *Proceedings of the Rabbinical Assembly of America* 22 (1958): 118–36.

"The Concept of Man in Jewish Thought," in S. Radhakrishnan and P. T. Raju (eds.), *The Concept of Man* (London: Allen and Unwin, 1960), pp. 108–57; reprinted in Neusner, 1990.

"The Values of Jewish Education," *Proceedings of the Rabbinical Assembly* 26 (1962): 83–100; comments, pp. 101–9.

"No Religion Is an Island," in *Union Seminary Quarterly Review* 21, 2 (January 1966): 117–34. Page citations to reprint in Harold Kasimow and Byron L. Sherwin (eds.), *No Religion Is an Island: A. J. Heschel and Interreligious Dialogue* (New York, 1991), pp. 3–22.

"From Mission to Dialogue," *Conservative Judaism* 21, 3 (Spring 1967): 1–11.

"The Moral Outrage of Vietnam," *Vietnam: Crisis of Conscience*, by Robert McAfee Brown, A. J. Heschel, David Novak (New York, 1967), pp. 48–61.

"The Jewish Notion of God and Christian Renewal," in L. K. Shook (ed.), *Renewal of Religious Thought* (Montreal, 1968), pp. 105–29.

"God, Torah, and Israel." Translated by Byron L. Sherwin, in Edward Long, Jr. and Robert Handy (eds.), *Theology and Church in Times of Change: Essays in Honor of John Coleman Bennett* (Philadelphia, 1970), pp. 71–90.

"On Prayer," *Conservative Judaism* 25, 1 (Fall 1970): 1–12.

"Hasidism as a New Approach to Torah," in *Jewish Heritage* 14, 3 (Fall–Winter 1972): 14–21.

Interviews with Heschel

"Abraham Joshua Heschel" with Patrick Granfield, O.S.B., *Theologians at Work* (New York: Macmillan, 1967), pp. 69–85.

"A Visit with Rabbi Heschel" with Arthur Herzog, *Think Magazine* (January–February 1964), pp. 16–19, with excellent photographs; condensed in *The Jewish Digest* (December 1968), pp. 15–19.

"Teaching Jewish Theology at the Solomon Schechter Day School," *The Synagogue School* 28, 1 (Fall 1969): 4–33; a fundamental presentation followed by a lively discussion. A concrete sense of Heschel as a person.

"Two Conversations with Abraham Joshua Heschel" with Harold Flender, NBC/Radio Network: part 1 (9 May 1971); part 2 (16 May, 1971). Copyright, The Jewish Theological Seminary of America, New York.

"A Conversation with Rabbi Abraham J. Heschel" with Frank Reynolds (aired 21 November 1971). Copyright American Broadcasting Company.

"A Conversation with Doctor Abraham Joshua Heschel" (December 1972) with Carl Stern, National Broadcasting Company (aired 4 February 1973). Copies available from The Jewish Theological Seminary of America.

Books in English on Heschel, Alphabetical Order

Conservative Judaism 28, 1 (Fall 1973). Memorial tribute to Heschel with important articles by Avraham Holtz, Fritz A. Rothschild, Edmond La B. Cherbonnier, Edward K. Kaplan, Seymour Siegel, Louis Finkelstein, and others.

Friedman, Maurice, *You Are My Witnesses: Abraham Heschel and Elie Wiesel.* New York, 1988. A personal and interpretive introduction to Heschel's personality and his philosophy.

Kasimow, Harold, *Divine-Human Encounter: A Study of Abraham Joshua Heschel.* Washington, D.C., 1979. Focus on religious experience and potentials for interfaith dialogue.

Merkle, John C., *The Genesis of Faith: The Depth Theology of Abraham Joshua Heschel.* New York, 1985. A remarkably detailed systematization of Heschel's entire theological system by a Catholic theologian. Merkle refers generously to other scholars in footnotes and incisively defines the context of Heschel's critics. Superb analysis of Heschel's basic concepts and phenomenology of faith. The basic reference work.

Merkle, John C. (ed.), *Abraham Joshua Heschel: Exploring His Life and Thought.* New York, 1985. An interreligious conference on Heschel at the College of Saint Benedict, Minnesota. Important papers by Bernard W. Anderson, Robert McAfee Brown, Samuel H. Dresner, Eva Fleischner, Edward K. Kaplan, Wolfe Kelman, John C. Merkle, Ursula M. Niebuhr, Fritz A. Rothschild. Expert responses to Heschel's many scholarly and public accomplishments.

Moore, Donald, *The Human and the Holy: The Spirituality of A. J. Heschel.* New York, 1989. A lucid summary of Heschel's basic ideas and values.

Perlman, Lawrence, *Abraham Heschel's Idea of Revelation.* Atlanta, Georgia, 1989. An important revised doctoral dissertation on Heschel's phenomenological method. Technical study for specialists.

Sherman, Franklin, *The Promise of Heschel.* Philadelphia, 1970. A useful introduction and overview.

Sherwin, Byron L., *Abraham Joshua Heschel.* Atlanta, 1979. A loving introduction by a disciple.

Major Articles on Heschel

Borowitz, Eugene. B. "A. J. Heschel," *A New Jewish Theology in the Making* (Philadephia: Westminster Press, 1968), pp. 147–60.

Cherbonnier, Edmond La B. "Heschel as a Religious Thinker," *Conservative Judaism* 23, 1 (Fall 1968): 25–39.

Dresner, Samuel H. "The Contribution of Abraham Joshua Heschel," *Judaism* 32 (Winter 1983): 57–69.

Eisen, Arnold. "Re-Reading Heschel on the Commandments," *Modern Judaism* 9 (February 1989): 1–33.

Fackenheim, Emil L. Review of *Man Is Not Alone,* in *Judaism: A Quarterly Journal* 1 (January 1952): 85–89.

———. Review of *In Search,* in *Conservative Judaism* 15, 1 (Fall 1960): 50–53.

Fox, Marvin. "Heschel, Intuition, and the Halakhah," *Tradition* 3, 1 (Fall 1960): 5–15.

Friedman, Maurice. "Divine Need and Human Wonder: The Philosophy of A. J. Heschel," *Judaism* 25, 1 (Winter 1976): 65–78.

Kaplan, Edward K. "Form and Content in Abraham J. Heschel's Poetic Style," *Central Conference of American Rabbis Journal* 18, 2 (April 1971): 28–39.

———. "Language and Reality in Abraham J. Heschel's Philosophy of Religion," *Journal of the American Academy of Religion* 41, 3 (March 1973): 94–113.

———. "Mysticism and Despair in Abraham J. Heschel's Religious Thought," *The Journal of Religion* 57 (January 1977): 33–47.

———. "Contemplative Inwardness and Prophetic Action," in Donald Grayston and Michael Higgins (eds.), *Thomas Merton: Pilgrim in*

Progress (Toronto, 1983), pp. 98–105, with correspondence between Heschel and Merton.

———. "Heschel's Poetics of Religious Thinking," in John C. Merkle (ed.), *Abraham Joshua Heschel: Exploring His Life and Thought* (New York: Macmillan, 1985), pp. 103–19.

———. "Abraham Joshua Heschel," in Steven T. Katz (ed.), *Interpreters of Judaism in the Late Twentieth Century* (Washington, D.C., 1993), pp. 131–50.

———. "Metaphor and Miracle: A. J. Heschel and the Holy Spirit," *Conservative Judaism* XLVI, 2 (Winter 1994): 3–18.

———. "Sacred versus Symbolic Religion: Abraham Joshua Heschel and Martin Buber," *Modern Judaism* 14, 3 (October 1994): 213–31.

———. "God in Exile: Abraham Joshua Heschel, Translator of the Spirit," in Amy Colin and Elizabeth Strenger (eds.), *Bridging the Abyss: Essays in Honor of Harry Zohn. Brücken über dem Abgrund: Festschrift für Harry Zohn* (Munich: Wilhelm Fink Verlag, 1994), pp. 239–54.

———. "The American Mission of Abraham Joshua Heschel," in Robert M. Seltzer and Norman J. Cohen (eds.), *The Americanization of the Jews* (New York, 1995), pp. 355–74.

Kasimow, Harold. "Abraham Joshua Heschel and Interreligious Dialogue," *Journal of Ecumenical Studies* 18 (Summer 1981): 423–34.

Katz, Steven T. "Abraham Joshua Heschel and Hasidism," *Journal of Jewish Studies* 31 (Spring 1980): 82–104. See the criticism by Zanvel Klein, "Heschel as a Hasidic Scholar," ibid. (1981): 212–14.

Petuchowski, Jakob J. "Faith as the Leap of Action: The Theology of Abraham Joshua Heschel," *Commentary* 25, 5 (May 1958): 390–97.

Rotenstreich, Nathan. "On Prophetic Consciousness," *The Journal of Religion* 54, 3 (July 1974): 185–98.

Rothschild, Fritz A. "Abraham Joshua Heschel," in Thomas E. Bird (ed.), *Modern Theologians* (Notre Dame, 1967), pp. 169–82.

———. "The Religious Thought of A. J. Heschel," *Conservative Judaism* 23, 1 (Fall 1968): 12–24.

———. "Abraham Joshua Heschel (1907–1972)," *American Jewish Yearbook* 74 (New York, 1973): 533–44.

Schachter, Zalman M. "Two Facets of Judaism," *Tradition* 3, 2 (Spring 1961): 191–202.

Seigel, Seymour. "Abraham Heschel's Contributions to Jewish Scholarship," *Proceedings of the Rabbinical Assembly* 32 (1968): 72–85.

Tanenzapf, Saul. "Abraham Heschel and his Critics," *Judaism* 23, 3 (Summer 1974): 276–86.

Weborg, John. "Abraham Joshua Heschel: A Study in Anthropopodicy," *Anglican Theological Review* 61 (October 1979): 483–97.

INDEX

DATE DUE

GAYLORD			PRINTED IN U.S.A.